Battle for
Hearts and Minds

New Media and Elections in Singapore

Battle for
Hearts and Minds
New Media and Elections in Singapore

Editors

Tan Tarn How
Institute of Policy Studies, NUS, Singapore

Arun Mahizhnan
Institute of Policy Studies, NUS, Singapore

Ang Peng Hwa
Nanyang Technological University, Singapore

Lee Kuan Yew
School of Public Policy
National University of Singapore

iPS Institute of
Policy Studies

World Scientific

Published by

World Scientific Publishing Co. Pte. Ltd.
5 Toh Tuck Link, Singapore 596224
USA office: 27 Warren Street, Suite 401-402, Hackensack, NJ 07601
UK office: 57 Shelton Street, Covent Garden, London WC2H 9HE

British Library Cataloguing-in-Publication Data
A catalogue record for this book is available from the British Library.

BATTLE FOR HEARTS AND MINDS
New Media and Elections in Singapore

ISBN 978-981-4713-61-0
ISBN 978-981-4730-00-6 (pbk)

In-house Editor: Sandhya Venkatesh

Typeset by Stallion Press
Email: enquiries@stallionpress.com

CONTENTS

LIST OF FIGURES

LIST OF TABLES

Chapter 10

RASHOMON EFFECT: INTRODUCTION

Arun Mahizhnan

"Rashomon Effect" is what comes to mind when we look back to the comments on and interpretations of the 2011 Singapore General Election (GE2011). As in the 1950 movie *Rashomon* directed by Akira Kurosawa, where different eyewitnesses to an event offer very different testimonies to what happened, the results of GE2011 led to a number of commentaries that, while based on the same events, differed in their summations. Some in the Singapore blogging community claimed that the new media,[1] especially the alternative media in cyberspace, which offered news and views often different from that in the old, traditional media, was the principal cause of what, by Singapore standards, was a dramatic reduction of popular votes for the ruling People's Action Party (PAP). The PAP suffered a 6.5 percentage-point swing from what it polled in the previous General Election in 2006, although it won GE2011 with a 60% majority. Some in the ruling party also felt the new media had done them in. Other observers even dubbed GE2011 as Singapore's First "Internet" election. On the other hand,

---

[1]"New media" is often used to refer to the online media as distinct from the traditional media of newspapers, radio and television but in Singapore's case there is also the connotation that it is the alternative media as distinct from the establishment media. These terms are explained in greater detail elsewhere in this book.

certain political commentators pointed to the real life problems that remained unresolved or exacerbated in recent times as the main reason for the sharp drop in popular support for the PAP. Yet others argued that the growing disenchantment with the ruling party and incumbency fatigue after 52 years of rule by the same party were the underlying reasons for the inexorable decline of the PAP.

This book is an attempt to mitigate the Rashomon Effect and make sense of conflicting testimonies on the battle for the hearts and minds of the Singapore electorate during GE2011. It focuses primarily on the effect of Internet-related electoral activities to influence or win over the voting public. It attempts to explain the different uses of the new media by different players in the media sphere and analyse their impact on electoral behaviour.

To ground the book on empirical evidence, the Institute of Policy Studies (IPS) took unprecedented steps to organise this particular study of a Singapore General Election and the role of the Internet and other technologies such as the mobile phone in the election. Though Singapore politics has been the subject of numerous studies, few have focused on the electoral process. Fewer still have examined the role and impact of the new media on elections. IPS itself has been paying attention to this phenomenon since 2001, when there were clear signs of Internet inroads into the body politic in Singapore and the elections in particular. However, they were nascent, if not simple, attempts at the use of new communication technologies by the government, the political parties, the public intellectuals, and ordinary citizens who sought to sway public opinion. The IPS research on the new media and GEs in 2001 and again in 2006 was also limited in scope. However, when GE2011 was announced early in 2011, IPS decided to mount the most extensive research to date covering several key aspects of Internet applications in electoral communications. It convened 15 scholars, at that time mostly from the National University of Singapore, the Nanyang Technological University and the Singapore Institute of Management University, specialising in media studies, information science and public communication. Each aspect of the study was designed to delve deep into the subject matter and provide hitherto unavailable understanding and insight.

The Institute of Policy Studies also launched the largest national survey to date of media use by the Singapore public in the electoral process. It covered 2,000 respondents and probed their media consumption patterns in gathering, using and disseminating political information related to GE2011.

When the initial findings from the 15 researchers were completed, they were presented to the public at a conference in October 2011. Those conference presentations were later revised and edited to form the current book. It represents the collective effort of concerned scholars who wanted to provide a better understanding of the role of the new media in the electoral process in Singapore. Hopefully, it would lead to further and deeper research into future elections.

Understanding New Media

One of the reasons why the Rashomon Effect is pervasive in discussions of the new media is the nature of the beast. It is so unlike any other media in human history that it poses tremendous difficulty in understanding what it is really about. Eric Schmidt and Jared Cohen, both from Google, start their book *The New Digital Age* with this telling observation: "The internet is among the few things humans have built that they don't truly understand."[2] Part of the problem is the term "media" itself. Because "media" has been used for almost a century to collectively refer to the mass media made up by newspapers, radio and television, it has also become the shorthand for the cyber medium and the cyber content this medium carries. Therein lies one of the fundamental problems in our media space: the expectation that this medium must function the way the other two media — print and electronic media — do, when, in fact, the new media is not at all like old media nor can it behave likewise. New media is a different species altogether. The difference is not unlike that between Neanderthals and Humans, though there are some similarities between the two.

---

[2]Eric, S. and J. Cohen, *The New Digital Age* (London: John Murray, 2013), p. 3.

To begin with, the Internet is vastly different from the traditional print or the electronic medium though they all are indeed communication channels. It is the first medium in human history that facilitated one to one, one to many, many to one, and many to many communication, through words, sounds and visuals, using the same device, at very low cost and with hardly any central control. Millions of people can now communicate with millions of others without intermediation by another person or organisation. Such a communication facility never existed until the arrival of the Internet. In the cyberspace, anyone can be an instant newspaper journalist, radio broadcaster or a television presenter. YouTube and Facebook are just two examples of global communication platforms that have enabled billions of people today to reach out to whom they choose without having to set up a newspaper office or a broadcast station. In many cases, the new media is blithely incognisant of the rules and norms of the old media. In fact, it has been developing its own rules and norms though it has not been possible — nor may it ever be possible — to have universally accepted rules or even norms in cyberspace. Much of the new media has no editor-in-chief, no censor-in-chief nor even owner-in-chief.

Second, the new found ability for horizontal communication — people to people communication — has empowered and encouraged the public to discuss events and issues in a way that was simply not possible with the old media which mostly facilitated vertical communication between the controllers of the media and the consumers of the media. One way of understanding this phenomenon is to think of the coffee shop, where dozens of people are engaged in unfettered conversations among themselves. Two may be gossiping in conspiratorial tones about a common foe, three may be discussing a family dispute and four others may be having loud and robust exchange of views on a public issue. There is a cacophony of voices, diversity of views and an endless list of subjects. The cyber media is the coffee shop writ large — extremely large.

Third, as with the coffee shop owner, in the new media, the owners of the infrastructure through which people communicate with each other are well advised not to control the content of the conversations any more than the coffee shop owner. If the coffee shop owner intervenes in the conversations, the customers simply move to another coffee shop. So too in cyberspace.

Fourth, it is important to note that even the coffee shop analogy reaches its limit quickly. Unlike the traditional mass media which has long established structures and systems, the new media has frequently changing structures and systems, which defy easy categorisation or definition. In this regard, another analogy — that of an amoeba — is helpful to understand the constantly changing and dynamic organism. Few anticipated the invention of Facebook, YouTube or Instagram, and each platform has added very different communication facilities and opportunities. Many more different approaches are already in the offing. The understanding of new media thus has to be continuously updated.

Fifth, the spread of content in new media is increasing at a rate no previous communication media was able to achieve. To give a sense of this capacity to convey content, see Figure 1 that tracks the growth of computing capacity.[3]

Computing power was less than one exaflop[4] in 2005, it was five exaflops in 2008, and by 2014 it had reached 40 exaflops. This phenomenal increase in capacity will greatly alter the way people gather and share information. The structures placed in their way will have to change continuously. Those who argue that technology will have minimum impact on how a community communicates may have to revise their view when they see how capacity for horizontal communication spreads so quickly and so extensively. Though we have observed what has been called the penetration-participation paradox in Singapore,[5] which suggests that technological availability of communication tools does not lead

---

[3]Richard, D., S. Ramaswamy, E. Stephenson, and S.P. Viguerie, "Management Intuition for the Next 50 Years", *McKinsey Quarterly* (September 2014).

[4]An exaflop is 1 quintillion (10 to the 18th power) floating-point operations per second.

[5]Cherian George, "The Internet's Political Impact and the Penetration/Participation Paradox in Malaysia and Singapore", *Media, Culture & Society*, no. 27 (November 2005): 903–20.

Annual additions to global business and consumer computing power, exaflops[1]

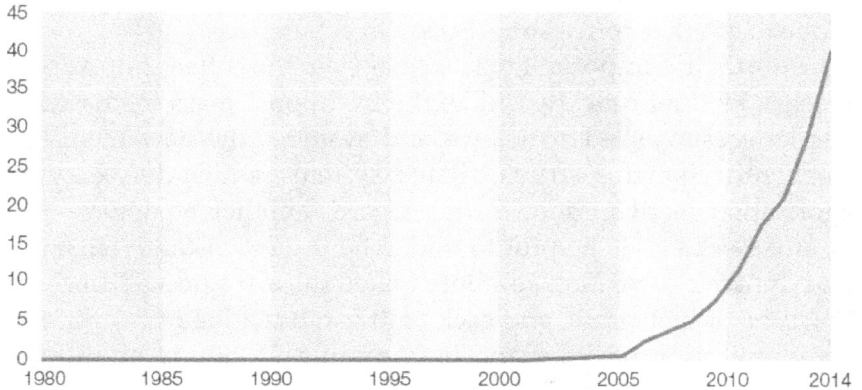

[1] An exaflop is 1 quintillion (10 to the 18th power) floating-point operations per second.

Source: William D. Nordhaus, "Two centuries of progress in computing," *Journal of Economic History*, 2007, Volume 67, Number 1, pp. 128–59; IDC; US Bureau of Economic Analysis; McKinsey analysis

Figure 1:   Annual growth of computing power

to actual communication, the future of horizontal communication may be vastly different from what it is today. The IPS's study of General Elections in 2001, 2006 and this one on GE2011 all show a slow take-off in terms of horizontal communication.[6] However, it might accelerate very rapidly when it reaches a tipping point in political communication in this country.

Finally, it is instructive to see the new media as part of the Fifth Estate, as defined by William Dutton.[7] He argues that the Internet affords individuals to network in ways that can enhance and reinforce the communicative power of networked individuals. Compared to what has been called the Fourth Estate — the

---

[6]Tan, T.H. and A. Mahizhnan, "Subverting Seriousness and Other Misdemeanours: Modes of Resistance Against OB Markers in the 2006 Singapore General Election", available at http://lkyspp.nus.edu.sg/wp-content/uploads/2013/06/pa_TTHAM_Subverting-Seriousness_AMIC_July-2008.pdf (accessed on 10 Month 2014).

[7]Dutton, W.H., "The Fifth Estate Emerging through the Network of Networks", *Prometheus: Critical Studies in Innovation*, 27(1), (2009): 1–15.

traditional mass media of the newspaper, radio, and television — the Fifth Estate "enables the networked individuals to move across, undermine and go beyond the boundaries of existing institutions, thereby opening new ways of increasing the accountability of politicians, press, experts and other loci of power and influence."[8]

Government and Media

In the context of Singapore, the locus of power and influence of the traditional mass media has long been subjected to government control, which is one of the most important factors in the analysis of Singapore media. Though Singapore was the home of rambunctious and pluralistic journalism during colonial times, once the PAP government came into power in 1959, the nature and practice of mass media began to change dramatically. Since the 1960s, the government has abided by what the first Prime Minister Lee Kuan Yew laid down as the fundamental basis of the role of the media. He made an unequivocal declaration that "freedom of the press ... must be subordinated to the overriding needs of the integrity of Singapore, and to the primacy of purpose of an elected government."[9] His successor Goh Chok Tong also rejected the concept of the media as the Fourth Estate in Singapore, because "an adversarial watchdog of government, goes against our goal of consensus politics, of getting Singaporeans to row as a team."[10] Over the decades, the government has introduced many laws and regulations to keep the traditional mass media within the boundaries defined by the government. Those media players who resisted government control went out of business and those who complied were eventually consolidated into the two media organisations that have dominated Singapore's

---

[8]*Ibid.*

[9]Address to the General Assembly of The International Press Institute, at Helsinki on 9 June 1971. National Archives of Singapore Document No. lky19710609b.

[10]*The Straits Times*, 16 July 1995.

media landscape since the 1980s: the Singapore Press Holdings and MediaCorp.[11] As is to be expected, the Singapore government's management of media has further spread the view that Singapore is an authoritarian state and the Singapore media is government-controlled.

As a consequence of government regulation and influence over media practice, the coverage of politics in general and electoral politics in particular occupied only a very narrow spectrum of political discourse. In liberal democracies, the mass media usually set the agenda that shaped what the public read, heard or viewed and it also framed the issues that influenced how the public discussed them. In such societies, in addition to media, there are other regular and strong sources of alternative discourses such as those offered by the civil society, the academia and the business community. However, in Singapore these sources had largely been muted. Even the mainstream media's role of agenda setting and framing has been conditioned and constrained not only by law but also by government-laid boundaries. In fact, it has led to the development of what is a peculiarly Singaporean media practice — to abide by the "OB markers." "OB markers", a term borrowed from the game of golf, refers, in this context, to the out-of-bounds areas that are considered to be taboo or sensitive subjects that the media should avoid or tread very carefully. However, these OB markers are not written down anywhere or passed on officially. Given its social responsibility obligations, media is expected to discern what these OB markers are and act accordingly. The media generally took the cues from the government and over time internalised them as standard practice.[12] In addition to the mass media, the above-mentioned sources of alternative discourse also took the OB markers to heart. The reasons varied from conviction in government positions

---

[11]The names of these organisations have changed over time but the core activities and management controls have remained essentially unaltered.
[12]For a thorough understanding of the media system and media practice in Singapore, refer to George, C., *Freedom From the Press: Journalism and State Power in Singapore* (Singapore: NUS Press, 2012) and Cheong Yip Seng, *OB Markers: My Straits Times Story* (Singapore: Straits Times Press, 2012).

to sheer fear of retribution. The overall effect of all the external constraints combined with self-censorship was that Singaporeans were exposed to more or less a monolithic mass media with a fairly homogenous political discourse over four decades lasting from the 1960s. Print and broadcast media in Singapore provided a predictable palette of news and views with only mild criticism of the government or the ruling party. While Singapore media was widely recognised for its professionalism and competence in many aspects of journalism, it was also believed to be biased towards the government and the ruling party.[13]

Old Media and New Media

It was into this milieu of a compliant media and constricted public sphere that the Internet brought a completely different "communicative power" through networked individuals — the beginnings of the Fifth Estate. As explained earlier, Singapore's new media developed and functioned in stark contrast to the old media. The role, the structure, the legal status and, most importantly, the content of the new media are all strikingly different from the old media and often defy the rules and norms set down for the old media.

The government, at first, adopted what it called a "light touch" approach to regulating new media. It introduced the Class Licensing scheme under which "Internet Service Providers and Internet Content Providers are automatically class licensed and must observe MDA's Class Licence Conditions . . . and the Internet Code of Practice."[14] By and large, the government has stuck to the light

---

[13]Karan, K., C.Y. Kuo and S.H. Lee, *Singapore General Elections, 2001: Study of the Media, Politics and Public* (Singapore: Asian Media Information and Communication Centre [AMIC] and WKW School of Communication and Information, Nanyang Technological University, 2010); Hao, X., "The Press and Public Trust: The Case of Singapore", *Asian Journal of Communication*, 6(1), (1996): 111–123; and Eddie, C.Y.K., D. Holaday, and E. Peck, *Mirror on the Wall: Media in a Singapore Election* (Singapore: Asian Mass Communication Research and Information Centre, 1993).

[14]http://www.mda.gov.sg/RegulationsAndLicensing/Licences/Pages/Internet-ServiceAndContentProviderClassLicence.aspx#sthash.ZTyBSWy2.dpuf (accessed in October 2014).

touch approach, though occasionally the light touch gave way to a steel fist as some were charged under the Sedition Act for inciting racial hatred. Very rarely are websites banned or asked to shut down on censorship grounds.[15]

On the whole, the new media landscape at the time of GE2011 was in sharp contrast to the old media landscape. Old media was well organised, well endowed, professionally run while still compliant of government rules and OB markers. The editorial viewpoints on politics and party coverage remained within the customary narrow spectrum. The new media, on the other hand, was challenging many OB markers, and while remaining conscious of strict media rules and regulations, tried to push the boundaries. As is natural in cyberspace, new media players were varied and unorganised. Their rules of engagement differed widely. Though their content was heterogeneous, most were critical of the PAP and the government. In terms of number of players, it was surprisingly small. Given the long-term frustration with the mainstream media and its alleged bias towards the PAP and the government, the actual number of political blogs and websites that provided critical and alternative analysis of Singapore politics was particularly small, totalling a dozen or so.

In sum, the Singapore case of Internet usage and impact on the GE2011 is in many ways untypical of what would be expected of such a situation and the following chapters provide an analysis of this phenomenon.

* * *

This book is laid out in 11 chapters, each of which focuses on a specific aspect of the role and impact of new communication technologies — especially the Internet — on the electoral process. They are not in any order of precedence as they can be read discretely. The essays examine the media activities of political parties and candidates, mainstream media and the alternative media, opinion makers and

---

[15]One example of a banned website is www.fluffboy.com, a gay website the government banned in 2005. Available at http://www.yawningbread.org/arch_2005/yax-504.htm (accessed in October 2014).

the ordinary voter. They also assess the impact on the voter in terms of their political knowledge, perceptions of issues, candidates and parties, reconciliation of conflicting information, and their voting behaviour.

However, it is instructive to note that the general public forms its views and impressions of the elections from a plethora of information sources and interactions based on them. In fact, the very first chapter by Tan Tarn How and Arun Mahizhnan, based on a national survey, reinforces that idea right at the outset. In their chapter on *Not Quite an "Internet" Election: Survey of Media Use of Voters*, Tan and Mahizhnan share their findings on three basic questions relating to media and GE2011:

- What is the impact of online versus offline media, and of mainstream versus alternative media during the election?
- What are the political traits of voters in terms of knowledge, interest, orientation, political efficacy, and political cynicism?
- What is the level of offline and online political participation among voters?

Their findings help answer one of the burning questions of the time: was the GE2011 really the "Internet" election it was widely claimed to be? The chapter also addresses another critical question: whether the alternative online media content during the election played a causal role in the significant decline of votes for PAP — as some PAP members lamented or as some bloggers had hoped for. This chapter also suggests the reasons for the Rashomon Effect in the diverse commentaries on the electoral outcome. The essay concludes that while the influence of the Internet in GE2011 did not turn out to be as large as many expected, there is clear evidence that "the power of the Internet is palpably on the rise."

The next chapter by Cherian George on *Legal Landmines and OB Markers: Survival Strategies of Alternative Media* specifically focuses on some socio-political bloggers who have emerged as potent voices in political debates. George points out that they are "not only active in circulating ideas but also in developing new norms of alternative online journalism in Singapore." The essay explores how these bloggers defined their roles during the election and the mechanisms through which they realised their goals. It also focuses on the way they navigated through the murky waters of legal and political restrictions, doing so with limited resources. George offers his critical assessment of the possibilities and limitations of these players in Singapore's political discourse.

The following two chapters by Debbie Goh and Natalie Pang, *"Untapped Potential: Internet Use by Political Parties"* and *"Pro, Anti, Neutral: Political Blogs and their Sentiments"*, provide detailed analysis of the blogosphere in general and the websites of political parties and candidates in particular. Their chapter on the blogosphere attempts to answer three basic questions through content analysis:

- What kind of political content was being produced about the elections?
- Who was generating content?
- What was the quality of the content?

They also examine how far Singaporeans went in redressing the frequently mentioned shortage of diverse and high quality discourse in mainstream media and whether they maximised the potential of the Internet in generating such content.

In the other chapter focusing on parties and candidates, Goh and Pang evaluate selected sites for the type of content including topics and issues published, format of content, volume of content, speed of delivery, and the presence of interactivity.

It has been a long held view among academics that the media sets the agenda for public discourse.[16] The gatekeepers in traditional media organisations decide what are the salient news and views of the day and inform their respective public accordingly. Even if the media does not tell the public what to think, it tells the public what to think about.[17] With the advent of new media, the question arises, naturally, to what extent it too sets the agenda of the public

---

[16]For a good discussion of agenda-setting theory, see Combs, M. and D. Shaw, "The Agenda-Setting Function of Mass Media", *Public Opinion Quarterly*, 36(2), (1972).
[17]See Cohen, B. *The Press and Foreign Policy*. New York: Harcourt, 1963.

discourse. In the case of Singapore, this issue is further complicated by the fact that the mainstream media has a strong presence in the new media with their online versions. The alternative media in Singapore, however, is mostly confined to online media. Besides, as is common to new media all over the world, the consumers are also producers of information and views, which role has a strong bearing on agenda setting. Therefore, it is especially important to understand the different agenda setting processes in the alternative online media on the one hand and the mainstream media — both online and offline — on the other.

Interestingly, early observations of the online content in Singapore suggested a certain co-relation between what was salient in the alternative media and the mainstream media, not so much as independent judgements on what is important but more as reactions to one another. In their chapter on *Who Calls the Shots? Agenda Setting in Mainstream and Alternative Media*, Paul Wu Horng-Jyh, Randolph Tan Gee Kwang and Carol Soon focus specifically on the interaction between the two. The study uses keywords and hyperlinks to discover the flow of ideas from one side to another. It is a pioneering study on inter-media agenda-setting in the context of an election and election-related topics.

In the next chapter, *Different but Not That Different: New Media's Impact on Young Voters' Political Participation*, Trisha Lin and Alice Y.H. Hong turn to the segment of the Singapore population that is most net-savvy — the youth. They analyse the responses of about 450 young Singaporeans aged 21 to 35 in the national survey mentioned above. They attempt to uncover patterns of political participation, attitude, voting behaviour, and media communication among the youth during the past election. As expected, the young Singaporeans engaged more in this election, thanks to the wide use of new media. On the other hand, almost 50% of them still trusted old media and a higher percentage of them supported the ruling party than supported the opposition. Again, this would surprise many analysts as it goes against conventional expectations. Lin and Hong offer some insights into what instigates the reactions of young Singaporeans in their essay.

Marko M. Skoric in his chapter on *The Leap from the Virtual to the Real: Facebook Use and Political Participation* sets out the patterns of use of social network sites (SNS) and mobile phones and evaluates their relationship with both traditional and online forms of political participation in Singapore during the election. His finding is that the use of mobile phones and SNS played a "predominantly positive role in promoting active participation in political life, both online and offline." However, the association of new media platforms with online participation was generally stronger than with traditional forms of engagement. The surprising finding, though, was that only fewer than one in five Facebook users belonged to a political or public affairs groups and that the generic Facebook user had "either no relationship or even negative relationship with the measures of participation." This finding prompts Skoric to caution that the common conception of social media platforms as inherently "participatory" might have to be reconsidered. He also raises the question of whether these new forms of political participation can lead to tangible political outcomes, or whether they simply represent "low effort, low yield" substitutes for genuine political engagement. While this is certainly a valid question, the ever increasing volume of political speech within the cyberspace in Singapore clearly indicates a marked change in public discourse. There are also an increasing number of political gatherings — often in opposition to the government — in designated public spaces like the Hong Lim Park, which is another measure of political participation. As pointed out earlier, the enormous capacity for horizontal communication among citizens is likely to reach a tipping point whereby political participation may increase at a much more accelerated pace than in the past few decades.

It was surprising to many researchers that despite deep penetration of computers and mobile phones in Singapore and despite wide reporting of the usage of new communication technologies in election campaigns elsewhere such as the United States Presidential Elections and the Indonesian General Elections, GE2011 saw so little of social media usage for political purposes. In his chapter on *David vs Goliath: Twitter's Role in Equalising Big-Party Dominance*,

Xu Xiaoge investigates the role and impact of Twitter in the context of GE2011. His particular concern was whether new media equalised the electoral playing field for opposition parties as predicted by equalisation theorists or merely reinforced politics as usual for the ruling party as postulated by normalisation theorists. Xu studied tweets, replies, hashtags, twitvideos, twitpics, and retweets among Twitter users before, during and after the general election in Singapore to see if either of those outcomes was prevalent. Interestingly, he found that Twitter was not fully utilised by either the ruling party or the opposition parties in normalising or equalising the electoral playing field. He sets out the patterns of Twitter use by parties and citizens and analyses the strengths and weaknesses of tweeting for political purposes. He closes with some specific recommendations for political parties.

One of the perennial accusations against the mainstream media in Singapore is that it is biased towards the government and the ruling party. The government mandates that the mainstream media be a partner in nation-building and some argue that its favourable coverage of the government and the ruling party are only natural to such partnership. The question then arises how much would Singaporeans know about the opposition parties if they only consumed mainstream media. It has been argued that if Singaporeans need to have sufficient knowledge of the opposition, they need to go to the alternative online media. In order to ascertain just how much of a knowledge gap — the difference in the knowledge of people who obtain political information from mainstream media and alternative online media — exists, Debbie Goh undertook a detailed study of the relationship between Internet use and political knowledge of opposition parties in Singapore. She shares her findings in the chapter on *Lifting the Veil of Ignorance: Internet's Impact on Knowledge Gap*. The study confirms that those who consumed mainstream media could only gain limited political knowledge of opposition parties. Goh also argues that "contrary to criticism that political discourse on the Internet is inaccurate and untrustworthy, this study shows that the Internet had been a reliable and effective source in helping citizens to be more knowledgeable about alternative parties, their candidates, and their policies and positions on issues." She provides a nuanced analysis of the knowledge gap between those who consume mainstream and alternative media.

An issue related to media consumption is how people cope with conflicting information. In addition to what professional journalists provide as news and views, there is a growing amount of user-generated content coming through blogs, social networks and discussion forums. Naturally, there are conflicting information or views on the same subject. It would be all the more so during an election campaign. Yet, little is known about how people deal with conflicting information. Natalie Pang, in her chapter on *Squaring Political Circles: Coping with Conflicting Information*, shares the findings of a study on how Singaporean voters reconcile the conflict. She also addresses the implications of such experiences for their views on media as information sources, their political beliefs, and their inclination for political participation. Pang argues that greater exposure to multifaceted information on multiple media platforms can lead to better-informed participants and to greater media literacy. She also points out that in their attempt to reconcile conflicting information, voters may also become active citizens by engaging in actions such as seeking expert opinions, attending rallies and political events, or discussing the issue with their personal networks.

In the final chapter on *The Silence of the Majority: Political Talk during Election Time*, Weiyu Zhang explores a particularly relevant subject in the electoral process — with whom and how people discuss politics during election time. Her research questions include how much did people talk about politics during election time; to whom did people talk to; how much did people disagree with each other when talking about politics; and how did people perceive the situation of their everyday political talk? Again, this subject is hardly researched in Singapore and Zhang's study throws out surprising and valuable insights. She found that during GE2011, Singaporeans, on average, did not talk much about the elections. If they did talk, it was usually with family and friends. Another interesting finding is that Singaporeans who talked about the elections seldom disagreed with their fellow discussants. The study also found that they talked least with people they met online. This may seem to go against conventional wisdom that the Internet enables frank and free discussions. However, there are studies elsewhere that confirm that people generally gravitate to their own ilk, creating an echo chamber effect. In fact, this is not unlike the gravitational pulls found in old media whereby readers of a certain political stripe tended to read papers of the same ideological bent. Zhang found that despite this lack of political talk, it was ranked as the second most important information source (after mainstream media) as well as the third most influential source (after mainstream media and political rallies) on voting decisions. All these findings show that the tapestry of political discourse in Singapore is a complex weave of disparate and diverse threads and we should be wary of easy labelling or quick conclusions.

* * *

We hope this collection of essays based on detailed surveys and studies provide a reasonable account of the use of the Internet and its impact on the GE2011 in Singapore. There is no question that the battle for hearts and minds during election time would continue to be a major challenge for political parties and an engaging event for voters. The advent of the new media has certainly complicated the long maintained status quo in the media space in Singapore. However, the distinction between new media and old media may indeed diminish over time as all new media become old media after some time and all old media were indeed new media at one time. What might remain undiminished is the distinction between self-owned media — media that is largely controlled by the user, and the other-owned media — media that is largely controlled by others — as that would make a significant difference in agenda setting and framing, two critical functions of media. Soon after the election in 2011, Prime Minister Lee Hsien Loong made a telling statement which portends the future of the media in Singapore politics. He said the PAP must strengthen its presence in cyberspace and learn to use the new media more effectively. "This meant not just going onto Facebook and Twitter but being on the same wavelength as the netizens and resonating with the Internet generation," he added.[18] Marshall McLuhan's dictum that medium is the message may still be the most valuable piece of wisdom.

---

[18]http://entertainment.xin.msn.com/en/radio/938live/singaporenews.aspx?cp-documentid=5246539 (accessed in October 2014).

1

NOT QUITE AN "INTERNET" ELECTION: SURVEY OF MEDIA USE OF VOTERS

Tan Tarn How and Arun Mahizhnan

Abstract

A national survey of voters after Singapore's 2011 General Election was carried out on their media use, political traits, political participation, and voting behaviour. The election had been dubbed by some as the country's first "Internet" election because of the high Internet penetration rate and the unprecedented rise in non-mainstream media such as blogs and party websites and Facebook pages. However, the results show the secondary importance of alternative media to traditional and online mainstream media during the election period in their use by and importance to voters. Most survey respondents also said they had already decided on their vote before the election period, which underlines the insignificance of all media in voting behaviour.

There are only a handful of quantitative surveys published on media and politics in Singapore. One of the key findings revealed by these studies is that Singapore over the years has seen increasing use of the Internet as a source of political and election information for voters. Kuo, Holaday and Peck's pioneering effort on media and the Singapore elections in the 1991 General Election came before the Internet era (Kuo, Holaday and Peck, 1993). It found that the most important source of election information in their sample of 434 voters from two constituencies was overwhelmingly the traditional mass media, especially newspapers, followed by television. The first published survey-based study which included the Internet was in 2001, which found that only a small segment — 5.8% of the 691 respondents — used the Internet as a source of election information (Karan, Kuo and Lee, 2010). Five years later, in the next election in 2006, Singaporeans still ranked the Internet as only the ninth most influential channel on how they voted, just before word of mouth (Koh, 2006.) The study unfortunately did not present findings on the proportion of voters using the Internet for election information. For the 2011 Singapore General Election (GE2011), which this chapter focuses on, one study found that the Internet had become the third main source of information on the elections, though it still trailed newspapers and television (Koh, 2011). This continuing preference of traditional mass media over the Internet, even as online sources rose in importance, was echoed in a second survey on GE2011, which found that 50% of 611 respondents named newspapers as their first choice of election information, followed by television (32%) and the Internet (11%) (Merdeka Centre, 2011).

One of the reasons for the rise in popularity of the Internet for election information is, of course, increasing penetration, with household access to the Internet climbing from 71% in 2006 to 85% in 2011 (Infocomm Development Authority of Singapore, 2013). In addition, the relaxation of rules in 2011 against election advertising (that is, expression of support for parties or candidates) by individual voters and the rise of social media in the preceding five years probably also played a large part. In 2006, only political parties could advertise through the Internet, subject to election advertising rules. Ordinary citizens were not allowed to promote or canvass for election candidates. However, some bloggers defied such restrictions and expressed their views openly on the Internet. But their defiance did not lead to any prosecutions by the authorities (Tan and Mahizhnan, 2008). Perhaps in response to this disregard of the laws and a tacit acknowledgment of the need for more active citizen participation in the electoral process, by 2011 election advertising rules were changed to allow anyone, not just political parties and candidates, to talk about election politics on blogs and social media and to even send chain emails and SMSes. Social media, especially Facebook, had also grown very popular by 2011, as our findings below show. As a result, some expected GE2011 to be Singapore's first "Internet" election, where social media buzz would influence swing votes (Wong, 2011).

The above studies also found that younger Singaporeans of higher socioeconomic class were more inclined to use the Internet as a source of political or election news. Such findings are further confirmed by an Institute of Policy Studies (IPS) survey in 2011 on Media Use and Political Traits (Tan, Chung, and Zhang, 2011). The study also found youth (those aged between 21 to 39 years old) to be a little less authoritarian than older people, to be more likely to participate in politics than older people, to be more likely to see government control of media and bias in media than older people, and to be less likely to say that they voted People's Action Party (PAP) in the past election (Tan, Chung, and Zhang, 2011). Youth also consumed more political news via both online mainstream media sources and Singapore-only alternative sources. Online alternative media use was also complementary to and not competitive with mainstream media use. The Internet is not a "ghettoising" force as many worried it might be. In fact, 93% who read alternative media also read print newspapers, 84% watched TV, and 89% read mainstream media online; hence they are not single source, "self-radicalising" media users. (Tan, Chung, and Zhang, 2011).

Our current study seeks to contribute to this body of literature on Singapore election surveys, specifically on the influence of media on the electoral process. The survey that forms the core of this study covered the largest sample to date (2,000 respondents), and provides the most comprehensive account of the use of new media and its many forms from blogs to Facebook, Twitter, e-mail and SMSes.

Also, most previous media surveys do not distinguish between finer categories of the Singapore media on the Internet such as online mainstream media and online alternative media (for example, The Online Citizen and Yawning Bread). The distinction is critical because researchers have found that Singaporeans consume more online mainstream media than online alternative news (Tan, Chung, and Zhang, 2011). Our current study yields more granular results on the relationship between media use and political traits. Additionally, one common shortcoming of many of the earlier studies was the confounding of terminology, namely, the failure to distinguish between media sources in two different dimensions, by content (mainstream versus alternative) and by the channel (offline versus online). The result is that, for instance, studies have assumed that newspapers and the Internet are exclusive categories when they are not, for newspapers are now increasingly also delivered and read online and not just in print form. This is discussed in detail in the following paragraphs.

Our study also contrasts the political traits of all media users with those who read blogs or Facebook. No election study has done this yet, possibly because Internet use was minimal in past elections.

Methodology

The survey was carried out by a reputable private company using Computer-assisted Telephone Interviewing (CATI). The final data consists of interviews with 2,000 respondents who were Singapore citizens aged 21 and above. The fieldwork was carried out from 24 May (two weeks after Polling Day) to 17 July 2011. Respondents met quotas set for race, gender, and age. Quotas for education and housing type were also used. The quotas were set based on Census of Population 2010. All set quotas (race, gender, and age) were achieved within a ±3% point difference. Soft quotas on education and housing type were achieved within a ±5% point difference. See Appendix 1 in this book for the breakdown of the sample.

The Questionnaire

The questionnaire comprises 50 questions, including screening questions for citizenship and age. The questions cover these categories:

1. Demographics: Age, sex, household income, and educational level

2. Political talk: Frequency of oral communication and disagreement in such communication with others about the election
3. Political traits: Political interest; political orientation (liberal versus authoritarian); political efficacy (belief that one can influence political affairs); political cynicism (belief that politicians care more about themselves than the public good)
4. Political knowledge: Knowledge of political parties and candidates
5. Political participation: Offline participation such as writing to mainstream media (MSM) and being member of and volunteering for political parties; online participation such as writing on the election in online forums, blogs or Facebook pages, and forwarding election related SMSes, e-mails or Twitter messages
6. Attitudes towards media: Whether respondents think there is too much control over media and political expression; and whether media is fair in reporting elections
7. Media use: Frequency and amount of use of different media; consumption of viral online media; use of party websites or Facebook pages; use of e-mail, Facebook, Twitter, mobile phone, and SMS for election purposes (some of the questions are used also to measure political participation)
8. Importance and trust of media for election information, and their influence on voting
9. Conflicting information: Whether and where they encountered conflicting information on the election
10. Voting: Who they voted for and when they decided who to vote for

The results and analysis from many of the questions are given below. However, responses to other questions are used for other chapters in the book, including those chapters dealing with Facebook, Twitter, political talk, youth and media, conflicting information, and knowledge gap. See Appendix 1 for the URL to access the survey questionnaire.

Research Questions

The research questions addressed in this chapter are:

1. What is the impact of online versus offline media, and of mainstream versus alternative media during the election? In particular:
   a. What media is used for election information, and what is the level of use?
   b. What proportion of the respondents consumed alternative online media and Facebook as sources of election information? How is this group different from the others?
   c. What is the influence of the different media on voting?
2. What are the political traits of voters in terms of political knowledge, interest, orientation, efficacy and cynicism?
3. What is the level of offline and online political participation among voters?

A Note on Classification of Media Types

In public as well as some academic discourse, there is some confusion about the terms used to describe the different media. This section seeks to clarify these terms and to define them for the purposes of this chapter.

First, academics and journalists often use interchangeably the two terms "mainstream media" and "traditional media" as well as the terms "alternative media" and "new media". This is wrong. Mainstream media refers to media that purveys mainstream views, that is, those that are generally accepted by a large part of the population at a particular time and place. These views are not necessarily consistent, or uniform, or undisputed. For instance, the mainstream media in the United Kingdom occupies a conservative to liberal spectrum that is not very far from the centre. The ideology of these media, though not necessarily held by a majority of the people, nevertheless has enough currency among a substantial minority, as can be seen by their wide circulation and viewership. Alternative media, on the other hand, refers to media holding views which are similar to those of a small minority of the population. Alternative media by definition have small circulations or viewerships, though not all media with low circulations or viewerships, such as an unpopular mainstream newspaper or radio station, is alternative. Hence, the difference between mainstream media and alternative media lies largely in their content. It should be also noted that some media lie in the middle of the spectrum between the mainstream and alternative.

Second, the difference between traditional media and new media lies in the channels or format of distribution. Traditional media (also called offline, old or legacy media) refer to print and broadcast media, while new media (also called online) refer to media distributed through digital networks like the Internet and on digital devices like the computer or mobile phone.

It is true that the preferred modes of transmission of mainstream media and alternative media are often different. For instance, alternative media owners often lack the economic resources needed to produce and distribute content for broadcast, and are confined to either new media or the cheaper old media such as pamphlets.

Based on the preceding discussion, it is, therefore, possible to create a table of the types of media categories according to whether they are mainstream versus alternative and traditional versus new (Figure 1). In Figure 1, we have included the actual names of the media entities in each category.

Several points of interest emerge from Figure 1:

1. Mainstream media now comes in old media channels (quadrant 1) as well as new ones (quadrant 3). First, old media content (quadrant 1) in newspapers is reproduced in new media. Hence there are online versions of *The Straits Times*, *The New Paper*, *Today*, etc. Second, old media broadcast content is reproduced in new media as text, and sometimes as video. Third, mainstream media has also created exclusively new media content, such as video websites Razor TV and Stomp, and also include multimedia in their websites.

2. Alternative media in the form of old media is a rarity in Singapore, especially political alternative media. There are no independent

Content \ Type of Channel	Mainstream Media	Alternative Media
Traditional or Old Media	**1:** - *The Straits Times, Today, The New Paper, Lianhe Zaobao* - CNA Broadcast - Radio via air	**2:** - *Hammer* - *The Democrat* - *Catholic Informer* - Election Posters - Party Brochures
New Media	**3:** - The Straits Times Online - Razor TV - Stomp - CNA Website	**4:** - The Online Citizen - Yawning Bread - Temasek Review Emeritus - Public House - Party Websites - Party SMS

Figure 1:　Mass media matrix

newspapers (licences to publish are required and may not be given), although some parties such as the Workers' Party and the Singapore Democratic Party print their own party newspapers.

3. Alternative online media come in the form of political blogs and aggregators. The most prominent ones are The Online Citizen, Temasek Emeritus and Yawning Bread. A few such as Singapore Election Watch were specially created just before the election, or revived from the 2006 election.

4. Media owned by foreign media conglomerates, whether Internet companies such as Yahoo! with its Yahoo! News portal or more traditional companies such as the *New York Times* and the British Broadcasting Corporation, occupy a space that is neither mainstream from the Singapore perspective nor truly alternative. They are best described as lying in the middle of the spectrum. In the past, access to foreign mainstream media such as newspapers was not easy, largely because of the expense of buying foreign newspapers, but that has changed with the Internet. Similarly social media platforms that are based on user-generated content such as Facebook and Twitter cannot be simply classified as mainstream or alternative. Media outlets, both alternative and

mainstream, also have Facebook and Twitter accounts, which are alternative or mainstream accordingly. Hence these media do not fall neatly into any of the four quadrants.

Findings

Media Penetration

Figure 2 shows the ownership of mobile phones, Facebook accounts and blogs. The data is given for all the respondents to the survey (labelled "all") and the sub-group of respondents who consumed election news via alternative online blogs and/or Facebook (labelled "non-MSM"). This non-MSM group did not consume blogs and Facebook content exclusively as they could also consume other media; this category will be explained more fully in a later section. As can be seen, mobile phone ownership is very high and Facebook account ownership is quite high among all the respondents.

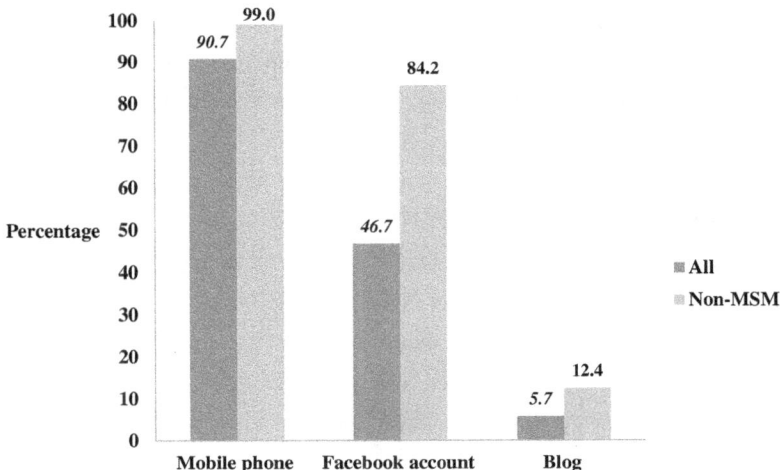

Figure 2: Media penetration

Notes: Breakdown of mobile phone ownership, Facebook account ownership and blog ownership among all respondents (all) and those who read alternative online media and Facebook for election news (non-MSM).

Consumption of Election News by Media

This section looks at the consumption of news by content (mainstream versus alternative) and channel (old versus new media). Respondents were asked how many minutes they spent a day getting election news from these seven channels:

- Mainstream media via traditional channels: (1) Reading print newspapers; (2) Listening to radio; (3) Watching television
- Mainstream media via new channels: (4) Reading online websites of Singapore mass media such as *The Straits Times*, *Today*, *The New Paper*, *Lianhe Zaobao* or Channel News Asia
- Foreign media: (5) Reading foreign news websites such as the BBC, CNN or the *New York Times*
- Facebook: (6) Learning about the election on Facebook.
- Alternative online media: (7) Reading Internet-only Singapore blogs or news websites such as The Online Citizen, Yawning Bread and Temasek Review.

Figure 3 shows the average number of minutes spent on the above seven types of media. It shows that consumption of news content was still mainly through mainstream sources, that is, print newspapers, television and radio, and their websites.

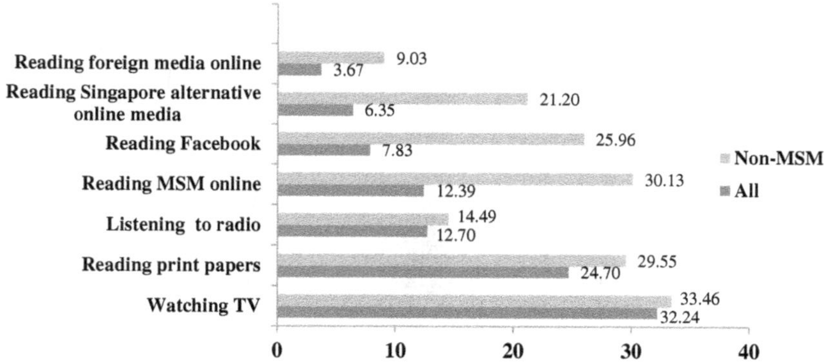

Figure 3: Time spent on different media

Notes: Respondents were asked to say how many minutes they usually spent a day consuming election news during the election period from the sources above.

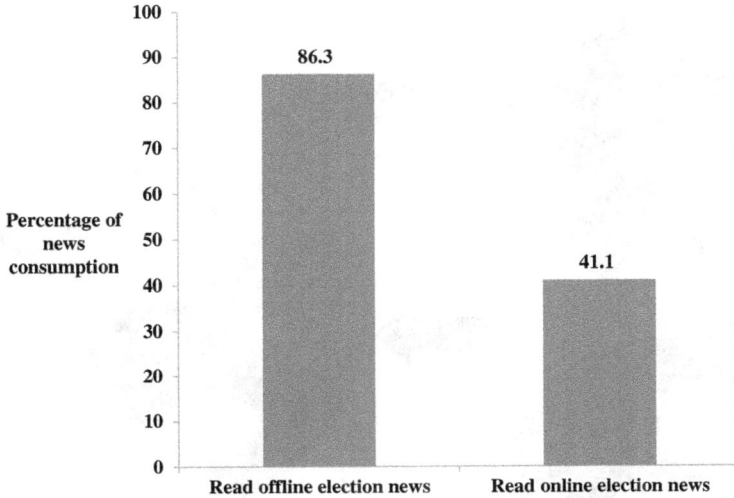

Figure 4: Offline and online consumption of elections news

Traditional Media Preferred Over New Media

Figure 4 shows the percentage of the sample who said they consumed at least some election news via old media (television, print newspapers, and radio) or new media (both mainstream and alternative content, and "neutral" content). As can be seen, old media was still twice as popular as new media as a channel for political news.

Consumption of election news still mainly mainstream

As can be seen from Figure 4, voters preferred mainstream news sources (print, television, radio, and MSM online) to the rest, that is, the non-mainstream sources irrespective of the channel. Even mainstream news delivered online was more popular than alternative online news sources.

Figure 5 shows the proportion of the sample who consumed non-mainstream election news. About a fifth consumed alternative online election news on blogs, and another fifth read about the elections on Facebook. Three in ten consumed one or both of these sources of election news — they will be known as consumers of non-MSM

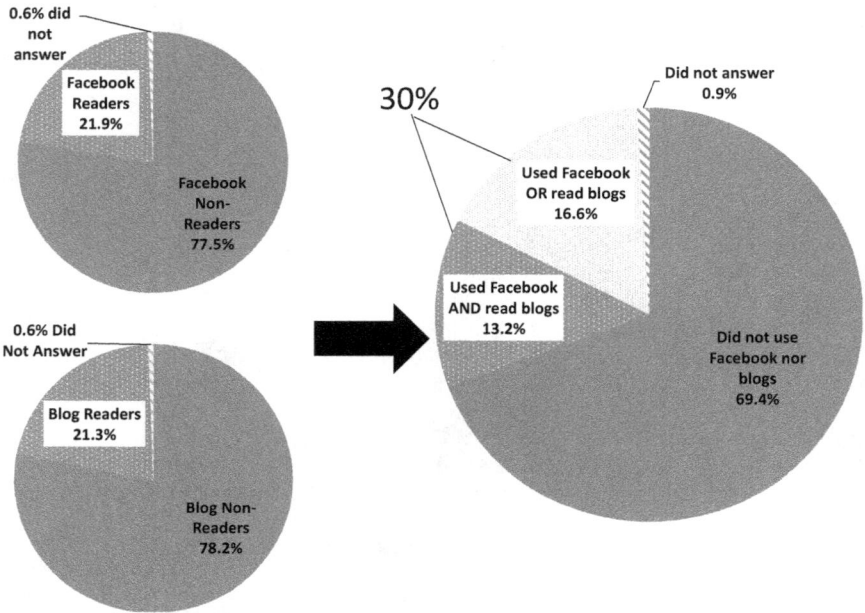

Figure 5: Consumers of non-mainstream media for election information

news in the rest of this chapter. This means that one in ten consumed alternative online news but not Facebook, another one in ten the other way round, and another one in ten used both alternative online news and Facebook for election information.

There appears to be a *rising trend of using blogs for political or election information* in the year leading up to GE2011. According to a nationwide representative survey in the third quarter of 2010, 12.8% of respondents read alternative online sources such as The Online Citizen and Temasek Review (Tan, Chung, and Zhang, 2011), while our GE2011 survey found that 17.3% read these sources on election issues in the last six months leading up to the election, and 21.3% read blogs on election issues during the election itself. This rise could be because of the heightened interest in political news as a result of the election or the increasing importance of alternative online blogs and websites or both.

Consumers of non-mainstream media (Facebook and alternative online media) election news were also users of mainstream media sources at the same time. In the sample, 95.5% of those who read Facebook and blogs for election news also consumed some mainstream media. This re-confirms a survey of 2010 which found that those who read alternative, online blogs for political information were also overwhelmingly consumers of mainstream media (Tan, Chung, and Zhang, 2011). Further, among consumers of non-mainstream media, 93% also read print newspapers, 84% watched TV and 89% read online mainstream media for election news. It needs to be emphasised, therefore, that when we refer to non-MSM consumers in this chapter, we do not mean that they did not consume MSM, when most of them, in fact, did.

Profile of the non-MSM consumers

As Figures 6 to 11 show, the *demographics of non-MSM consumers* are different from the rest of the sample. To a statistically significant degree, they were younger, were more educated, came from households with higher incomes, and were male.

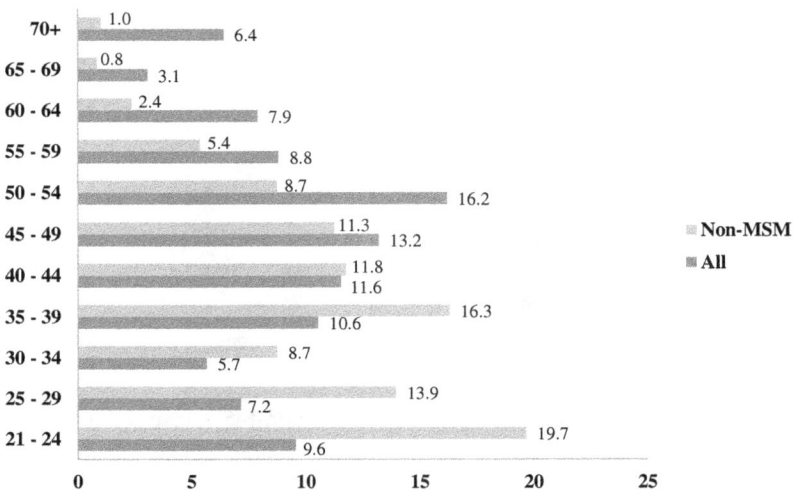

Figure 6:   Age of all and non-MSM respondents

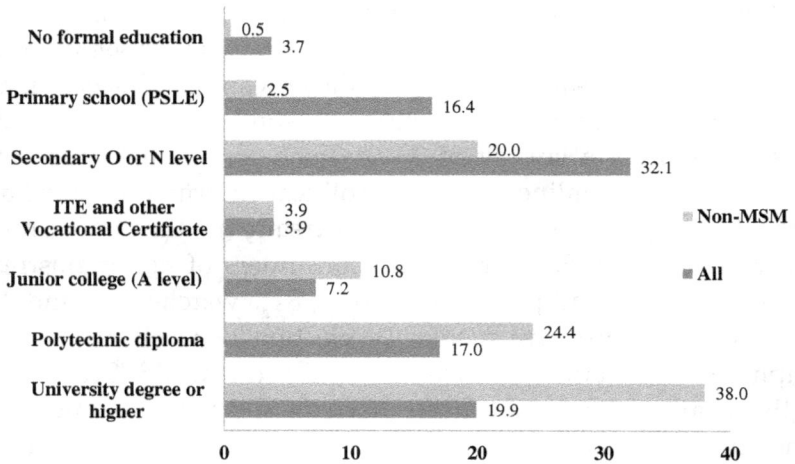

Figure 7: Level of education of all and non-MSM respondents

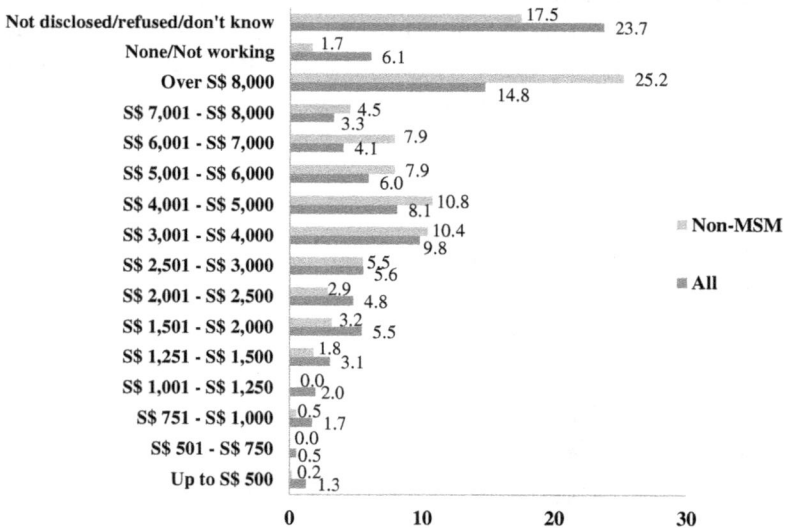

Figure 8: Household income of all and non-MSM respondents

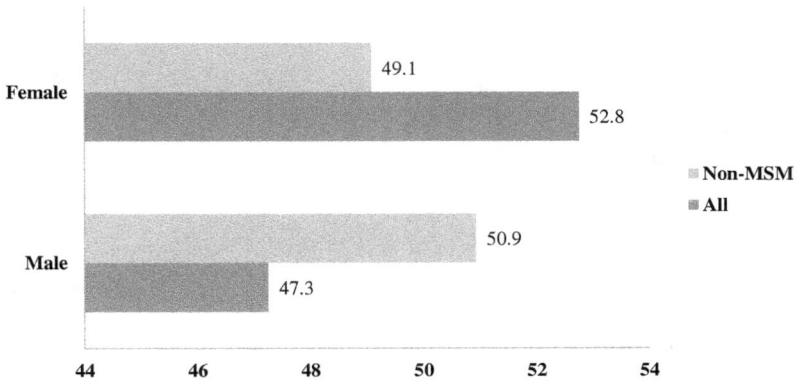

Figure 9: Gender of all and non-MSM respondents

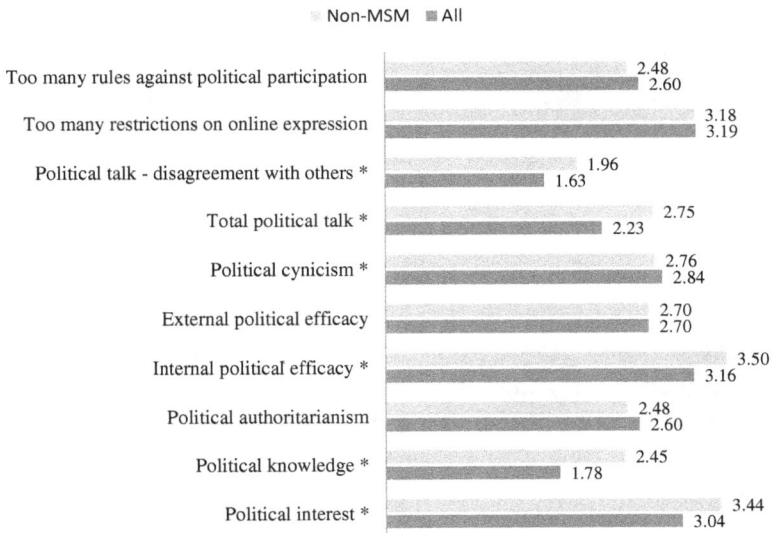

Figure 10: Political traits of all and non-MSM respondents

Notes: Political knowledge scale is from 0–5, and all others are from 1–5.
*Indicates a statistically significant difference between all and non-MSM.
External efficacy = belief that government responds to one; Political authoritarianism = does not believe in political freedom.

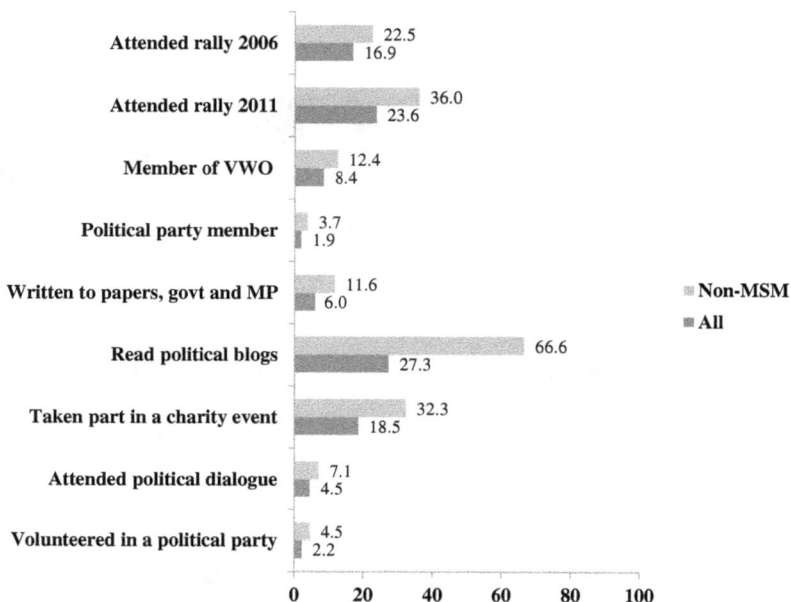

Figure 11: Percentage of all and non-MSM respondents who took part in various political activities

In terms of *political traits* (Figure 10), non-MSM users also tended to talk more about the election with others; to disagree more with others about the election when they talked; to be more politically knowledgeable and interested; to be less politically cynical (that is, less distrustful of politicians' motives); and to have higher political internal efficacy (belief that they could understand and hence take part in politics). They were not significantly different for the other variables.

In terms of *political participation*, the non-MSM consumers tended to have higher offline and online political participation (Figure 11). They were more likely to take part in online forums and write comments online, be members of voluntary welfare organisations (VWOs) and take part in charity events, attend election rallies and dialogues. But their participation, like the general population, was still low in absolute terms.

Media Importance and Trust

Respondents were also asked about the importance of various media as sources of election information, and how much they trusted them. The media categories were: TV, radio, newspapers, party websites, party brochures, rallies, Facebook, Twitter, YouTube, blogs, SMSes, talking with others. As can be seen from Figure 12, the most important sources for the whole sample were newspapers and television and the least were SMS and Twitter. Compared to the 70% who did not use Facebook or alternative online media as sources of election news, the 30% who were non-MSM users rated all the above media (except for TV and radio) as more important sources of election information.

Figure 12 also shows that the most trusted sources for both the non-MSM users and the other 70% were newspapers and TV while the least were SMS and Twitter. However, a higher proportion of the 70% trusted mainstream sources such as newspaper and TV than that for non-MSM users. Both groups trusted radio about equally.

Other Attitudes Towards Media

The non-MSM consumers were more likely than the rest to be influenced by all the above categories of media in how they voted (Figure 13). They were more likely to think there was too much government control of mainstream media but not more likely to think there were too many restrictions on online expression. Among the whole sample, mainstream media were seen to be slightly less fair than Facebook, blogs, and Twitter when reporting the election (Figure 14). The 30% were also less likely than the rest to think MSM was fair when reporting the election. Interestingly, they were also a little less likely than the rest to think blogs, Facebook, and Twitter were fair in reporting the elections.

Voting Behaviour

Figure 15 shows that only 50.5% of respondents were willing to reveal how they voted. Table 1 shows how the votes went on Polling Day.

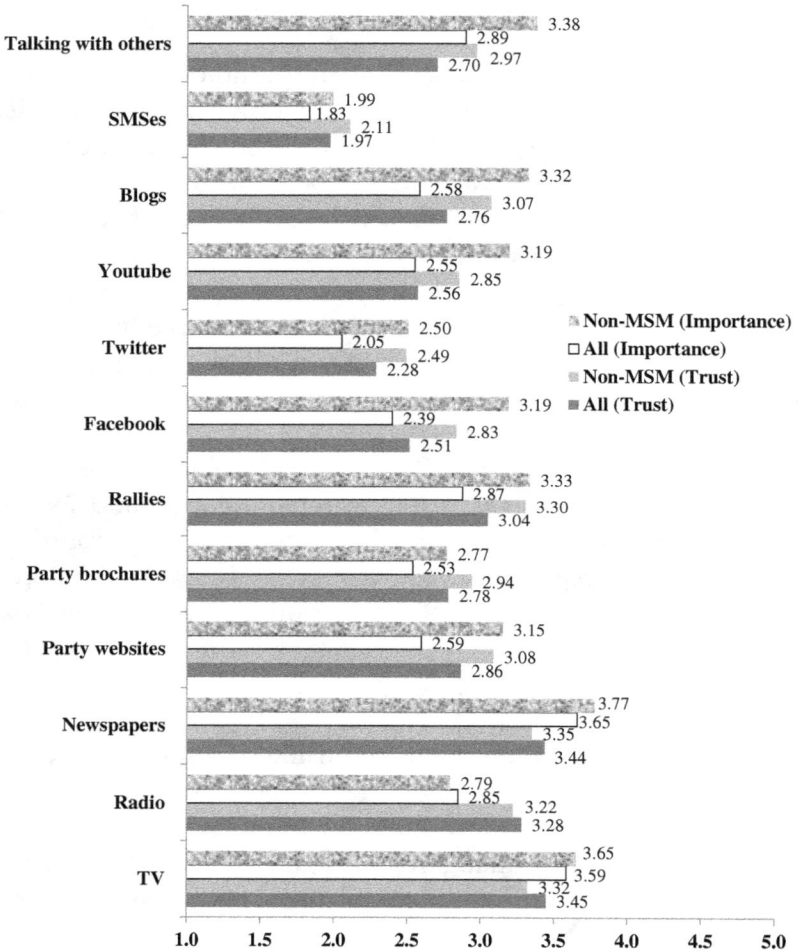

Figure 12: Importance of and trust in various media types for all and non-MSM respondents

Notes: Respondents were asked these questions:

How *important* was each of the following as a source of information about the recent election? 1 = Unimportant; 5 = Very Important. "I don't Knows" range from 7% to 36%.

How *trustworthy* was each of the following as a source of information about the election? 1 = Untrustworthy; 5 = Very Trustworthy; "I Don't Knows" range from 10% to 45%.

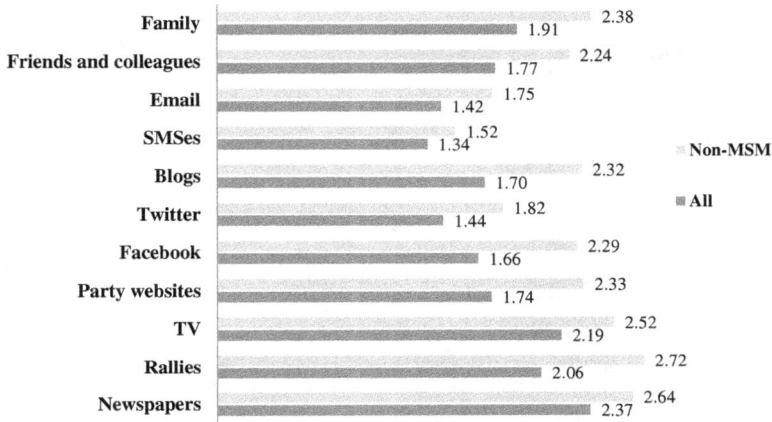

Figure 13: Influence of different sources on voting

Notes: Respondents were asked: "During the election, how much did the following influence how you decided to vote? 1 = no influence at all; 5 = a lot of influence. "I Don't Knows" range from 7% to 28% of all.

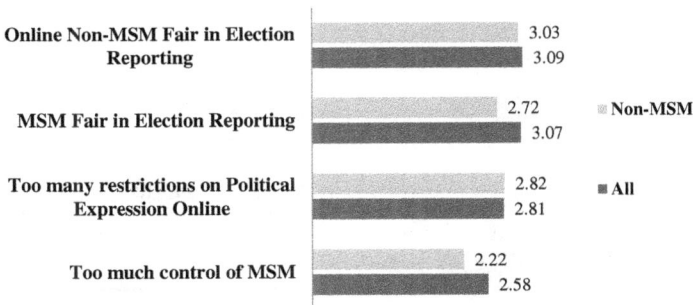

Figure 14: Media fairness and control

Notes: Respondents were asked whether different media were fair in reporting the election and whether there were too many restrictions on different media (on a scale of 1 to 5).

Compared to the actual voting figures it should be noted that:

1. Among all the respondents, the ratio of those who said they voted for the PAP over those who said they voted for the opposition was

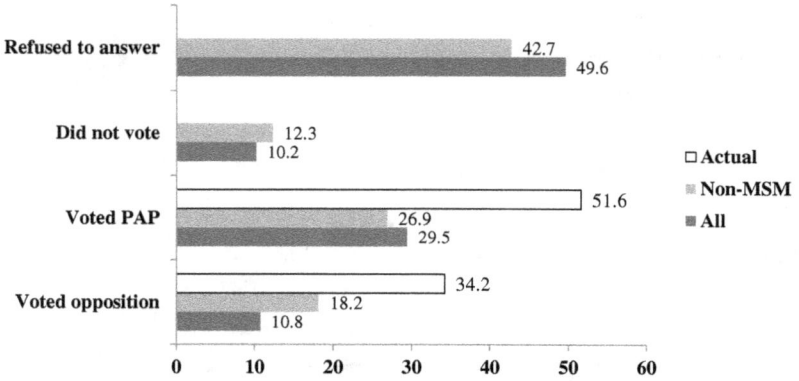

Figure 15: How respondents voted

Table 1. How the votes went in GE2011

Electoral Roll 2,350,875				
In Walkover Constituency 139,771	In Contested Constituencies 2,211,102			
	Voted 2,060,874			Did Not Vote 150,729
	Valid Votes 2,016,159		Spoiled Votes 44,715	
	Voted PAP 1,212,154	Voted opposition 804,005		
As Percentage of Electoral Roll	5.90%	85.80%		1.90% 6.40%
		51.60% 34.20%		
As Percentage of Valid Votes		60.10% 39.90%		

2.73, compared to the ratio of the actual votes for the PAP over those for the opposition on Polling Day, which was 1.51. This suggests fear or other reasons on the part of those who voted for the opposition to reveal their vote.

2. Among the non-MSM consumers, the ratio of those who said they voted for the PAP over those who said they voted for the opposition was 1.47, compared to the ratio of 1.51 of the actual votes for the PAP over those for the opposition on Polling Day.
3. The non-MSM users were less likely than the rest to refuse to say how they voted.

SMS

Despite the high penetration rate of mobile phones, only 13.2% received election-related information via SMS and just 4.6% shared those election-related messages with others via SMS. Some 6.5% wrote election-related SMSes of their own. Only 9.9% shared election material by e-mail, Facebook or Twitter.

Visits to Party Websites

Surprisingly, party websites were not much used (Figure 16) for election information. Even the two most popular websites (PAP and WP's) were visited by less than half of the respondents during the election fortnight.

Viral Material

During the elections, there were a number of instances when content became viral, circulating via e-mail and other platforms such as Facebook and blogs. For the survey, we chose four such instances from various media:

1. Satirical videos of the controversial PAP candidate Tin Pei Ling.
2. A mock e-mail in which political parties were compared to domestic maid agencies.
3. Collages where the faces of candidates were superimposed over those of superheroes in movie posters.
4. Videos of candidates speaking at rallies.

Figure 17 shows that all of these "viral" content were seen by less than half of the sample.

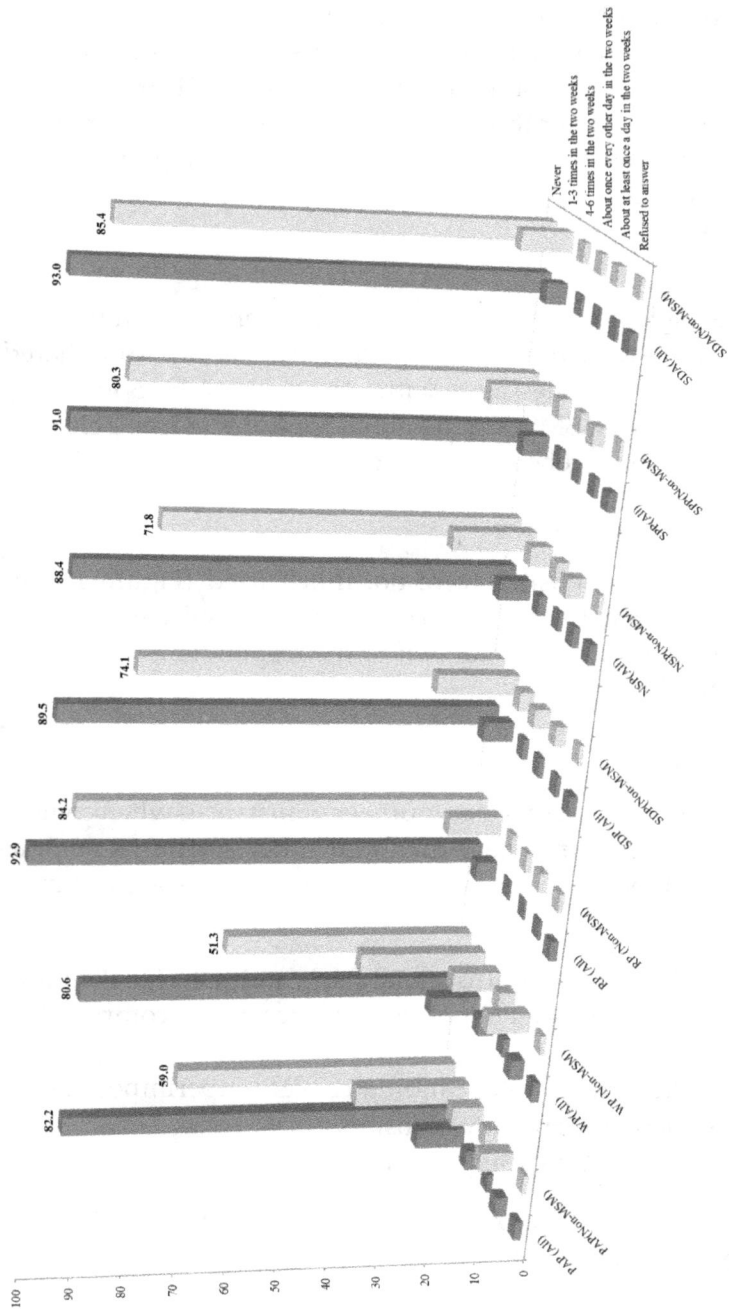

Figure 16: Visits to party websites during the election period
Note: See Appendix 2 for the names of these political parties.

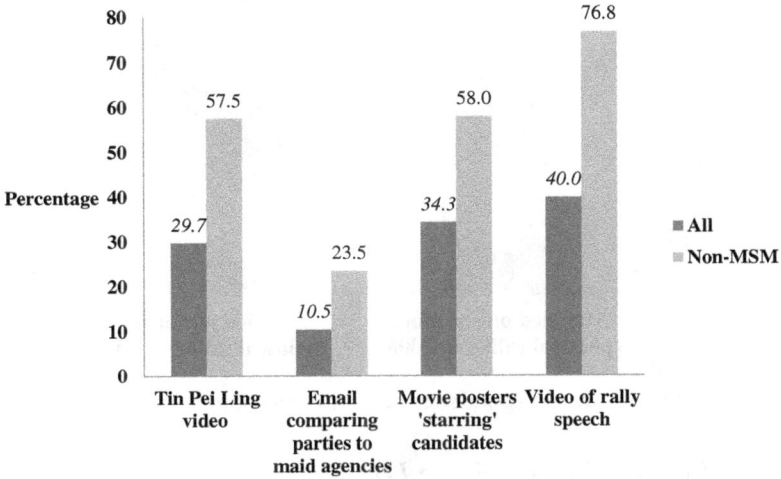

Figure 17:   Respondents' exposure to viral material

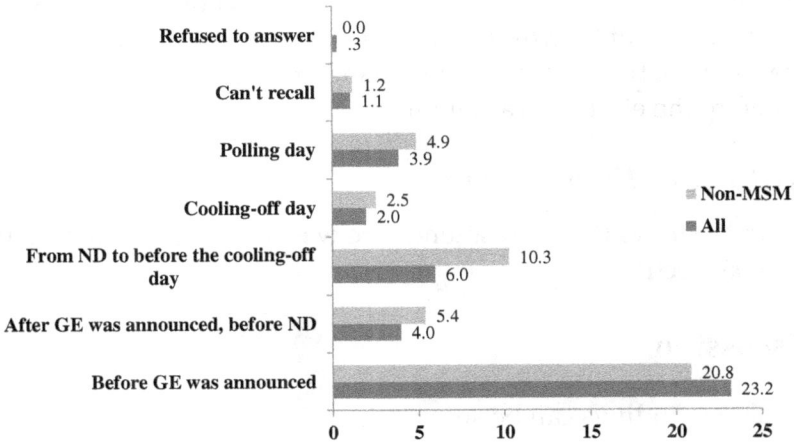

Figure 18:   When the mind was made up

Notes: All and non-MSM respondents were asked when their mind was made up on who to vote for.
ND: Nomination Day
GE: General Election

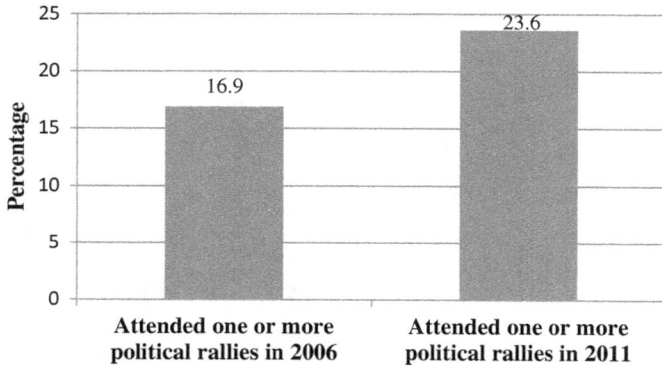

Figure 19: Respondents' attendance at political rallies

When the Mind was Made Up

The 51.4% of the interviewees who revealed who they voted for were asked when they decided who to vote for. Figure 18 shows their responses, given as percentages of the whole sample. As can be seen, 23.2% of the whole sample (that is, 57.6% of the 51.4% who revealed who they voted for) had made up their mind whom to vote for before the election was announced.

Political Rally Attendance

Figure 19 shows that rally attendance was higher in GE2011 than in the 2006 election.

Discussion

The above findings can be summarised thus:

1. The consumption of non-MSM election content (alternative online media and Facebook) was considerably lower than that of MSM content.
2. Consumption of election content via online channels was much lower than offline.
3. Almost all consumers of non-MSM election content also consumed MSM content.

4. Voters rarely visited party websites.
5. E-mail and SMS were not widely used by both parties and voters as channels for election information.
6. Non-MSM had a low influence on how people voted, and that influence is lower than that of MSM.
7. Non-MSM media was less trusted and less important than MSM as sources of election information.
8. Most respondents did not see the most popular online viral material.
9. Voters decided on their vote before the election, implying that there was little impact of all media during the campaign period.

In sum, the findings show that during the campaign period the direct influence of the Internet (indeed of all media) on voting outcome was limited.

However, two concerns need to be addressed here. First, although the direct influence of the Internet was not large, there is the possibility of a two-step flow of information (Katz and Lazarsfeld, 1955), that is, election information did not travel directly from the media to most individuals but arrived via opinion leaders who had consumed the media. This study does not explore this question directly. However, several findings from this survey indicate that the two-step flow might not be a major factor. First, there was very little political/election talk among voters, so the information was not flowing between people. Second, voters did not send that many things they saw online to others, either via e-mail or SMS.

The second concern is that while the Internet had little influence during the short election period, it probably had an important influence in the two or three years leading up to the election. In particular, the Internet allowed political issues to be aired and to remain on the political agenda on an unprecedented scale. Issues brought up by online alternative media about the increasingly high number of foreigners, the crowded public transport system and the rising cost of housing were kept alive longer both on MSM and on alternative media sites and they probably contributed to the erosion of support for the PAP.

In addition, over the last few years and in particular during the election, the Internet could also have had important and lasting psychological effects on the public at large. Even if it changed few people's minds during the campaign, it led to a range of impacts which include changing the experience of participating in an election; enhancing engagement of citizens with the election process; breaking through psychological barriers of fear, self-doubt and of being alone; establishing a sense of community; engendering or increasing the democratic impulse; and empowering by nurturing political mobilisation and action. These are long-term impacts that should not be downplayed.

However, these concerns do not distract from the basic and clear findings of this study. Thus it may be concluded that the 2011 GE was not the "Internet" election it was predicted to be by many observers. It should also be noted that there is little or no evidence that the alternative online media content during the election or just earlier played a causal role in the significant decline of votes for PAP — as some PAP members lamented or as some bloggers had hoped for. Equally importantly, the study also shows a clear increase in the use and influence of the Internet in the political life of Singapore compared with the previous General Election. The power of the Internet is palpably on the rise.

References

Infocomm Development Authority of Singapore. "Infocomm Usage — Households and Individuals (Household Access to Internet, 2003–2011)". Available at http://www.ida.gov.sg/Infocomm-Landscape/Facts-and-Figures/Infocomm-Usage-Households-and-Individuals#2 (accessed 5 August 2013).

Karan, K., E. Kuo, and S.H. Lee *Singapore General Elections, 2001: Study of the Media Politics and Public*. Singapore: Asian Mass Communication Research and Information Centre, 2010.

Katz, E. and P. Lazarsfeld. *Personal Influence*. New York: Free Press, 1955.

Koh, G. "IPS Post-Election Survey 2006". Available at http://www.lkyspp.nus.edu.sg/ips/Survey_Report_postelection.aspx (accessed 19 March 2013).

Koh, G. "IPS Post-Election Survey 2011". Available at http://www.spp. nus.edu.sg/ips/docs/events/pops/POPS%204_May%2011_slides.pdf (accessed 19 March 2013).

Kuo, E., D. Holaday, and E. Peck. *Mirror on the Wall: Media in a Singapore Election*. Singapore: Asian Mass Communication Research and Information Centre, 1993.

Merdeka Centre. "Singapore General Election Public Opinion Poll 2011". Available at http://www.merdeka.org/v2/index.php?option=com_jotloader&section=files&task=download&cid=85_57e59045fc9302600d0c6bfb9f889441&Itemid=68 (accessed 13 March 2013).

Tan, T. H. and A. Mahizhnan. "Subverting Seriousness and Other Misdemeanours: Modes of Resistance Against OB Markers in the 2006 Singapore General Election". (2008) Available at http://www.spp. nus.edu.sg/ips/docs/pub/pa_TTHAM_Subverting%20Seriousness_AMIC_July%202008.pdf (accessed 12 November 2011).

Tan T.H., S.Y. Chung and W.Y. Zhang "Survey of Media Use and Political Traits". (2011). Available at http://www.spp.nus.edu.sg/ips/ACM_Survey_on_Political_Traits_and_Media_Use_2011.aspx (accessed 19 March 2013).

Wong, T. "Will GE2011 be a social media election?" *The Straits Times*, 18 March 2011, retrieved 19 March 2013 from Factiva database.

2

LEGAL LANDMINES AND OB MARKERS: SURVIVAL STRATEGIES OF ALTERNATIVE MEDIA

Cherian George

Abstract

The general election was an opportunity seized by "citizen journalism" websites to showcase the contribution they could make as alternative media in Singapore's political landscape. It was also a moment of choice. With little institutional baggage and few organisational restraints, bloggers could pick from a wide range of political stances and editorial strategies. This chapter examines the choices made by four leading websites: The Online Citizen (TOC), Temasek Review, Yawning Bread and the Singapore General Election Portal. It analyses where they situated themselves in relation to partisan politics, to other media, and to the electorate at large. It finds that while some adopted more populist approaches, others were more wary of ground sentiments and tried to maintain some professional distance from the public. These differences suggest that citizen journalism has not resolved the fundamental tensions between popular and elitist conceptions of democracy, and among competing normative notions of journalism's role. Rather than a failure to conform to some unitary professional norm, citizen journalism's diversity should perhaps be seen as a reflection of these tensions inherent in journalism's relationship to democracy.

Singapore's 2011 General Election (GE2011) was an opportunity for the country's alternative online media to stake their respective claims in an increasingly crowded public sphere. Although often talked about as if it is a homogeneous mass, the Internet in fact sustains a wide diversity of forms, with individuals and groups using cyberspace in myriad ways. Some engage in what has been loosely called "citizen journalism", but even this term obscures an array of distinctive approaches. Alternative media that plant themselves online start almost from scratch-facing low barriers to entry, little institutional baggage, and few organisational restraints, giving them multiple approaches to choose from. While most studies on the media and elections focus on voters' reception of media and the impact this makes on their behaviour — the demand side, as it were — this chapter is devoted to the supply side. It examines the strategic choices made by Singapore bloggers. While apparently united in their aim to compete with or complement established news organisations' influence over the national agenda, they were also divergent in their strategies and philosophies. In particular, this study focuses on their responses towards regulatory and resource obstacles, their approach towards fairness and balance, and where they situated themselves in relation to public opinion. Such decisions have consequences for the media landscape and the social construction of politics, not just during the General Election but also well beyond.

The four sites studied here are in a category of news media that usually call themselves independent socio-political blogs. They can be distinguished from various other websites that also played active roles in the General Election: the online platforms of news organisations such as newspapers and broadcasters, large Internet-only commercial organisations such as Yahoo!, the websites of political parties, online forums, and social networking sites. As I will elaborate in the next section, independent socio-political blogs tend to have explicitly journalistic missions, defining their roles in opposition to mainstream news organisations. Most of them are run by individuals. Prominent ones include Diary of a Singaporean Mind by "Lucky Tan"[1] and Ng E-Jay's SGPolitics.[2] Probably the best known and longest running, though, is Yawning Bread by

---

[1]http://singaporemind.blogspot.com

[2]http://www.sgpolitics.net

Alex Au.[3] Yawning Bread was accordingly selected for this study. Among group-run blogs, The Online Citizen (TOC) is the leading website that operates in the open.[4] It was another obvious choice for inclusion in this study. Although sympathetic to the opposition and various progressive causes, it has no formal affiliations with any party or civil society organisation. Two other notable group blogs were run by political organisations: Singaporeans For Democracy[5] and Think Centre.[6] Neither site was particularly active during the elections, perhaps because their activists were more directly involved in election work for opposition parties. Another type of group blog is the anonymously-run website, the most active of which was Temasek Review. An introductory message to Temasek Review's editors inviting them to take part in this research elicited a positive reply, but subsequent e-mails containing specific questions were unanswered. The site was taken down soon after the Presidential Election of 27 August 2011, but a Temasek Review Facebook page remained active. Although its editors were uncontactable, Temasek Review remains an important case and is included in this study. A final category of independent socio-political blogs is made up of aggregators, of which the most popular were probably Singapore Surf,[7] Singapore News Alternative,[8] and Singapore Daily.[9] The oldest is Singapore Window.[10] However, for this study, the Singapore General Election Portal (SGEP) was selected because it was set up specifically for the election. Its editors were, therefore, likely to have given the most thought to the issues explored here.[11] Editors of SGEP, Yawning Bread, and The Online Citizen were interviewed and their election output read closely

---

[3] http://www.yawningbread.org

[4] http://www.theonlinecitizen.com

[5] http://www.sfd.sg

[6] http://www.thinkcentre.org

[7] http://www.myapplemenu.com/singapore/

[8] http://singaporenewsalternative.blogspot.com

[9] http://singaporedaily.net

[10] http://www.singapore-window.org

[11] http://www.easyapps.sg/sgep

for insights into their editorial stances. For reasons already cited, Temasek Review was studied through its content alone.

Key Concepts and Concerns

The websites featured in this study were not expected to attract the biggest audiences. By that measure, large commercial news organisations' websites were likely to dominate — a prediction that subsequent surveys confirmed beyond any doubt (see Chapter 1 in this volume). Instead, this chapter's interest in independent socio-political blogs arises from their potential to add to Singapore's media diversity. They are able to practise journalism in a qualitatively different way from the mainstream, admitting voices and issues into the public sphere that might otherwise be marginalised (George, 2006). Indeed, their approach to journalism can be so distinct from the more familiar professional form that their status as "journalism" is often disputed. This, however, is mostly due to a lack of conceptual clarity about what journalism actually is. For decades, the term has been used without explication. Precise definitions were unnecessary because the field was dominated by narrow forms of practice, allowing them to be defined tautologically — journalism was what journalists did, and journalists were people who did journalism. The Internet has opened up access to previously restricted domains, demanding more precision in language. I define journalism as the use of observation, investigation, and analysis, to report and comment on current affairs, in order to help people comprehend change and engage in collective self-determination. Under this definition, journalism is not limited to the work of full-time professional journalists; it can be produced by amateurs. The term "citizen journalism" has been used to refer to ground-up practices such as blogging. However, it is a muddy term, sometimes used by traditional news organisations to describe their user generated content, and sometimes for projects that emerge from outside of the established media. Another weakness is that it suggests that journalism minus the "citizen" qualifier is restricted to top-down professionalised communication. In fact, journalism has always included diverse practices, ranging from the more elite and industrialised to the more amateur and small-scale (Schudson, 2003).

A more meaningful distinction has been drawn in media scholarship between mainstream and alternative media, based on where they stand in relation to the centres of political, economic, and cultural power in any given society. Alternative media are distinguished not just by their missions and content, but also by their forms: they tend to be small, less dependent on capital and labour, informally organised, and less bound by professional norms and standards (Atton and Hamilton, 2008; Downing, 2001). While these seem like weaknesses, such attributes remove barriers to democratic participation that afflict the mainstream, such as large news organisations' dependence on advertising revenue, their hierarchical newsrooms, and the arms-length relationship they maintain with the public. Alternative media are a broad category, covering newsletters of minority groups and political parties, fanzines, and the student press. One subset is what I have termed "contentious journalism" (George, 2006). It is contentious in two senses. First, it is deliberately transgressive towards the political status quo. Second, it challenges the norms of mainstream journalism, such as the way professionals interpret objectivity. The websites featured in this chapter are all examples of alternative media, and — in different ways — all practitioners of contentious journalism.

There is, however, no single or obviously superior formula for practising contentious journalism. Media activists heading in an "alternative" direction must still choose from among different routes. This study examines three specific choices that faced sociopolitical blogs in the General Election. They are as follows:

1. How would they manage practical constraints such as government regulation and a lack of resources? Alternative media have the quality of a social movement. They tend to possess a can-do spirit that finds openings where most see only obstacles. However, their formulae for overcoming hurdles can vary significantly.

2. What position would they adopt towards the different political parties? Partisan journalism has a tradition as long as the press itself. In the modern era, though, mainstream professional journalism in many countries has aspired to an image of fairness and balance, betraying no obvious bias towards one party or another. This study asks bloggers if they hold similar norms, and if not, why not.
3. How would they relate to the broader public? Again, there is a spectrum of possible strategies. Editors and writers can consider themselves as organically entwined with their constituency, or try to keep a professional distance from the readers they serve. They can lean towards a more representational role, or a more guiding function.

The blogs studied here may all engage in contentious online journalism, but the choices above were not predetermined. Each represents a fork in the road. Collectively, such decisions will shape the emerging online public sphere.

Regulatory and Resource Restrictions

Alternative media have found the Internet to be a radically open platform compared with earlier modes of communication. It is the only medium for mass communication in Singapore that does not require producers and distributors to apply for government permits. Singapore-based websites are brought within the regulatory fold en masse through a so-called "class licence", but this does not amount to a system of prior censorship, unlike the discretionary licensing systems for operating newspapers and television or radio stations. Internet service providers are required to observe a code of practice, and must block websites if instructed to do so by the regulator. However, the authorities have refrained from using these powers against any political site, largely keeping their promise to manage the Internet with a "light touch". Singapore websites can be ordered to register themselves as political or religious sites, requiring them to declare their editors' identities, sources of funding and other details. Only a handful of political sites — none of them individual blogs — have been asked to register. Registration is supposed to make such sites more accountable, which in theory could have a chilling effect. In practice, however, much depends on the attitude of a site's owners. The Online Citizen — the only one of the four studied websites that was asked to register — took it on the chin, even organising a party to celebrate the event.

More worrisome for blogs than the class licence and registration regime were the various post-publication actions taken by the government since 2001 under laws concerning defamation, sedition, political films, and other offences. Election advertising regulations have also been used to dampen the impact of the Internet during the campaign period. By and large, though, bloggers in previous elections showed that they were undeterred by the lack of guaranteed freedoms. In 2006, for example, the use of online video was rampant despite some confusion over whether it was or was not permissible under the election advertising rules. Perhaps acknowledging that some of the restrictions were redundant and unenforceable, the government significantly liberalised online campaigning regulations in time for the 2011 poll. Online videos, for example, were expressly permitted. Restrictions specific to registered political sites' activities during the campaign period were also removed. In 2006, a registered political site like TOC, as well as political parties, would have had to confine itself largely to static content during the campaign period. By 2011, most of such restrictions were lifted and TOC's coverage of the campaign was not noticeably hampered by its registration.

However, 2011 did see a newly-imposed restriction, in the form of a "Cooling Off Day". This extended the long established ban on any fresh election advertising on Polling Day, to cover the eve of Polling Day as well. The law defined "election advertising" in typical catch-all terms. In addition to explicit calls to vote for this or that party, "election advertising" was deemed to include any material that could "reasonably be regarded as intended" to "enhance the standing of" any of the contenders — "even though it can reasonably be regarded as intended to achieve any other purpose as well and even though it does not expressly mention the name of any political

party or candidate" (Section 2). To allow news media to do their job
of carrying campaign reports on Polling Day and its eve without
being caught by this driftnet provision, the law states that the
ban on election advertising does not apply to the publication of
election news (Section 78B). Going by the spirit of the law, it could
be argued that coverage by socio-political blogs should enjoy the
same exemption from the ban as established news organisations,
since both are directed at fulfilling the same social function of
informing and educating voters about their choices. However, the
letter of the law provided no such refuge for the blogs. The news
exemption applied only to news "in a newspaper in any medium"
licensed under the Newspaper and Printing Presses Act (essentially,
mainstream newspapers and their websites) or in licensed radio or
television broadcasters' programmes. Technically, therefore, a blog
that posted campaign articles on "Cooling Off Day" or Polling Day
could be deemed to have the intention of enhancing a candidate's
standing, thus violating the Act and facing a fine of S$1,000 and up
to a year in jail.

Temasek Review, unsurprisingly, ignored the rule. Run anony-
mously, with editors widely assumed to be based overseas, the site
evidently relished its impunity. In contrast, SGEP decided that it
would observe the letter of the law. The Singapore General Election
Portal was owned by Tan Kin Lian, the former chief executive
of NTUC Income who became a champion of the common man
after the Lehman Brothers collapse left small investors in the lurch.
While listing courage among his key values, Tan stated categorically
before the election that his site would observe "Cooling Off Day."
It duly stopped posting at 11 p.m. the night before, resuming
only after the close of polling. However, SGEP's policy was not
typical of the blogs, even those run by real-named individuals
within easy reach of the authorities. Alex Au, for one, published
a 1,600-word review and commentary on "Cooling Off Day," clearly
advocating a vote for the opposition. The respective policies of
SGEP and Yawning Bread may not have been due to differing
appetites for confrontation — Tan went on to contest the Presidential
Election, after all. Au, considerably more experienced, probably had

more self-confidence in assessing the risk. Furthermore, they were engaged in a different kind of struggle. While Tan was a relative newcomer to blogging and probably saw the Internet as peripheral to his wider political mission, Au and many other established bloggers are more passionate and protective about the online space that they occupy. For example, Au had been one of the leaders of the "Bloggers 13" network (of which this author was also a member) lobbying for greater Internet freedom a few years earlier. Such individuals may be more likely to resist, on principle, Internet restrictions that they consider unjust.

This was certainly the stand of Andrew Loh of TOC. Interviewed before the GE, he said that he was inclined to challenge the election advertising moratorium. "On principle, it's ridiculous that there are media that are not subject to the rule while ordinary citizens are not allowed to speak up," he said. Under Loh's editorship, TOC posted one article on "Cooling Off Day" and another on Polling Day. Such behaviour in 2011 was in line with what had already been observed in 2006: while there was a frenzy of online indignation when election restrictions were announced, most simply ignored rules that they considered to be unclear or unreasonable when the campaign got under way. As the government has so far shown no desire to criminalise the behaviour of large numbers of Singaporeans, bloggers have found some safety in numbers.

More clear-cut are the well-established limits relating to defamation and contempt of court. Those who operate openly and within Singapore's jurisdiction tend not to take chances with these laws. However, as careful as such blogs may try to be with their own articles, they may find it hard to police readers' comments. The Online Citizen received a lawyer's letter claiming that a People's Action Party (PAP) politician was defamed in an article that a reader had posted in a TOC comments section. The comment, when eventually located by the TOC editors, was duly removed. The same comment, though, had been circulating in Temasek Review, which was harder for regulators and lawyers to reach. When its successor site, TREmeritus, decided that one of its editors should come out into the open in early 2012, he was instantly served with a lawyer's letter threatening a defamation suit over a contributor's commentary that cast aspersions on the high-level appointment of the prime minister's wife.

Along with being asked to register, The Online Citizen was gazetted as a political association to bring it within the ambit of the Political Donations Act, a law enacted to prevent money politics infecting the electoral process. The action against TOC marked the first instance of the Political Donations Act being used to restrict a media operation (fundraising restrictions were later incorporated into a new regulatory regime introduced in 2013). The Registry of Political Donations said that TOC had "the potential to influence opinions and shape political outcomes in Singapore" and that it had to be gazetted to ensure that it was not funded by foreign elements. This law blocks gazetted groups from accepting anonymous donations above a total amount of S$5,000 a year, as well as banning foreign funding entirely. Since the site had already given up on its dreams of becoming Singapore's Malaysiakini — an online news operation that had enough funds from subscriptions and overseas grants to employ more than 20 full-time journalists — the new restrictions did not impede TOC's plans to cover the election. Indeed, insiders said that the government action was, overall, probably a windfall. The move in the run-up to the polls implicitly anointed TOC as the leading alternative website. The attention galvanised its existing volunteers and attracted new ones. It mustered around 40 volunteers in total, with 20-odd working each day of the campaign. This was less than half of what Loh had hoped for before the election. But, it was enough to provide video, tweets, Facebook postings and original reporting throughout the campaign. Its volunteer technical support was able to cope with the increased traffic, unlike Temasek Review, whose service was interrupted by overloading early in the campaign. Donations also streamed in. The Online Citizen's coffers were sufficiently healthy for it to treat volunteers and well-wishers to a thank-you dinner soon after the election.

The Online Citizen was the only site that encountered shots across its bow as it approached the May 2011 election. Temasek

Review was outside the regulators' reach, while Yawning Bread and SGEP received no direct warnings. Overall, the legal fairways had widened for socio-political blogs since 2006, even for TOC. What continued to choke socio-political blogs, though, were their resource constraints. None of them were commercially viable; all depended on volunteer labour. Professional journalism's commercial basis is double-edged. On the one hand, it can compromise professional autonomy by forcing publishers and editors to make commercial calculations that may deviate from the public interest. On the other, a healthy revenue stream gives media the wherewithal to employ large teams of full-time journalists. The alternative websites' vows of poverty — whether voluntary or imposed — limited what they were able to do. Lacking even a small fraction of the resources needed for comprehensive news coverage of the election, they aimed to supplement rather than substitute the work of mainstream news organisations. Each project tried to carve a niche that would make best use of its resources.

Like other one-man-operated blogs, Yawning Bread focused on commentary. However, Alex Au, a 59-year-old businessman, was able to take advantage of his flexible schedule to attend rallies and report directly from a nomination centre. He had discovered the value of original reporting by accident. Having a habit of taking copious notes at civil society events he used to attend, he found that these were sometimes the most detailed or only public record of meetings that were sketchily reported or completely ignored by mainstream media. This realisation developed into a more conscious strategy of supplementing commentary and armchair analysis with first-hand reportage. Au averaged one substantive post a day from Nomination Day to Polling Day. His posts included standard bloggers' fare of critiquing mainstream media coverage and PAP statements as reported in the press, but most were based on attending rallies, following parties on their constituency visits and interviewing candidates. Unable to provide comprehensive coverage of the campaign, he selected topics that he felt would add value to the political debate, including themes of personal interest to him, such as sexual politics.

Another 59-year-old, Gerald Ho, ran Tan Kin Lian's SGEP from home, spending as much as 18 hours a day during the election period to sift through others' coverage and select and summarise the best articles. Ho, who had no previous journalism experience or training, devised his own techniques for single-handedly dealing with the large volume of information out there. Realising that noteworthy articles consistently came from the same set of online sources, he set up RSS feeds to compile what he called a "Division 1" folder of articles from those sources. This would receive his immediate attention. Later, he would scan other bloggers and aggregators to check if he had missed anything significant. His daily work cycle was also planned to maximise his effectiveness. Ho grew familiar with when to expect new postings from which sources. The *Today* newspaper would upload its daily edition before 6 a.m., while some individual bloggers such as Alex Au had a habit of posting after midnight, he noted. Accordingly, he went to bed after 1 a.m. and woke up before 5 a.m. every day, with a short afternoon nap and brief breaks for meals.

Fairness and Balance

The principles of fairness and balance have been at the core of professional journalism for around a century. However, their centrality to journalism's mission has always been problematic and contested, as there is an even longer tradition of partisan journalism that prevails to greater or lesser extents in different societies (Stephens, 1988; Hallin and Mancini, 2004). It should not be surprising, therefore, if alternative media do not conform to professional journalism's dominant paradigm of non-partisanship. The most striking characteristic of Singapore's political blogs is that they are all on the same side of the ideological fence: all identify with the opposition underdogs. They see mainstream media as biased against the opposition and try to level the political playing field.

"The mainstream media covers more establishment views. We try to balance it with other views," said SGEP owner Tan Kin Lian. Added Gerald Ho, "The field is lopsided. Even if we don't put out the mainstream media view, you'll still get to know it." Such blogs are not necessarily pro-opposition by policy, but believe that the best way they can contribute is to provide a platform for voices that are neglected by mainstream media. Lacking the resources to provide comprehensive coverage, they have identified a niche that they believe is under-served. Said Andrew Loh, "We are not supportive of any opposition party, but we recognise that they don't have a platform." These websites do not believe it is their responsibility to aim for balance within their websites, claiming instead to provide a counterweight on an already unbalanced media landscape. "We have never claimed to be 'balanced'," noted Loh. Joshua Chiang, who was TOC editor shortly before the election, added, "We *are* the balance."

Thus, critics who accuse the blogs of being unfair or one-sided are right, but may fail to realise that their criticism is unlikely to cause bloggers sleepless nights. Their goal is not necessarily more balance within their individual blogs, but a more balanced media system. Such a vision is not unique to bloggers. A major school of thought within media scholarship shares the view that "societies' media reforms should strive to develop media diversity" — achieving balance of perspectives and approaches across media — rather than investing all hope in supposedly balanced and comprehensive media outlets from the same mould (Curran, 2002; Baker, 2002).

The bloggers are similarly unimpressed by the norm of profes-sional disinterest or objectivity so carefully cultivated by the press for over a century. In a 2010 survey of journalists at Singapore Press Holdings and MediaCorp, most were uncomfortable with the role of shaping public opinion: under 6% of respondents said it was extremely important to set the political agenda for their society. Instead, they prized their informant role: the majority (58.6%) rated it as extremely important to get information to the public (Hao and George, 2012, pp. 91–103). In contrast, bloggers interviewed in this study refer spontaneously to the values that drive them, seeing no conflict between these and their roles as writers and editors. Alex Au, Tan Kin Lian, and the founders of TOC pointed out that they were activists before they were journalists. They continue to have clear ideas of what they want to achieve through their journalism. TOC's website says:

> Advocacy journalism champions causes and values like civic participation, open government and free media. The advocacy journalist makes no attempt to be "even handed" with the injustices of their day. He or she has seen through the illusory "objectivity" and has assumed partisan positions from every point on the socio-political spectrum. He or she is more of an activist with a blog and hence the name "blogivist" (The Online Citizen).

While it does not explicitly state which issues it champions, it has a record of supporting various progressive causes, such as free speech, gender equality, gay rights, and worker rights. Andrew Loh and Joshua Chiang described the kind of impact they desired: they could take up important social issues that mainstream media were neglecting, such as mistreatment of foreign workers and homelessness in Singapore. "We can stick with an issue," Loh said. "We are like a small, commando unit; we can fight for things." As for Alex Au, he first emerged in the public sphere as a gay activist and saw no need to conceal his ideological stand in his election writing. One of his posts tracked candidates' statements on gay rights. His broader mission and "strategic purpose", though, was to raise the level of political discourse, including within the opposition. Temasek Review did not explicitly state where it stood, but its opposition sympathies were clear from its postings.

Public Opinion

Most professional journalists say that their first duty is to the public. And most blogs present themselves as representing a more authentic discourse than the mainstream media. Yet, it is clear that the blogs are not a mirror on society. Middle-of-the-road opinion in Singapore is either neutral or pro-PAP — as would be shown yet again in GE2011 — while, as noted in the previous section, the blogs speak up for the opposition and other progressive causes. The blogs' relationship to public opinion is thus not straightforward. In a society dominated by a hegemonic party, alternative media are forced to confront the reality that many of the readers that they are trying to serve do not share their values or visions. Accordingly, the editors interviewed in this study expressed misgivings about the public. They were not comfortable with simply following public opinion because they did not trust prevailing popular sentiments on some of the issues they cared about. And they were under no illusions that the majority of Singaporeans wanted radical democratisation. If only because of decades of indoctrination, the public was resistant to deep political change.

For this reason, most of the bloggers saw themselves engaged in a long-term ideological struggle, more than in a scrap for votes in the election. Winning seats for the opposition was less important than opening people's minds to democratic ideas, as only the latter would lay the foundations for a more just society. "It's pointless to change the government if the people are still the same," as Joshua Chiang put it. Raising the political maturity of Singaporeans meant refusing to pander to them just to increase their viewership. In Gerald Ho's view, the goal was to incrementally grow the audience for quality debate. He said, "Even if it's just 1%, let's make that 1% secure."

The Online Citizen and Yawning Bread, which have both championed progressive causes — gay rights, economic justice, migrant worker issues, freedom of expression, and capital punishment, in particular — know from experience that these are not particularly popular with the majority of Singaporeans. Such issues are closest to these bloggers' hearts but do not usually generate the most positive response from their readers, who instead seem to prefer articles that simply poke fun at the government. Indeed, articles that stand up for the rights of migrant workers sometimes bring out the reactionary right-wing tendencies within Singapore's netizens. Describing some readers as "simplistic" and "xenophobic", Au said candidly, "I'm engaging in a war with my readers. It annoys me to no end."

Therefore, these sites did not think of themselves as taking part in a popularity contest. They of course tracked their page views and unique visitors — and drew immense satisfaction from rising numbers during the campaign — but they were reluctant to let this dictate their sense of what is important. Their ambiguous and fraught relationship with mass opinion was most apparent in their policies on reader comments. At one extreme, Temasek Review appeared to practise no moderation of comments, implicitly adhering to the principle that every member of its reading public deserved to have his opinion aired on its platform, regardless of what he or she said. In contrast, for SGEP editor Gerald Ho, off-the-wall comments risked diluting the website's own content. Indeed, he did not put it past agents of the government or ruling party to pump blogs with wildly anti-government comments, in order to distract readers from the ideas being presented in the original articles and, at the same time, to tarnish the site's credibility. Like most aggregators, SGEP carried no comments. The Online Citizen had an active comments section, with editors practising post-moderation. The high volume of comments, though, was hard for them to cope with. As a result, most comments remained on the site. For Yawning Bread, Alex Au was firmly in favour of pre-moderation: comments were only cleared for posting after he had made a positive decision to allow them. "I want to raise the IQ level of political discourse," he said.

Such diversity in approaches to managing public opinion should not be surprising — the distinction between mass-market popular tabloids and the elite press, with the former essentially following public opinion while the latter aimed to lead it, was found in journalism long before the arrival of new media. Indeed, this is a symptom of a deeper, unresolved tension at the heart of democratic theories of journalism. In striving for more democratic journalism, various critiques have oscillated between two opposing views of the public, notes Muhlmann (2010). On one side, an innocent public is seen as let down by guilty journalists — but this fails to consider the public's role in sustaining mediocre journalism. On the other side, the public is blamed for the poor state of the media — but this slips into an elitist position that sounds dangerously anti-democratic. Thus, how we conceive of the public turns out to be central to the exercise of critiquing journalism.

No Convergence

The online space provided Singaporeans with an intense experience during the election. While many appreciated the work done by independent alternative media, it was less clear where this momentum would or should lead. The starkest choice is between the underground approach of Temasek Review and the open engagement of The Online Citizen. The anonymously-edited Temasek Review's survival strategy was to stay out of reach rather than within the law. It was able to channel a regular stream of patently defamatory anti-PAP material into the public sphere. With no apparent policy of fact-checking, it became Singapore's de facto rumour site. Temasek Review's guerilla, hit-and-run operation is the most common mode of operation for online dissidents in authoritarian regimes, so the wonder is that it is not more widely used in Singapore, where whatever freedom bloggers enjoy is not legally guaranteed.

It is noteworthy that when Singapore's first group-run independent online magazine, Sintercom, was required to register as a political website before the 2001 election, it chose to wind up in protest. It resurfaced overseas, showing that extra-territoriality is always an option for Internet activists. However, Sintercom's subsequent swift decline from being Singapore's most influential alternative online project to oblivion also showed that such a strategy comes with a cost. Thus, when TOC was asked to register ten years later, it responded by throwing a party, signalling to its supporters that it was here to stay.

The Online Citizen, more exposed to political risk, has had to be more careful. Arguably, however, this limitation is outweighed by the benefits of being able to network face to face with the wider community. The Online Citizen founders decided that they would operate transparently in order to build credibility. Being seen as trustworthy was important not only to develop a loyal audience, but also to build a team of volunteer reporters. In addition, TOC's out-in-the-open approach enabled it to work with like-minded civil society organisations on various campaigns, and to hold events involving established political groups and individuals. The clearest sign of the benefits of TOC's transparency was its success in organising the pre-election inter-party forum in December 2010, followed by a presidential debate in August 2011.

Temasek Review's ethereal existence meant that it was disconnected not just from the authorities but also from other Singapore groups pushing for democratisation. It was unusual in carrying no links or references to other blogs — almost all other sites exchange links and acknowledge others' contribution to the political debate. Its deliberately individualistic stand could be why its mysterious closure in September 2011 generated no significant expressions of concern or solidarity in the rest of the blogosphere. When it was resuscitated as TREmeritus, one editor outed himself as the face of the editorial team. He said that this step was taken to increase the confidence of sources who might have tip-offs for the site. Given that there has always been a layer of hardcore anti-government Singaporeans, the closure of Temasek Review website did not spell the end of its particular brand of no-holds-barred contentious journalism. New underground websites as well as anonymous posts on forums and social networking sites eventually filled the gap.

For decades, Singapore was served by a dominant model of journalism, which was simultaneously empowered by its commercial success and constrained by legal and political restrictions. The Internet has opened up the field to more diverse forms of journalism. Several of these were on show in the General Election of 2011. One common question that has greeted the rise of citizen media is whether they will ever replace mainstream journalism. But that line of enquiry is based on a mistaken expectation of convergence or substitution. Even within the blogosphere, there is no homogeneity. This study helps to explain why. The editorial choices faced by Singapore bloggers are ultimately dilemmas with no obvious answers. They involve trade-offs, reflecting unresolved tensions in the democratic role of journalism. We can be sure that alternative media will continue to evolve in Singapore, and we can be equally sure that they will not converge around a set of common norms. They will continue to be fragmented and diverse in their interpretations of their journalistic missions.

References

Atton, C. and J.F. Hamilton. *Alternative Journalism* (London: Sage, 2008).

Baker, C.E. *Media, Markets, and Democracy* (Cambridge: Cambridge University Press, 2002).

Curran, J. *Media and Power* (London: Routledge, 2002).

Downing, J.D.H. *Radical Media: Rebellious Communication and Social Movements* (Thousand Oaks, CA: Sage, 2001).

George, C. *Contentious Journalism and the Internet: Toward Democratic Discourse in Malaysia and Singapore* (Singapore: National University of Singapore Press, 2006).

Hallin, D.C. and P. Mancini. *Comparing Media Systems: Three Models of Media and Politics* (Cambridge, UK: Cambridge University Press, 2004).

Hao, X. and C. George. "Singapore Journalism: Buying into a Winning Formula". In *The Global Journalist in the 21st Century*, David H.W. and L. Willnat (New York, NY: Routledge, 2012).

Muhlmann, G. *Journalism for Democracy* (Cambridge: Polity, 2010).

Schudson, M. *The Sociology of News* (New York: Norton, 2003).

Stephens, M. *A History of News* (New York: Viking, 1988).

The Online Citizen. "About Us". Available at http://www.theonline-citizen.com (accessed 1 Feb 2011).

3

UNTAPPED POTENTIAL: INTERNET USE BY POLITICAL PARTIES

Debbie Goh and Natalie Pang

Abstract

Singapore opposition parties have always been marginalised because of a pro-ruling party mainstream media and restrictions on election advertising and campaigning. Even the Internet failed to help opposition parties in their campaigning in previous elections as parties encountered resource limitations and legal constraints on online campaigning. The 2011 General Election in Singapore, however, saw extremely high levels of expectation on the Internet's potential to enhance the campaign efforts of opposition parties. Such buoyant sentiments rested on new legislation liberalising Internet election advertising in 2010, as well as on a large percentage of young voters participating in the election for the first time. This study examines functions and strategies of Singapore political party websites and Facebook pages during the 2011 General Election to determine whether the Internet helped opposition parties level the playing field.

Singapore's mainstream media have a long-established reputation for either not providing sufficient coverage of opposition parties, or reporting critically and negatively about them (Gomez, 2008; Kavita *et al.*, 2003; Kluver, 2004; Cenite *et al.*, 2008). It is thus unsurprising that much hope was placed on the Internet as a medium for alternative political information and dissenting political views. Baber (2002) argues that the Internet's interactivity contributes to an emerging alternative public sphere in Singapore, letting opposition parties use their websites to contest dominant discourse and seek political power. Indeed, Gomez (2002) finds that it provides opposition parties an avenue for highlighting political harassment and reaching voters previously limited to largely pro-ruling party information in the mainstream media. Literature on new media use and election campaigns elsewhere highlights the use of the Internet to provide timely and accurate party information, raise campaign issues and facilitate political dialogue with voters, generate resources by recruiting volunteers, members and fundraising, capture voter demographics, build political communities, and organise and mobilise grassroots efficiently (Cogburn and Espinoza-Vasquez, 2011; Hooghe and Vissers, 2008, pp. 171–96; Kluver, 2004; Strandberg, 2009). Compton (2008) shows that social networking software enables people to get to know politicians better. Comparatively lower costs of Internet campaigning can also benefit minor and fringe parties that often lack the financial and human resources of major parties (Norris, 2001; Strandberg, 2009).

Research over the past decade on the use of the Internet by Singapore opposition parties to level the political playing field, however, proved these forecasts optimistic (Kluver, 2004; Gomez, 2008; Lee and Kan, 2009). Kluver's (2004) detailed content analysis comparing informational and interactive functions of political party websites during the 2001 General Election and in 2003 found that the opposition parties were not harnessing the potential of the Internet. He found content and applications on the People's Action Party (PAP) websites to be richer in information and interactive features. The opposition party websites also lacked political discussions and interactivity. Kluver concludes that laws against Internet campaigning may have dampened the potential of dissenting political discussions on opposition party websites. He adds that the absence of interactivity suggests political parties in Singapore were more comfortable with top-down organisation, and that face-to-face contact between politicians and voters was preferred. Kluver's findings concur with other studies conducted in the United States and Europe that found that while party websites did a fair job in providing political information, most fared poorly in interactivity (Lusoli and Ward, 2005; Trammell *et al.*, 2006). Studies also found that politicians do not fully optimise the dialogic characteristic of the Internet, including social networking sites (SNS), as they found the conversational style of SNS burdensome and difficult to control (Endres and Warnick, 2004; Fernandes *et al.*, 2010; Postelnicu and Cozma, 2007; Sweetser and Lariscy, 2008). Most rarely respond to comments on their SNS (Sweetser and Lariscy, 2008).

Gomez (2008) asked opposition parties why their sites were largely static and non-interactive. He found that prohibitive costs of hiring professionals to develop their websites made opposition parties dependent on volunteers or use a "do-it-yourself" approach. As a result, parties did not fully harness features that could make their campaigning more effective. His findings mirror those of studies conducted in Western democracies where major parties could afford the professional help to run more sophisticated websites (Strandberg, 2009). Singapore's political climate also discouraged Internet use. Lee and Kan (2009) observed that bloggers defied regulations in the 2006 election by blogging, but exercised self-restraint and self-censorship when doing so. Gomez (2008) found a similar caution among opposition parties, in particular with regard to potential defamation of PAP politicians. Parties such as the Workers' Party (WP) thus installed centralised control over their website and limited content to general text-based party information, avoiding news that would "raise socio-political issues in a rigorous manner" (p. 608). Gomez concludes the political climate and limited resources prevented them from exploiting the web for significant electoral advantage.

The 2011 General Election in Singapore saw extremely high levels of expectation on the Internet's potential in rallying opposition supporters and providing platforms for party members and voters to raise alternative views. Opposition candidates said they still saw the Internet as an important campaigning tool (Leong, 2011; Ng, Saad and Ismail, 2011; Wong, 2010, 2011). Web 2.0 applications, including

Facebook and Twitter, have lowered even more both the cost and technical skills required for Internet campaigning, which would most benefit resource-strapped minor opposition parties (Norris, 2001).

Such buoyant sentiments rested on legislative and regulatory changes liberalising Internet election advertising in 2010. Political parties could now campaign using more new media platforms including mobile phones, chain e-mail, podcasts, videos, blogs, photo-sharing sites, and social networking sites (Elections Department Singapore, 2011; Shanmugam, 2010). Videos of campaigning, such as political rallies, also were allowed to be uploaded (Saad, 2011). Moreover, amendments to the Films Act in 2009 had lifted the prohibition on the distribution of party political films, allowing parties to upload videos including live recordings of events, anniversary and commemorative films, factual documentaries and biographies, manifestos, and candidate declarations of policies and ideology (Tan, 2011). The 2011 elections also saw an increase in the number of younger first-time voters who were more likely to turn to the web for political information and discussion.

Another reason for high expectations of the Internet in this election is the popularity of social networking sites in the last few years. Studies of the role of social networking sites such as Facebook in elections have demonstrated that SNS offer another avenue for information dissemination, and facilitate political dialogue and civic engagement among young voters (Cogburn and Espinoza-Vasquez, 2011; Fernandes *et al.*, 2010; Woolley, Limperos and Oliver, 2010; Wu, 2009). Benoit (1999) found three types of messages were used to construct a candidate's image: acclaims or self-praise, attacks, and defences. Applying Benoit's (1999) framework, Compton (2008) found that politicians use their SNS mainly for self-acclamation, enabling people to get to know site owners better rather than for attacking others. The quality of political discourse on SNS varies from shallow but friendly posts demonstrating support (Sweetser and Lariscy, 2008) to robust discussions between fans (Wu, 2009). Wu's (2009) analysis of Facebook pages of supporters of United States President Barack Obama found that fans use the SNS to express support, opine on issues, and respond to comments posted by others. Social networking sites have proven effective in allowing open and active political dialogue between election candidates and voters, and are particularly effective in nurturing political engagement among young voters (Fernandes *et al.*, 2010).

The preceding discussion lays out several changes that point to greater use of the Internet as a campaigning tool for Singapore's 2011 General Election: liberalisation of campaigning laws, ease of use of new Web 2.0 applications, and younger and digitally savvy party supporters and voters. Since political parties had declared their intent to engage new media for the 2011 election, this study will examine how the parties used the Internet for campaigning, and whether opposition parties were able to level the playing field through online means. Our research questions are:

1. How did opposition parties' campaign strategies on their websites and Facebook pages differ from those of the ruling PAP?
2. To what extent were opposition parties able to use their websites and Facebook to break through barriers that prevented effective online campaigning in previous elections?

The Study

We conducted content analysis of the websites and Facebook pages of all contesting political parties during Singapore's 2011 General Election. The parties with websites were the ruling PAP, and opposition Reform Party (RP), Singapore Democratic Alliance (SDA), Singapore Democratic Party (SDP), Singapore People's Party (SPP) and WP. Another opposition party, the National Solidarity Party (NSP), made its website unavailable and redirected traffic to its Facebook page during the election period. All the parties had active Facebook pages. While some parties also had separate websites and Facebook pages for the constituencies and candidates, we limited our study to the main party websites and Facebook pages. For more about the participation of the parties in the election, refer to Appendix 2 of this book.

Party Websites

Types of content

The websites were coded for their content on 26 April 2011, the day before Nomination Day. We also conducted daily analyses of the updates on these websites between 27 April 2011 (Nomination Day), and 8 May (the day after Polling Day). We adopted Norris' (2001, 2003) and Kluver's (2004) frameworks that measured information and interactive/communicative features of political websites. Informational features refer to general and election information about the party, including its history, manifesto, candidate biographies, and news. Interactive/communicative features refer to elements that help the party recruit members and volunteers, mobilise voters to participate in focus groups or dialogue sessions, or enable voters to contact party candidates. We further updated the framework to accommodate the new media tools that parties were now allowed to use following the liberalisation of Internet election advertising. Table 1 shows the list of features in each website as of 26 April 2011 (the features not included in Kluver's study but which we have added in this paper are indicated by "NEW").

Table 2 shows the number of informational and interactive features available in party websites as of 26 April 2011. Table 3 compares informational and interactive features in the websites in the election years 2001, 2003, and 2011. The ruling People's Action Party (PAP) and the Reform Party (RP) had the highest number of party information elements (19). The PAP had seven interactive elements, making it third in total number (26) of elements (Table 2). The RP website, with a total of 33, had the highest number of informational and interactive elements in 2011 (Table 2). It was followed by the Singapore Democratic Party (SDP) (27 elements). Compared with 2001 and 2003, the PAP had almost doubled their number of interactive elements, while the SDP had almost doubled their information elements and tripled their interactive elements (Table 3). The RP was a new party established only in 2008, but it had the richest mix of elements on its websites. The PAP website had always been rich in information (Kluver, 2004), likely due to its vast

Table 1.   List of informational and interactive features in political party websites, 26 April 2011

Informational Features	PAP	RP	SDA	SDP	SPP	WP
Party information						
History	X			X	X	
Organisation/leadership structure	X	X	X	X	X	
Manifesto/principles	X	X	X	X	X	X
Leader interviews	X					
Press releases/media section	X	X	X	X	X	X
Archived news	X	X		X	X	
Party constitution and rules	X					
What's new section/page		X				
Website in English	X	X	X	X	X	X
Links to external websites	X	X		X	X	X
Other affiliated organisation			X			
Youth section	X	X		X		
Multimedia video or audio	X	X	X	X		X
Links to social media *NEW*	X	X		X	X	X
Non-party content				X		
Women's section	X	X				
Updated news	X	X		X	X	
Election period updates	X	X		X	X	X
Search capability	X	X		X	X	X
Election Information						
Separate election site			X			
Parliamentary candidate information	X	X	X		X	X
Rally announcements		X				
Rally highlights		X				
Schedule of events	X	X				
Constituency information	X	X				X
Interactive/Communication Features						
Recruitment/Activism						
Join party	X	X		X	X	X
Submit message form		X	X			
Join discussion/listserv		X		X		
Comment *NEW*		X				
Volunteer services		X		X	X	X
Sign up for e-newsletter		X		X		
Donate to party *NEW*		X		X	X	
Purchase party goods/products *NEW*		X		X		

(Continued)

Table 1.   *(Continued)*

Informational Features	PAP	RP	SDA	SDP	SPP	WP
Mobilisation						
Forums and dialogue session						X
Ad for candidate				X		X
Polls				X		X
Games		X				X
Advisory team						
Focus group						
Interest groups						
e-communities						
Internet chat and e-forum						
Contact						
Ability to e-mail	X	X	X	X	X	X
Central e-mail	X	X	X	X	X	
Party officials	X					
Candidates	X					X
Webmaster						
Party mailing address	X	X	X	X		X
# of e-mail addresses	1	2	1	2		

Table 2.   Number of informational and interactive features in party websites, 26 April 2011

	Informational		Interactive			
Party	Party Information	Election Information	Activism/ Recruitment	Mobilisation	Contact	Total
PAP	16	3	1	0	6	26
RP	14	5	8	1	5	33
SDA	6	2	1	0	4	13
SDP	14	0	6	2	5	27
SPP	11	1	3	0	2	17
WP	8	2	2	4	3	19

resources. In this election, the PAP not only continued providing rich informational content, but also added more interactive components. The SDP since the late 1990s had been a strong believer that the Internet is a vital conduit for reaching out to citizens, and actively

Table 3. Features of Singapore political party websites in 2001, 2003, and 2011

Party Name (28 items)	Informational			Interactive		
	2001* (22 items)	2003* (25 items)	2011 (17 items)	2001* (17 items)	2003* (24 items)	2011
PAP	22	18	19	4	4	7
RP	NA	NA	19	NA	NA	14
SDA**	NA	8	8	NA	3	5
SDP	9	8	14	3	4	13
SPP	NA	12	12	NA	7	5
WP	10	9	10	3	7	9

*2001 and 2003 data from Kluver (2004).
**Several opposition parties including the Singapore Malay National Organization (popularly known as PKMS for Pertubuhan Kebangsaan Melayu Singapura) merged to form the SDA in 2001. Hence, the 2011 findings were compared with findings on the PKMS website from Kluver's (2004) study.

deployed multimedia including podcasts and videos in all elections (Gomez, 2008). This continued in 2011 (Lee, 2011), with a website rich in information, multimedia, and interactivity. The RP — in 2011 was still in its infancy and with its limited resources and young team (five of its 11 candidates were in their 20s) — very likely saw the Internet as one of its main campaigning tools. The remaining opposition parties, however, did not ramp up their websites from previous elections. They mainly provided informational features. As in previous elections, the WP viewed traditional media as more effective and new media as not key to winning votes (Lee, 2011; Gomez, 2008).

Updating of Websites

All parties except the SDA and SPP updated their websites daily. As required by law, no updates were made on 7 May 2011, "Cooling Off Day." These updates included rally speeches, news releases, and announcements. As this study also compares the parties' use of websites and Facebook, we adopted Wu's (2008) typology to code for six functions that website updates and Facebook posts enable parties to do: (1) expressing support for the party and its

Table 4. Frequency of updates on party websites

	Express Support	Raise Issues	Respond to Comments	Monitor Media	Network/ Mobilise Voters	Provide Rally or Campaign Updates	Total Updates
PAP	2	21	0	0	7	1	31
RP	2	1	0	0	5	1	9
SDP	6	4	1	3	6	3	23
SPP	2	0	0	0	7	0	9
WP	0	8	1	0	9	5	23

Table 5. Issues raised on party websites

Issue	No. of Updates
Governance	5
Cost of living	4
Candidate's quality	4
Political system	4
Housing cost	3
Minister's salary	2
Generation Y	2
Singapore's identity	2
Foreigners' unease	1
Leadership quality	1
Number of seats contested	1
Hearing people's voices	1

candidates; (2) raising election issues; (3) responding to comments posted by fans; (4) monitoring and responding to media reports; (5) networking or mobilising voters and volunteers; and (6) providing rally and campaign updates. Table 4 shows the frequency of type of updates by party and Table 5 shows the issues raised by them (see Chapter 4 for the procedure on how issues were identified).

The PAP had the most number of updates, followed by the SDP and WP (Table 4). All the parties used their websites frequently to network or mobilise voters by announcing rally venues and times, and calling for volunteers and supporters to attend election events.

Only the PAP was active in using their site to raise issues. The SDP was the only party to use their website for all six functions. However, none of the parties responded to public comments on their websites, as other studies elsewhere had found. The issues posted most often were about governance — the effectiveness and quality of the government and its policy (raised by the PAP, RP, SDP, WP); cost of living (raised by the PAP, SDP, WP); candidate quality, history, and background (raised by the PAP); and the political system in Singapore (raised by the PAP, WP).

Party Facebook Pages

All the parties had Facebook pages, and we captured wall posts by the parties by archiving them three times daily between 27 April and 8 May: at 8 a.m., 4 p.m. and midnight. As the study focuses on how the parties used the wall posts, we only analysed the party posts, and not the posts of their fans. (We also considered the comments of fans to the posts by the parties; in Facebook, posts are articles put up by someone, which others can then add their comments to.) There were 1,380 wall posts in all. The literature shows that politicians rarely respond to fan posts on their SNS, but given Singapore's limited outlets for opposition parties to engage with voters, did they turn to Facebook to build relationships and discuss politics? To answer this, wall posts with the highest number of comments were examined to determine what types of messages drew the most reaction from voters, and whether the parties engaged in two-way communication with voters on these popular posts. We also analysed what types of issues were most commented upon by fans. A total of 165 such most-commented-on posts were captured. Table 6 shows the number of "Likes" for each party, number of posts by each party, and the number of comments received for their most-commented-on posts.

Between Nomination Day and the day after Polling Day, the SDP posted the most frequently, followed by the RP and the NSP. The PAP posted the least frequently, while the WP — the only opposition party that eventually won seats — was the third least frequent poster.

Table 6. Party Facebook posts and comments received

Political Party	No. of Posts	No. of "Likes"	No. of Comments Received
SDP	481	11,342	712
RP	365	4,726	324
NSP	171	8,265	503
SPP	145	5,863	663
WP	102	48,014	3,279
SDA	69	2,528	158
PAP	47	31,704	3,309
Total	1,380	112,442	8,948

The number of posts by parties did not reflect their popularity or the number of comments from voters. Specifically, the WP had the most "Likes" (48,014) followed by the PAP (31,804). The PAP also received 3,309 comments for its most-commented on posts while the WP received 3,279 comments. The SDP, with the highest number of posts, was third in number of "Likes" (11,342) and third in number of comments received. The RP was second in number of posts, but had the second least number of "Likes", and received only the second lowest number of comments. The NSP, which replaced its website with its Facebook page for campaigning, ranked third in number of posts, and was the fourth in "Likes". The SDA was second from the bottom in number of posts with 69 messages and last in "Likes". The SPP, the only other opposition party in Parliament before the election, narrowly lost its sole seat, and the relatively large number of "Likes" and comments it received can most likely be attributed to existing supporters.

The Buzz on Facebook

Rally and campaign updates drew the most comments (41%), followed by posts promoting political participation (24%), and posts about election issues (22%). The three issues that drew the most comments were on governance (12%), candidate quality (15%), and hearing the voice of the people (18%). Table 7 shows verbatim the posts from each party that received the highest number of comments.

Table 7. Party posts that received the highest number of comments

Party	N	Post with Most Comments
PAP	1,364	I would like to hear new ideas from u on how to make Singapore a better place. – Lee Hsien Loong
WP	771	Thank you to all supporters and everyone who made this possible. Let us work together towards a First World Parliament!
NPS	103	SM Goh says we stand for No Substance Party. We urge our supporters not to indulge in similar name-calling.
SPP	80	SPP teams will be holding our "thank you" parades today starting from 4pm from Potong Pasir. Will move to Toa Payoh and Bishan as well.
SDP	71	Singapore Democratic Party candidate Dr James Gomez said the party's main outreach effort is online. Links to a CNA article.
RP	34	Osman Bin Salaiman: Old lady in AMK told him that she will rather die than to fall sick. Her reason? She could not afford to stay at a nursing home.
SDA	24	Thank [sic] for those who have voted us! I hope the other results will bring change to Singapore.

The post with the most comments (1,364) was by the PAP. This was a call by PAP leader Lee Hsien Loong for people to send their views for a one-hour web chat. Follow-up posts on the web chat by the PAP continued to draw comments from fans. For NSP and RP, it was also posts on issues that drew the most comments. Thank-you posts to voters the day after Polling Day by the WP, SPP, and SDA drew the most comments for these parties. For the SDP, it was a post about their election strategy. Interestingly, SDP's proclamation of an online campaign drew a number of comments from their supporters advising the SDP that it needed to have face-to-face campaigning and not limit its efforts to the web.

The comments were largely one-way: from voters to parties. There were 8,948 comments to the 165 posts with the most comments, but only 25 responses to them from the parties, a dismal 0.2%. While voters used Facebook to have their voices heard, parties themselves used it mainly to broadcast messages rather than for dialogue. The discussions occurred between the fans, not between party and fans.

So while Facebook is more interactive, parties still used it like their websites — for top-down information broadcasting.

Originality and Media Type

To determine if the parties were taking advantage of the new ruling that has greatly expanded the range of new media platforms, we coded each Facebook post for media type (video, podcast, photo, text, and/or illustration) and originality (primary, secondary, or both). Primary content refers to content that is created by the parties, secondary content to content from other sources, such as mainstream media or non-party websites. "Both" refers to posts with both primary and secondary content. Tables 8 and 9 show the originality and types of posts put up by the parties.

Table 8.   Originality and type of posts on party Facebook pages

	Primary	Secondary	Both	Total (%)
Text	950	127	47	1,124 (82.4%)
Photograph	105	12	0	117 (8.6%)
Video	8	102	0	110 (8.1%)
Illustration	11	0	0	11 (0.8%)
Podcast	1	1	0	2 (0.1%)
Total	1,075 (78%)	242 (17.5%)	47 (3%)	1,364*

*16 posts could not be identified, so these were excluded from the analysis.

Table 9.   Media types of Facebook posts by political parties

	Text	Video	Photograph	Podcast	Illustration
SDP	383	59	32	0	7
RP	329	11	22	2	1
NSP	139	24	8	0	0
SPP	131	7	4	0	3
WP	46	15	40	0	1
SDA	58	3	8	0	0
PAP	38	4	5	0	0

Text was the most common media used (found in 82.4% of all posts), followed by photographs and videos. Illustrations and podcasts made up less than 1% of the posts. The SDP posted the most videos, mostly of their rallies. Workers' Party posted the most photographs, generally of their candidates interacting with voters at walkabouts. Almost 80% of all posts had primary content, indicating that parties spent time crafting messages. Overall, the Facebook pages were not particularly multimedia-rich. Text and photographs made up the majority of primary content, indicating that the parties most easily produced these formats. The WP, for example, would upload hundreds of shots taken by their own photographers at walkabouts.

The high use of text and photos shows that parties likely saw Facebook as useful for sending short messages and updates quickly and efficiently. As with the websites, we also coded Facebook posts for their functions and types of election issues. As Table 10 shows, the parties used Facebook most often to provide updates on what their candidates were doing and saying during rallies and campaign walkabouts (41% of posts). These included photographs and videos. Posted videos were largely from secondary sources such as mainstream news media's recordings of rallies. While easy to post, the production of party political film requires equipment and people skilled in videography and video editing. Our findings suggest that parties very likely lacked the resources to produce these videos, despite revisions to the Films Act. Only the Reform Party uploaded podcasts, again indicating either lack of resources or the belief that this format is less effective. The RP was also the only party that used all five media formats.

Function of Facebook Posts

Table 10 shows what parties used Facebook for, with updates on campaign activities (41.2%) topping the list as the most common function for the PAP, SDP, and WP. This indicates that parties see Facebook as a means to disseminate information quickly and en masse. The second most popular function was to present election

Table 10. Campaign functions of party Facebook posts

Purpose of Posts	PAP	RP	NSP	SDA	SDP	SPP	WP	Total posts by all parties
Updates on candidates campaigning	18 (38.3)*	109 (29.9)	56 (32.7)	23 (33.3)	251 (52.2)	41 (28.3)	70 (68.6)	**568 (41.2)**
Present issues	17 (36.2)	157 (43)	63 (36.8)	14 (20.3)	156 (32.4)	55 (37.9)	17 (16.7)	**479 (34.7)**
Promote participation	4 (8.5)	75 (20.5)	46 (26.9)	23 (33.3)	42 (8.7)	43 (29.7)	11 (10.8)	**244 (17.7)**
Express support for own party	5 (10.6)	9 (2.5)	5 (2.9)	5 (7.2)	20 (4.2)	3 (2.1)	2 (2.0)	**49 (3.6)**
Media surveillance	1 (2.1)	5 (1.4)	0	2 (2.9)	5 (1.0)	1 (0.7)	0	**14 (1.0)**
Respond to posts	2 (4.3)	1 (0.3)	0	0	0	0	0	**3 (0.2)**
Others	0	9 (2.5)	1 (0.5)	2 (92.9)	7 (1.5)	2 (1.4)	2 (2.0)	**23 (1.7)**
Total posts by each party	47	365	171	69	481	145	102	**1,380**

*( ) denotes percentages across all functions.

issues (35% of posts). The top three issues raised were hearing people's voices (17.5%), candidate quality (15%), and governance (12% of posts). Using Facebook to present issues was the most-used function by the RP, NSP, and SPP. Promoting political participation was the third most popular function, with 18% of posts announcing rallies and calling for volunteers. Again, the RP was the only party to use all functions. Only the PAP and RP responded to their fans, but a mere three times in total.

Discussion

The Internet was extolled as an alternative channel for opposition parties to overcome mainstream media bias and level the playing field against the PAP in disseminating party information and positions. Indeed, as we have found, the opposition parties, particularly newer ones such as the RP, were able to develop Internet platforms for campaigning. The PAP still presented a better and more sophisticated website than most of the opposition parties. It maintained the types of content carried in previous elections, and also beefed up interactive elements. Opposition parties SDP and RP, however, did not fall behind, each maintaining websites with more interactive features than the PAP's, and were equal in presenting informational elements.

All the parties also had Facebook pages, with the SDP and RP again being most active on Facebook and engaging more media types than the PAP. Their intense online campaigning efforts may have resulted from a history of little or negative coverage, particularly for the SDP, in the mainstream media. Opposition parties used Facebook and party websites to publicise their campaigns, detail their positions on issues and arguments left out by the mainstream media, and drew voters to discuss these issues.

Parties were less active on their websites. The NSP used its website only to redirect visitors to its Facebook page. The SDA, SPP, and WP did not greatly enhance their websites for the 2011 elections, and were not highly active on Facebook. Furthermore, all Singapore political parties — ruling and opposition — used their websites and Facebook mainly to disseminate information. Websites were channels for in-depth information about the parties, but they were largely static, updated only once a day, if at all. Facebook became their primary channel for immediate and frequent broadcast of campaign updates, issues, and rally information.

The two most successful parties in electoral results were the ruling PAP (winning 81 of the 87 seats) and the WP (winning six seats), even though they were among the least active parties online. Both parties, one being the ruling party and the other a long-time parliamentary member with a high potential of winning a Group Representation Constituency (GRC), received more news coverage than other parties. Consequently, they viewed the mainstream media as more important. Moreover, a squabble over the behaviour of WP members on Internet forums in 2006 led to the resignation of its members and put the party's reputation in question. This led to the WP being even more cautious in its engagement of the Internet. The SDP and RP, the most active parties online, were unsuccessful in the elections. However, both parties did receive a reasonable share of the votes (at least 30% in all the wards contested), suggesting that the Internet might have contributed to their campaigning efforts.

The parties did capitalise on Facebook's easy-to-use information dissemination feature and to allow feedback from fans. Yet election content remained limited to brief textual announcements, updates on activities, and wholesale uploading of photos. The parties did not use different media formats online or maintain dynamic websites, suggesting that even with easier-to-use Web 2.0 platforms such as Facebook, the opposition parties were still restrained by barriers. These constraints were very likely due to the lack of staff to update the sites and pages, lack of professional multimedia skills for posting primary videos, podcasts, and illustrations, and also lack of time for candidates to respond to voters during the intensive week of campaigning. The parties did not, or possibly could not, take advantage of the Internet's potential for them to network with voters, have dialogue with voters, generate resources, or mobilise and organise their supporters.

The survey of media use habits during the election established that only 30% used new media resources such as party websites, blogs, Facebook, Twitter, and mobile phone for election-related information and discussion (Tan and Mahizhnan, Chapter 1 this volume). The survey also found that during the fortnight of campaigning, the party websites attracted very little traffic. Only 1 in 5 voters said they had visited at least one political party website or used Facebook for election information (the number of voters who visited party Facebook pages was not measured), and that the mainstream newspapers, television, and radio still trumped the Internet in garnering voters' trust, being an important source of information, and voting influence.

Since digital access is not a major impediment in Singapore, it is likely that content and what parties were doing on these sites did not sufficiently engage voters. Research abroad has shown that voters do understand logistical, ethical, and strategic problems that could arise from candidates interacting directly with voters online, and hence do not expect greater exchanges with them on policy matters (Stromer-Galley and Foot, 2002; Fernandes *et al.*, 2010). However, they still appreciate and hope for some interaction with candidates, either through an acknowledgement of their comments or even a "poke" back on Facebook (Stromer-Galley and Foot, 2002; Sweetser and Lariscy, 2008). More interactivity and engagement with voters through websites and social media may encourage them to access the parties' Internet sites more.

Tan and Mahizhnan's survey (Chapter 1, this volume) found that alternative online media still lags behind mainstream media as voters' sources of information. But the present group of young voters has demonstrated their trust and use of new media for election information and discussion. It is unlikely that voters were apathetic online. Thousands flocked to the prime minister's web chat, and at least 40% of those surveyed had seen a video of a candidate speaking at a political rally. Discussions about governance, candidate quality, and hearing people's voices were the most prolific on Facebook, again indicating the voters did go online to discuss election-related matters more so than bread-and-butter issues such as cost of living or healthcare. Gaffs and spoofs of candidates, as well as party political video clips including two videos produced by the SDP, also went viral online, suggesting the potential of an active citizenry waiting to be engaged. Future elections will see a higher percentage of people using the Internet, so political parties should continue to focus on engaging Internet users.

The low entry barrier of online campaigning was evident through the parties' web presence. Yet, having Internet platforms require resources to maintain them, make them dynamic and engaging, and to employ the tools the Internet offers. Apart from posting updates, rally information, and brief comments, the parties failed to involve and mobilise supporters and potential voters. In Obama's 2008 presidential campaign, his campaign team used e-mail, Facebook, SMS, and their website in personalised ways, sending messages directly to targeted voters encouraging donations and purchase of campaign buttons, t-shirts, car decals, and so on. Supporters could submit campaign-related articles and personal stories on the website, making it interactive and relevant. The campaign also capitalised on social networks to disseminate information and mobilise supporters. Another key success factor in the Obama campaign was the early introduction of social media tools, which allowed campaign staff to use them often (Cogburn and Espinoza-Vasquez, 2011). With a population of smartphone and advanced Internet users, the 2012 U.S. Presidential Elections saw campaign content garnering tens of thousands of "Likes", reposts, retweets, mashed-up, and made viral across social media platforms (Wortham, 2012). Similar phenomena occurred in Singapore, with parodies and memes of the election going viral daily. It was clear during Singapore's 2011 General Election that the social network was present, and waiting to be engaged. Singapore's political parties only stepped up their online campaigning in 2011. They need to invest a longer period of time and develop activities that will build a self-sustainable network of supporters who can provide the resources to maintain a successful campaign in an election. Cogburn and Espinoza-Vasquez point out that the Internet may not be the "silver bullet" in campaigning, but paired with an understanding of the political climate and campaign issues, they are critical elements to a successful campaign.

References

Baber, Z. "Engendering or Endangering Democracy? The Internet, Civil Society and the Public Sphere", *Asian Journal of Social Science*, 30(2), (2002): 287–303.

Benoit, P.J. *Seeping Spots: A Functional Analysis of Presidential Television Advertisements, 1952–1996* (New York: Praeger, 1999).

Cenite, M., S.Y. Chong, T.J. Han, L.Q. Lim and X.L. Tan. "Perpetual Development Journalism? Balance and Fairness in the 2006 Singapore Election Coverage", *Asian Journal of Communication*, 18(3), (2008): 280–95.

Cogburn, D.L. and F.K. Espinoza-Vasquez. "From Networked Nominee to Networked Nation: Examining the Impact of Web 2.0 and Social Media on Political Participation and Civic Engagement in the 2008 Obama Campaign", *Journal of Political Marketing*, 10(1/2), (2011): 189–213.

Compton, J. "Mixing Friends with Politics: A Functional Analysis of '08 Presidential Candidates Social Networking Profiles". Paper presented at the annual meeting of the NCA 94th Annual Convention, San Diego, CA, 2008.

Elections Department Singapore. *Parliamentary Elections Act (Chapter 218, Sections 78, 78A and 102): Parliamentary Elections (Election Advertising) Regulations.* Available at http://www.elections.gov.sg/agc/parliamentarySubLeg3.htm (accessed 13 October 2011).

Elections Department Singapore. *Total Votes Cast for the General Election 2011*, 11 May 2011. Available at http://www.elections.gov.sg/pressrelease/ParE2011/2011_05_11%20Press%20release%20on%20total%20voter%20turnout.pdf (accessed 15 October 2011).

Endres, D. and B. Warnick. "Text-Based Interactivity in Candidate Campaign Web Sites: A Case Study from the 2002 Elections", *Western Journal of Communication* 68, (2004): 322–42.

Fernandes, J., M. Giurcanu, K.W.V. Bowers, and J.C. Neely. "The Writing on the Wall: A Content Analysis of College Students' Facebook Groups for the 2008 Presidential Elections", *Mass Communication and Society*, 13, (2010): 653–75.

Gomez, J. *Internet Politics: Surveillance and Intimidation in Singapore* (Singapore: Think Centre, 2002).

Gomez, J. "Online Opposition in Singapore: Communications Outreach Without Electoral Gain", *Journal of Contemporary Asia*, 38(4) (2008): 591–612.

Hooghe, M. and S. Vissers. "Belgium: Websites as Party Campaign Tools — Comparing the 2000 and 2006 Local Election Campaigns". In *Making a Difference: A Comparative View of the Role of the Internet in Election Politics*, Ward, S., D. Owen, R. Davis, and D. Taras. Lanham (eds.) (MD: Lexington Books, 2008).

Kavita, K., E.C. Kuo and S. Lee "Where is the Opposition? Media Coverage, Political Interest and Voting Behaviour in Singapore's 2001 Election". Paper presented at the annual meeting of the International Communication Association, San Diego, CA, 2003.

Kluver, R. "Political Culture and Information Technology in the 2001 Singapore General Election", *Political Communication*, 21, (2004): 435–58.

Lee T. and Kan C. "Blogospheric Pressures in Singapore: Internet Discourses and the 2006 General Election", *Continuum: Journal of Media and Cultural Studies*, 23(6) (2009): 871–86.

Leong, W.K. "Opposition Parties Raise their Internet Profiles". *Today*, 22 April 2011.

Lusoli, W. and J. Ward. "Politics Makes Strange Bedfellows: The Internet in the 2004 European Parliament Election", *Harvard International Journal of Press/Politics*, 10(4), (2005): 71–97.

Ng, E., I. Saad and S. Ismail. "A Game-Changer for the Polls?" *Today*, 15 March 2011. Retrieved from Factiva database.

Norris, P. *Digital Divide: Civic Engagement, Information Poverty, and the Internet Worldwide* (Cambridge, UK: Cambridge University Press, 2001).

Norris, P. "Preaching to the Converted? Pluralism, Participation and Party Websites", *Party Politics*, 9(1), (2003): 21–45.

Postelnicu, M. and R. Cozma. "From MySpace Friends to Voters: Campaigning Strategies on MySpace during the 2006 U.S. Congressional Elections". Paper presented at the National Communication Association Conference, Chicago, November 2007.

Saad, I. "Cyberspace: The Next GE Battleground". *Channel News Asia*, 11 November 2010. Available at http://www.channelnewsasia.com/stories/singaporelocalnews/view/1092878/1/.html (accessed 17 October 2011).

Saad, I. "Singapore Eases Rulings on Internet Election Advertising". *Channel News Asia*, 14 March 2011. Available at http://www.channel-newsasia.com/stories/singaporelocalnews/view/1116396/1/.html (accessed 13 October 2011).

Shanmugam, K. *Second Reading Speech: Parliamentary Elections (Amendment) Bill 2010. Delivered by Mr K. Shanmugam, Minister for Law and Second Minister for Home Affairs*. Available at http://www.elections.gov.sg/mediarelease/Second_Reading_by_Law_Minister_ K_Shanmugam_on_the_Parliamentary_Elections_Amendment_Bill.pdf (accessed 12 October 2011).

Singapore Elections Department. *Press Release: Total Votes Cast for the General Election 2011*, 11 May 2011. Available at http://www.elections.gov.sg/

pressrelease/ParE2011/2011_05_11%20Press%20release%20on%20to-tal%20voter%20turnout.pdf (accessed 17 October 2011).

Strandberg, K. "Online Campaigning: An Opening for the Outsiders? An Analysis of Finnish Parliamentary Candidates' Websites in the 2003 Election Campaign", *New Media and Society*, 11(5) (2009): 835–53.

Stromer-Galley, J. and L. Foot. "Citizens' Perceptions of Online Inter-activity and Implications for Political Campaign Communication", *Journal of Computer Mediated Communication*, 8(1), (2002). Avail-able at http://jcmc.indiana.edu/vol8/issue1/stromerandfoot.html (accessed on 11 October 2011).

Sweetser, K. and R. Lariscy. "Candidates Make Good Friends: An Analysis of Candidates' Uses of Facebook", *International Journal of Strategic Communication*, 2, (2008): 175–208.

Tan, Bryan "Laws on Blogging during the Singapore General Elections". Presentation at the SiRC workshop on Blogging the General Election, 12 March 2011. Available at http://isoc.sg/wp-content/uploads/2013/03/Election-blogging-laws-in-Singapore_Bryan-Tan.pdf (acce-ssed 7 February 2014).

Trammell, K.D., A.P. Williams, M. Postelnicu and K.D. Landreville. "Evo-lution of Online Campaigning: Increasing Interactivity in Candidate Website and Blogs through Text and Technical Features", *Mass Com-munication and Society*, 9(1), (2006): 21–44.

Wong, T. "The Battle for Eyeballs is on". *The Straits Times*, 4 December 2010. Retrieved from Factiva database.

Wong, T. "Easing of Rules on New Media 'Inevitable'". *The Straits Times*, 15 March 2011. Retrieved from Factiva database.

Woolley, J.K., A.M. Limperos, and M.B. Oliver. "The 2008 Presidential Election, 2.0: A Content Analysis of User-Generated Political Facebook Groups", *Mass Communication and Society*, 13, (2010): 631–52.

Wortham, J. "Campaigns Use Social Media to Lure Younger Voters". *The New York Times*, 7 October 2012. Available at http://www.nytimes.com/2012/10/08/technology/campaigns-use-social-media-to-lure-younger-voters.html?_r=0 (accessed 1 February 2013).

Wu, J. "Facebook Politics: An Exploratory Study of American Youths' Political Engagement During the 2008 Presidential Election". Paper presented at the annual meeting of the International Communication Association, Chicago, IL, 2009.

4

PRO, ANTI, NEUTRAL: POLITICAL BLOGS AND THEIR SENTIMENTS

Natalie Pang and Debbie Goh

Abstract

This study focuses on political content of blogs belonging to the online alternative media during the 2011 Singapore General Election. In all, 764 blog posts were coded and analysed for their originality, media type, parties mentioned, issues addressed, and politicians mentioned. For issues addressed and parties and politicians mentioned, we also studied their valence. Our findings show that online media was used to create mostly original content, largely in the forms of text and photos. The People's Action Party (PAP) was the most mentioned party, followed by the Workers' Party (WP) and the Singapore Democratic Party (SDP). Most mentions about political parties were neutral in nature, but mentions about issues took on greater nuances in terms of positive or negative valence. Results also show that the electorate was using the blogosphere to engage in political issues, with the top three issues relating to governance, candidate's quality, and the political system of Singapore.

The birth of the Internet and its accompanying communication tools has been described as empowering citizens and spreading democratic values (Chadwick, 2001). However, this claim is not made without caution, with critics arguing against the Internet as being inherently democratising and all-empowering (Resnick, 1998, pp. 48–68). Instead, it should be understood as operating in its political, cultural, and technological environments. Shapiro (1999, cited in Lee, 2010) suggested that it should come as no surprise then "to see governments and corporations trying to shape the code of the [Internet] to preserve their authority or profitability" (p. 105).

It is not hard to understand why much attention has been paid to the potential impact of the Internet and its relationship with citizens, political leaders, and democracy, given perceptions of Singapore as a "highly regulated society" (Lee, 2010, p. 105). As Lee (2010) posited, "against such a backdrop, it would be interesting to see how certain groups in Singapore attempt to employ the Internet to find their voice and seek their desired social, cultural and political ends" (p. 106). Other scholars such as Baber (2002) argued for the viability of spaces on the Internet in building up alternative public spheres for deliberation on issues of concern.

Since blogging was invented in the mid-1990s, the number of blogs has grown significantly, with Technorati reporting that the "blogosphere" doubles in size every five months (*The Economist*, 2006). Blogs have distinct cultural ethos — essentially, it is about the voice and style each blog carries. In other words, each blog usually has an authentic and unique voice, reflective of its creator(s). In Singapore, there are generally two kinds of sociopolitical blogs: the first is driven by an individual, and the second is formed by a collective.

For instance, blogger mrbrown has a distinct identity, and his name and interests are known from a quick glance at his site. However, in The Online Citizen, which calls itself "a community of Singaporeans", it is not immediately obvious who are accountable and are lending their voices to the blog. This is, of course, a coarse generalisation. In reality, blogs are different from each other, especially those formed by collectives of individuals since the make-up of each group would shape the character of each blog.

Since the 2006 Singapore General Election, the Internet — specifically blogging — has risen in popularity and use amongst the electorate (Tan and Mahizhnan, 2008). Yet the Parliamentary Elections (Elections Advertising) Regulations at that time prohibited the use of blogs for the purpose of political campaigning. Although bloggers could write about the elections, they must not be "persistently political" by expressing support for candidates or parties or they would be asked to register with the regulator, the Media Development Authority, and submit information about "its editor, publisher, and financial backers". Additionally, they "could not take part in electioneering campaign" (Tan and Mahizhnan, 2008, p. 4). During the 2006 General Election, blogs openly defied the regulations, challenging the sanctions imposed upon them. This may have made the regulations unsustainable, as suggested by Tan and Mahizhnan (2008), thereby resulting in the amendment in 2010 removing the prohibitions on blogs. Internet election advertising rules were, indeed, amended in 2010.

Some background on how the blogosphere is situated against the backdrop of the media environment in Singapore would provide greater clarity on the significance of such events. As Rodan (2000) observed, Singapore is known for its controlled media environment where speech is often curtailed. The 2011 General Election was the first election since the rules changed to permit cyber campaigning by voters for candidates and parties. Specifically, we wanted to address these questions: (1) Were bloggers raising issues through the blogs that were different from those raised by mainstream media, what were these issues, and in what forms were they being pursued? (2) Given the backdrop of curtailed speech in mainstream media, were blogs used effectively to present a diversity of views? To answer this question the valence of blog posts needs to be understood. As Lee (2010) suggested, whether different groups use the Internet to fulfil different purposes would be a significant question to address. These motivations drove us to conduct a content analysis of blog posts written during the 2011 General Election.

Methodology

First, we collected all the 833 blog posts listed in two well-known blog aggregators, Singapore Daily and the Singapore General Election Portal (SGEP), between Nomination Day (27 April 2011) and a day after the elections (8 May 2011). As the focus of this study is the online content by voters rather than online mass media content, those posts from mainstream news sources, such as *The Straits Times* and Yahoo! News were excluded, resulting in a final 764 blog posts. These posts came from 200 blogs (see Appendix 4.1 for the list of top twenty blogs and the number of posts from each blog used in the study). It is interesting to note that all of the posts were in English, and none in the other three official languages: Mandarin, Malay, and Tamil. English is the language of instruction in schools, the *lingua franca*, and is the language of choice amongst almost all bloggers. All posts were coded and analysed for their originality, media type, parties mentioned, issues addressed, and politicians mentioned. For posts on parties, issues, and politicians, we also studied their valence.

The Satay Club, The Online Citizen, Singapore Election 2011, Singapore Notes, and mrbrown generated a significant number of posts. The most prolific blogs tended to be collective, presumably because they had more resources available to create new content. In looking at the distribution of the posts coming from respective blogs, a "long tail" is also evident (Figure 1). That is, a small number of blogs had many posts, whilst many blogs had very few posts. The long tail distribution will be used to examine the data later on in the chapter.

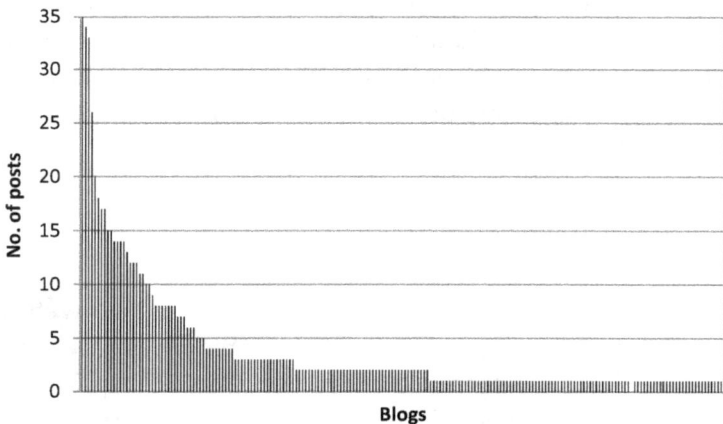

Figure 1: A long tail of blog posts

The final list of issues used to analyse the blog post for content was derived in this manner. The initial list was derived from one compiled by *The Straits Times* on 20 April 2011 as "hot button" topics of concern to the electorate (Table 1). Then we tested the relevance of these issues with three samples of blog posts randomly selected from the archive of posts we had already collected, with three researchers in the first round, and then with six researchers in the second round. In each round researchers coded the blog posts separately, and then came together to discuss the applicability of the issues, and to suggest new ones.

As a result of these discussions, some of the initial issues were further broken down into sub-categories. In the final coding template we also included an "others" category to allow coders to code issues not in the list and yet addressed by blog posts. If a certain issue kept coming up in the "others" category a new category would be created to accommodate the issue being raised. One example of issues raised by the blogs but was not in *The Straits Times* list is the issue of governance, the top issue raised by the blogs. In the course of coding, researchers frequently encountered blog posts that raised questions about the effectiveness of the Singapore government and the policies made, through the discussions of examples such as single mothers and the elderly as groups that have not been well-served by existing policies. Such blog posts were initially coded with labels such as "effectiveness" or "policy lags" in the "others" category. However, in the final analysis they were listed under a new code "governance". The final list of issues, ranked in order of frequency, can be found in Table 2. Explanations for each issue can be found in Appendix 4.2. It should be noted that a blog may sometimes contain more than one issue and that each issue in that blog will be coded separately.

Findings and Discussions

The Pursuit of Issues

The final list of issues in our study turned out to be quite different from the list compiled by *The Straits Times*. The top three issues

Table 1. Preliminary list of issues (*The Straits Times*, 2011)

No.	Issue	Brief Description
1	Scholars in opposition	Emergence of quality candidates in the opposition camp, such as Mr Chen Show Mao, Mr Tony Tan, Ms Hazel Poa, Mr Benjamin Pwee, and Mr Jimmy Lee.
2	Hot seats	With a line-up of potential match-ups, this election could be the most intense, with opposition parties also trying to work together to avoid three-cornered contests.
3	4G leadership	Amongst the new candidates introduced by the PAP, a number of them exhibit ministerial potential.
4	"Y-Fi" access	With the introduction of young candidates such as Tin Pei Ling, 27, the PAP is out to engage the younger, "Gen-Y" voters.
5	New benchmarks	The election is setting itself up as a test for both the PAP and the opposition, with the latter wanting to win a GRC and the former looking to see if their past winning margins would change.
6	Online and offline	The relevance and influence of online media in campaigning by parties.
7	Cost of living	The rising cost of living may also present itself as a significant issue for the electorate.
8	Housing woes	The escalation of prices of both HDB and private housing may cause significant concerns for the electorate, especially young couples who are anxious about their finances and the affordability of housing in the long run.
9	Foreigner unease	Tensions about the influx of foreigners may be causing unhappiness especially in the competition for jobs, schools/university places, and over-crowded trains.
10	Buying "insurance"	The Workers' Party argued that voting for the opposition is like taking out an insurance policy against the possibility of a government that could fail without adequate checks and balances.
11	Wildcards	As the name implies, wildcard issues could also emerge, which may override any or all of the issues above.

Note: Based on *The Straits Times*, 20 April 2011.

Table 2. Issues and their prominence amongst bloggers

Issue	No. of Mentions	Percentage of Total Issues Mentioned
Governance	307	14
Candidate's quality	302	13
Political system	247	11
Hearing people's voices	170	8
Housing cost	127	6
Media surveillance	116	5
Fair play	115	5
Foreigners' unease	114	5
Elections online	111	5
Minister's salary	103	5
Cost of living	99	4
Number of seats contested	96	4
Singapore's identity	74	3
Generation Y	51	2
Healthcare	32	1
Election strategy	29	1
Transport	25	1
Leadership quality	15	1
Education	14	1
Party quality	12	1
Others	90	4
Total	2,249	100

addressed by the blogs were those relating to political issues such as governance, candidate's quality, and the political system. The blogosphere was used to raise a slightly different set of issues from those highlighted by *The Straits Times*. In this context, our findings resonate with those of McKenna and Pole (2004), whose study found that bloggers in the United States used blogs to improve political participation and encourage interactions amongst readers. Through the issues pursued by the blogs, our study suggests that bloggers have an impact in creating awareness and significance around issues of interest, thereby shaping public opinion at least amongst their readers.

They also found that individuals who were moderately politically active also became politically more active through blogging.

In other words, blogs can also be understood to strengthen political participation. Even though it was not our intention to find out if individuals in Singapore indeed became politically more active via blogging, our study demonstrates that amongst bloggers, higher order issues such as democracy and governance took greater precedence over more self-oriented issues such as bread-and-butter issues (for example, housing and cost of living). The finding is consistent with the 2006 election survey by the Institute of Policy Studies (IPS) (IPS, 2006), which highlighted that respondents saw political issues as being more important than issues such as cost of living. However, the finding is at odds with reports arguing that bread-and-butter issues were still the main concerns of Singaporeans (Shafawi, 2011). At this point it is pertinent to note that those who actively blog are a very small subset of Singapore's population, identified by the post-election survey done after the election (see Chapter 1 this volume). Of 2,000 participants surveyed, only 113 (approximately 6%) said that they have a blog. Out of these 113 surveyed, only 46 of them (approximately 41%) wrote about the election or matters relating to the election. In terms of demographics, significant differences for age and education can be noted between those who have blogs, and those who do not (Figure 2). For those with blogs, 69% are below 40 years old, and 58% of them have either a diploma or university degree. No significant differences were found for other demographics such as race, gender, and dwelling type (which may also be understood as a proxy for household income).

Significant differences can also be found in the political traits of those with blogs. Some 62% of those with blogs indicated that they were interested in political issues, compared to 44% of those who do not have blogs. As suggested by McKenna and Pole's (2004) study, individuals are more politically active through blogging. In the context of Singapore, it could be that bloggers were already interested in political issues and used blogs to further their interests or to extend public discussions in these issues. In Singapore where speech is controlled in mainstream media, the availability of blogging as a means to further issues of interest becomes even more important.

Blog Ownership by Education

University Degree or higher — 19% / 36%
Polytechnic Diploma — 17% / 21%
ITE and other Vocational Certificate — 4% / 4%
Junior College (A level) — 7% / 12%
Secondary O or N level — 25% / 33%
Primary school (PSLE) — 0% / 17%
No formal Qualification — 2% / 4%

⊟ Have a blog   ⊞ Do not have a blog

Blog Ownership by Age

21–24 — 8% / 31%
25–29 — 7% / 14%
30–34 — 5% / 12%
35–39 — 10% / 12%
40–44 — 8% / 12%
45–49 — 9% / 13%
50–54 — 6% / 17%
55–59 — 3% / 9%
60–64 — 3% / 8%
65–69 — 2% / 3%
70+ — 1% / 7%

⊟ Have a blog   ⊞ Do not have a blog

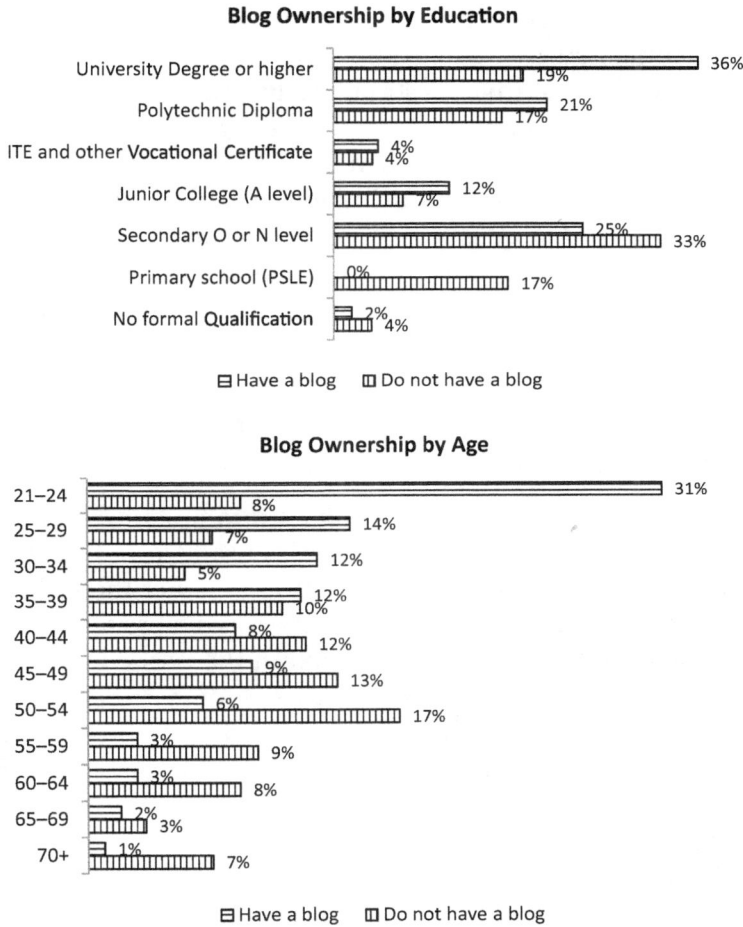

Figure 2: Demographic differences by age and education

Individual interests aside, the fact that the blogs were raising different issues (and potentially inspiring public deliberation on them in the comments and responses to the posts) also highlighted the function of the blogs as alternative platforms for deliberation on issues of concern. Even if the issues raised may not actually be representative of the opinions of the general electorate as a whole, one could argue that the blogosphere may be critical for sustaining democracy and active citizenship. It could also serve to create greater awareness about issues of concern, and lead to more informed public opinion on the issues.

In addressing our first question, we thus conclude that bloggers were using blogs to pursue a different set of issues from the ones raised by mainstream media, and argue that such pursuits can work to strengthen their political participation and citizenry. On this note, we want to raise the question of whether online discourse or the mainstream media represent the voices of the electorate. One could argue that it is both, or neither. From our study, they are definitely different in their aims.

Were the Bloggers Using Blogs to Pursue a Diversity of Views?

To understand if the blogs were being used to pursue a diversity of views, we analysed the valence of each issue addressed by the blog posts (whether it was pro, anti, or neutral to either the PAP or the opposition). Table 3 shows results for the top five issues. The issue of governance was the most mentioned in the posts, with most of them being anti-PAP (60%), followed by 27% of them being neutral. Very few posts raised this issue about the opposition parties (0% being anti and 2% being pro-opposition) — and understandably so, as there were only three (including Non-Constituency Members of Parliament) opposition members then in Parliament, and so little could be said about their governance. On the issue of candidate quality, most of the posts were supportive of the opposition (43%), reflecting the favourable attitudes shown towards the "scholars in

Table 3. Top five issues and valence

Issue	Pro-PAP	Anti-PAP	Neutral	Anti-Opp	Pro-Opp
Governance (14%)	20 (10%)	123 (60%)	56 (27%)	0 (0%)	5 (3%)
Candidate's quality (13%)	7 (5%)	47 (31%)	19 (13%)	12 (8%)	64 (43%)
Political system (11%)	2 (1%)	66 (37%)	99 (56%)	2 (1%)	8 (5%)
Hearing people's voices (8%)	16 (12%)	70 (54%)	21 (16%)	3 (2%)	21 (16%)
Housing cost (6%)	3 (3%)	60 (57%)	36 (34%)	2 (2%)	4 (4%)

opposition", the name given by *The Straits Times* to those with high academic credentials.

The analysis of the valence shows that within each issue a mix of views, which were not always negative towards the ruling party as is often presumed (Paulo, 2006), were represented. However, this also indicated much scepticism within the blogosphere towards the PAP on issues such as governance, the political system, and cost of public housing. In other words, blogs were being used to pursue and generate public discourse that was alternative to those issues generated by the mainstream media controlled by the ruling party.

In What Forms Were Issues Being Raised?

To understand how the issues were being pursued, blog posts were also coded for their originality (primary, secondary, or both) and the types of media found within each post (whether video, audio podcast, photographs, text, and/or illustration). Primary content refers to content that is created by the blogger, whilst secondary content refers to links to other sources, such as mainstream media, websites, or other bloggers. Blog posts may also contain multiple media and content types (such as a secondary video with original text). Text was the most prominent media type generated across all blog posts studied, comprising 53% of all posts but photographs topped the list for secondary content. In other words, photographs were the most common media amongst blog posts that focused on posting only secondary content. Text, however, accounted for 54% and 54% of posts consisting of primary content and both primary and secondary content respectively. Table 4 shows the breakdown by media type. For instance, many posts used photographs extracted from other sources in the production of their own narrative and analysis on various issues. While the photograph used was not original (i.e. created by the blogger), the textual content created was original and primary. Such posts inspired readers to engage in the topic (shown by the number of comments).

Out of 84 posts comprising only secondary content, 29% were links from local mainstream media. Links from alternative online

Table 4.   Number of posts by originality and media type

	Originality		
	Primary	**Secondary**	**Both**
Videos (2%)	13 (1%)	11 (13%)	10 (3%)
Podcasts (1%)	5 (0%)	1 (1%)	3 (1%)
Photographs (32%)	344 (33%)	33 (39%)	80 (25%)
Texts (53%)	560 (54%)	28 (33%)	176 (54%)
Illustrations (12%)	109 (11%)	11 (13%)	56 (17%)
	1,031	84	325

Table 5.   Sources of secondary content

	Local Media	Foreign Media	Other Blogs	Alternative Online Media	Social Media	Party Websites	Elections Department	Others
Video	11							
Podcast			1					
Photographs	5	1		18	3	4		2
Text	8	3	1	3	3	1	2	7
Illustrations				2	6			3
	24	4	2	23	12	5	2	12
	(29%)	(5%)	(2%)	(27%)	(14%)	(6%)	(2%)	(14%)

media (defined as user-generated media such as Temasek Review and The Online Citizen) followed closely as the second most widely circulated amongst blog posts consisting of secondary content (27%). Links from social media (Facebook and Twitter) accounted for 14% of secondary content. For instance, when Prime Minister Lee Hsien Loong made a speech to apologise for mistakes that the ruling party may have made in the past, links to the story carried by mainstream media were posted by many blogs as secondary content. Table 5 shows the breakdown of secondary content by source. Although blogs can generally be considered as social media together with portals such as Facebook and Twitter, for analytical reasons of showing what secondary types of content were the most common in blog posts, we came up with the following categories: local media (links to content from local mainstream media), foreign media (links to content from foreign mainstream media), other blogs (links to blogs other than the blogger's own blog), alternative online media (links to citizen-generated collective blogs, such as Temasek Review, The Online Citizen), social media (links to Facebook or Twitter pages or accounts), party websites (links to websites of political parties), elections department (links to pages of the elections department website), and others (links to other pages on the World Wide Web, such as Wikipedia, online forums, and quotations).

There were surprisingly few audio podcasts — but this might be because bloggers were now more sophisticated in their use of other media, such as videos. The videos posted as secondary content were mostly of rallies carried by local mainstream media such as Channel News Asia. More sophisticated use of technologies took the form of comics, illustrations, or digitally modified pictures that were circulated as secondary content.

Significance of Online Discourse

What was really the role of online discourse reflected in the blogs, given that the issues and valence highlighted here did not show overwhelming support for the ruling party? Did it really influence actual voting behaviour? It is difficult to tell, given the outcomes of the election. On one hand, the PAP still won 60.14% of all votes, followed by the WP (with 12.8% of the votes), National Solidarity Party (NSP) (with 12% of the votes), SDP (with 4.8% of the votes), Reform Party (with 4.3% of the votes), and the Singapore People's Party (SPP) (with 3.1% of the votes). On the other hand, support for the PAP waned, with a loss of 6% percentage points of votes compared to the last election, the highest loss in the most recent decade. Still, the number of times each party was mentioned may provide a different perspective on party popularity, given that the PAP was the most mentioned party (558 times) across all blog posts, followed by the Workers' Party (WP) (285 times). If the number of mentions is used as a proxy for assessing the prominence of each party, the election results show that the number of mentions needs to be taken seriously, as two parties most mentioned (the PAP and WP) also performed the best.

However, qualitative evaluation of the mentions matters as well. For this, we examined the valence of the mentions in six categories: purely positive, purely negative, purely neutral, positive and negative, positive and neutral, or negative and neutral, or all three together. For the PAP, the highest number of mentions were neutral in nature (39.1%) and likewise for all other parties. Posts mentioning the PAP that were negative and neutral in valence followed, with 26.3%. For the WP, which was the second most-mentioned political party, most of these mentions were neutral as well (66%), but this was followed by positive mentions (16.1%). From this analysis the net effect of positive versus negative talk may be calculated for each party. Looking at the net effects, WP showed the greatest gain in terms of positive support (a positive gain of 18.9% across all posts), whereas the PAP showed the largest loss of positive support (2% positive posts against 22.6% negative posts, resulting in a net effect of 20.6%). However, the PAP is not the only party with more negative than positive posts: the Singapore Democratic Party (−2%) and Reform Party (−2.2%) also showed negative effects. Table 6 shows the analysis of party mentions according to their respective categories of valence as well as their corresponding net effects.

These results demonstrate that mentions of political parties were not always one-sided with either a positive or negative view of each party. Across all political parties mentioned, the references were mostly neutral in nature (defined as mentions that were stating factual details and what the parties were saying or doing without expressing a positive or negative valence). Out of 1,219 mentions of political parties, only 151 were purely negative in nature. In other words, our study shows that the blogosphere was projecting multiple views of political parties. However, it is still notable that the proportion of posts that were negative for the PAP was much higher than all other parties, although this might also be due to the prominence of the party or that the blogosphere was the place

Table 6. Party mentions by party and valence*

Party	Actual Votes	No. of Mentions	Pos.	Pos.+Neu.	Pos.+Neg.	Neutral	Neg.+Neu.	Neg.	Net Effect (Positive–Negative)
PAP	60.1%	558	11 (2%)	12 (2.2%)	26 (4.7%)	218 (39.1%)	147 (26.3%)	126 (22.6%)	–20.6%
WP	12.8%	285	46 (16.1%)	39 (13.7%)	1 (0.4%)	188 (66%)	0 (0%)	8 (2.8%)	+18.9%
SDP	4.8%	148	9 (6.1%)	12 (8.1%)	2 (1.4%)	110 (74.3%)	3 (2%)	12 (8.1%)	–2.0%
NSP	12%	105	10 (9.5%)	6 (5.7%)	1 (1%)	83 (79%)	1 (1%)	1 (1%)	+8.5%
SPP	3.1%	48	3 (6.3%)	5 (10.4%)	0 (0%)	37 (77.1%)	1 (2.1%)	1 (2.1%)	+4.2%
RP	4.3%	45	1 (2.2%)	1 (2.2%)	0 (0%)	39 (86.7%)	2 (4.4%)	2 (4.4%)	–2.2%
SDA	2.8%	30	1 (3.3%)	1 (3.3%)	0 (0%)	26 (86.7%)	1 (3.3%)	1 (3.3%)	0.0%
		1,219	81	76	30	701	155	151	

*Mentions of parties with unclear or ambiguous valence, and with all three valences (positive, neutral and negative) are omitted from this table because they were insignificant in number.

where people chose to, or the main place where they could, express these views. Nevertheless our study shows an encouraging trend that bloggers actually seek and offer multifaceted views, and were not as anti-establishment as perceived (Li, 2007; Lee and Kan, 2009). The negative perception could have stemmed from the fact that a number of prominent blogs were anti-establishment, or perhaps the very tone of online discourse is different from the mainstream media. This also implies that bloggers were using the space in pursuit of diverse speech and deliberation.

To understand the analysis of valence further in the context of blog post content about political parties, we also sought to understand how they contributed to the overall discourse generated during the General Election. To do this we return to Figure 1 (a long tail of blog posts). From Figure 1, it can be inferred that although there were many bloggers involved in producing the entire discourse (during our period of study), there were key bloggers (as represented by the ones towards the left end of the curve, who were responsible for generating a greater number of posts). Applying the well-known Pareto principle in economics (also known as the 80–20 rule, or the law of the vital few), this could also mean that 80% of the discourse is contributed by 20% of the bloggers. From the number of posts generated it can already be inferred that this principle is somewhat valid (see Appendix 4.1), that is although 200 blog sites generated 794 posts, up to 48 of them contributed a total of 532 posts (67% of the total number of blog posts). What can be observed from the discourse generated by these opinion shapers in terms of valence? The answer to this question may have implications for perhaps predicting how future discourse may be understood in terms of their valence.

Figure 3 illustrates the nature of the discourse of the top contributors (approximately 20% of bloggers) on the top two most mentioned political parties. From the figure it can be seen that there was a mix of sentiments for both parties, although actual percentages

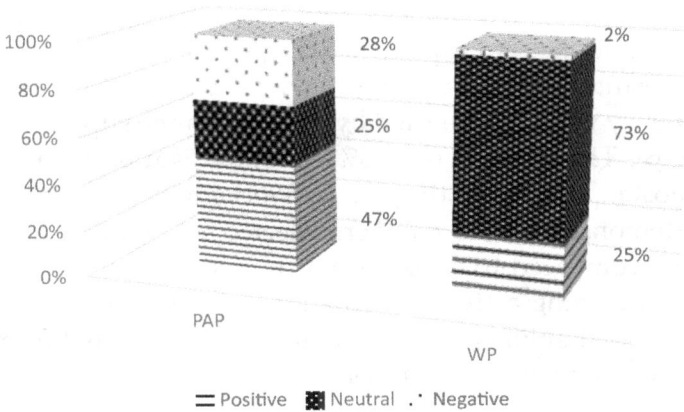

Figure 3: Valence of discourse generated by top contributors

may vary within each party. None of the purely negative mentions about political parties actually came from these top contributors, that is, their discourse offered balanced views.

Conclusion

Blog posts make up the key unit of analysis in the content analysis here. Although comments to the blogs were also collected, they did not form part of the analysis as these comments were not equally distributed between blog posts (i.e. some blogs attracted a lot more comments than others), and at the same time, may not always be related to the content of the posts they were tagged to. Including them in our analysis thus may not be useful since the purpose was to examine the blogosphere — and the "blogging electorate".

The project marks the first study of blogging content since amendments to the Parliamentary Elections (Elections Advertising) Regulations were made in 2010. Our results show that the blogosphere, when taken as a whole, is robust and diverse in its perspectives, issues generated, and sentiments. When analysed for their valence, net gains or losses can be reflected for each party, and may help to explain actual gains and losses in terms of election results. The Workers' Party win of a Group Representation Constituency was also reflected by positive online support (+18.9% in Table 6). The net loss (−20.6%) in online support for the PAP was almost equivalent to the gain by Workers' Party (Table 6). This project demonstrates that bloggers selected slightly different issues to pursue compared to those raised by mainstream media. Other than strengthening active participation and citizenry, our analysis also shows that online public opinions may be different from those reflected in the mainstream media.

Appendix 4.1.   List of blogs and number of posts contributed

No.	Blog Name	Number of Posts
1	The Satay Club	35
2	The Online Citizen	34
3	Singapore Election 2011	33
4	Singapore Notes	26
5	mrbrown: L'infantile terrible of Singapore	20
6	Diary of a Singaporean Mind	18
7	Hun Boon's Blog	17
8	Thoughts of a Cynical investor	17
9	The Owl	15
10	Yawning Bread	15
11	Singapore Election Watch	14
12	SpotlightOnSingapore	14
13	Yee Jenn Jong	14
14	Yours Truly Singapore	14
15	New Asia Republic	13
16	Molitics Writing Silence	12
17	pressrun.net	12
18	Sgpolitics.net	12
19	life one degree north, one-o-three degrees east	11
20	Think Happiness	11

Appendix 4.2. List of issues mentioned and their descriptions

Issue	Description
Governance	Effectiveness, and/or quality of the Singapore government and its policies.
Candidate's quality	The quality of candidates fielded from both PAP and opposition parties, who they are, the quality of their backgrounds, and competencies.
Political system	Details about political and parliamentary system in Singapore, including the GRC, such as its purpose, views about it, its history of candidates, and voting secrecy.
Hearing people's voices	Details about a party's connection/disconnect with the people, the government not attending to people's concerns, need for more voices to speak up on policies, and whether or not people's voices are being heard.
Housing cost	Rising or high cost of housing, particularly HDB flats and their affordability.
Media surveillance	Discussions on how the media is covering the elections, their objectivity or biasness and how they are working with politicians and parties. Also addresses what other media sources are reporting about the elections, and also includes praises or criticisms of those reports.
Foreigners' unease	Unease or unhappiness with competition from foreigners for resources such as jobs, transportation, housing and education.
Elections online	Details about what's going on in cyberspace pertaining to GE2011, such as what people are posting, saying, doing online.
Fair play	Issues relating to the playing field, such as access to facilities by opposition and PAP MPs, perceived "shielding" of new candidates, unfavourable conditions, and lack of upgrades or public programmes for opposition wards.
Number of seats contested	Details on the large number of seats contested, who's contesting and why.
Minister's salary	Posts talking about the high salaries of Singapore ministers.
Cost of living	Concerns about the rising cost of living in Singapore.
Singapore's identity	Details about what it means to be Singaporean, characteristics of a Singaporean/Singapore citizen, and being "one people, one nation, one Singapore".
Generation Y	Discourse about the younger generation of Singaporeans and their concerns or interests.

(Continued)

Natalie Pang and Debbie Goh

Appendix 4.2. *(Continued)*

Issue	Description
Healthcare	Posts addressing the issue of healthcare costs and policies in general, and its affordability for the elderly.
Election strategy	Addresses strategies taken by political parties during this election.
Transport	Posts relating to the costs and overcrowding of public transport.
Education	Education costs in Singapore and perceptions of education policies in favouring the elites.
Leadership quality	The next generation of leaders (4G) that the government is grooming for Singapore.
Party quality	The quality of parties, including their track records, competencies, and ability to stay relevant.

References

"11 Issues for GE '11". *The Straits Times*, 20 April 2011, p. A9.

"It's the Links, Stupid". *The Economist*, 20 April 2006. Available at http://www.economist.com/node/6794172 (accessed 4 September 2011).

Baber, Z. "Engendering or Endangering Democracy? The Internet, Civil Society and the Public Sphere", *Asian Journal of Social Science*, 30(2), (2002): 287–303.

Chadwick, A. "The Electronic Face of Government in the Internet Age", *Information, Communication & Society*, 4(3), (2001): 435–57.

Institute of Policy Studies (IPS). "IPS Post-Election Forum 2006". 2 June 2006. Available at http://www.lkyspp.nus.edu.sg/ips/Survey_Report_postelection.aspx (accessed 23 August 2011).

Lee, T. *The Media, Cultural Control and Government in Singapore* (London: Routledge, 2010).

Lee, T. and C. Kan. "Blogospheric Pressures in Singapore: Internet Discourses and the 2006 General Election", *Continuum*, 23(6), (2009): 871–86.

Li, Xueying. "PAP Moves to Counter Criticism of Party, Government in Cyberspace". *The Straits Times*, 3 February 2007.

McKenna, L. and A. Pole. "Do Blogs Matter? Weblogs in American Politics". Paper presented at the American Political Science Association's Annual Meeting, Chicago, IL, 2 September 2004. Available at http://www.allacademic.com/meta/p60899_index.html (accessed 9 September 2011).

Paulo, D. A. "PAP must Address 'Negative' Internet". *Today*, 24 May 2006.

Resnick, D. "Politics on the Internet: The Normalization of Cyberspace". In *The Politics of Cyberspace: A New Political Science Reader*, Toulouse, C. and T. W. Luke (eds.). (New York: Routledge, 1998).

Rodan, G. "Asian Crisis, Transparency and the International Media in Singapore", *The Pacific Review*, 13(2), (2000): 217–42.

Shafawi, M. "Bread-and-Butter Issues Remain Top Concerns: REACH Survey". *Channelnewsasia*, 31 January 2011. Available at http://www.channelnewsasia.com/stories/singaporelocalnews/view/1107998/1/.html (accessed on 1 October 2011).

Shapiro, A. L. "Think again: The Internet", *Foreign Policy*, 115, (1999): 14–27.

Tan T.T. and A. Mahizhnan. "Subverting Seriousness and Other Misdemeanours: Modes of Resistance Against OB Markers in the 2006 Singapore General Election". Paper presented at the 17th Annual Conference of the Asian Media Information and Communication Centre (AMIC) on Changing Media, Changing Societies: Media and the Millennium Development Goals, Manila, Philippines, 14–17 July 2008. Available at http://www.spp.nus.edu.sg/ips/docs/pub/pa_TTHAM_Subverting %20Seriousness_AMIC_July%202008.pdf (accessed 7 September 2011).

5

WHO CALLS THE SHOTS? AGENDA SETTING IN MAINSTREAM AND ALTERNATIVE MEDIA

Paul Wu Horng-Jyh, Randolph Tan Gee Kwang and Carol Soon

Abstract

New technologies are shaping government-electorate communication and civic engagement in Singapore, a consequence of Singapore's pro-IT policies. While blogs stimulated online discourse and served as alternative news sources during the 2006 General Election, social media such as Facebook and Twitter are emerging as new forces that the ruling elite and mainstream media have to contend with. The overarching questions for this study are: What inter-media agenda setting between traditional and new media occurred during the General Election? What were the patterns pertaining to the directionality of agenda setting between traditional media and new media? Almost 1,200 relevant online media sites were archived between 1 February to 16 May 2011 and posts were crawled and archived based on 48 topics. A time series analysis and Granger causality test showed that the overall agenda-setting effect operated in both directions between traditional and new media. Thus, agenda setting is no longer the sole province of traditional media.

The progression of online technologies from Web 1.0 to Web 2.0 involved the shift from personal websites to blogs and from publishing information to participation in information creation (Flew, 2005). Such a participatory approach in both the consumption and production of web content, characterised by an ongoing and inter-active nature, led to the emergence of "citizen-governors" (Winner, 2003) and "produsers" (Bruns, 2008). Observations of how users of new media such as blogs, Facebook, and Twitter are influencing political landscapes are not limited to countries in the West, as evident from the recent Arab Spring and Jasmine Revolution. Closer to home, Malaysian bloggers' criticism of the government's alleged mismanagement of the country's economy and the government's failure to tap into the blogosphere saw unprecedented gains made by opposition parties in the 2008 Malaysian General Election (Sani, 2009). During the Singapore General Election in 2006, the Singapore blogosphere was described as putting up "politics of resistance" when bloggers leveraged the easy-to-access technology to challenge and push the boundaries of accepted norms in societal discourse (Ibrahim, 2009). During the 2011 General Election (GE2011), the topic of our study, journalists from mainstream press such as *The Straits Times* as well as media scholars observed how social media catalysed the exchange of political quips, photographs and videos of election rallies, and opinions during the days leading up to the General Election (George, 2011; Ng, 2011).

Scholars and media observers have lauded the democratisation effects of new media technologies and how they enable marginalised or alternative voices to participate and shape public discourse (George, 2006; Kluver, 2007). There is a growing body of work which examines how new media are exerting unanticipated influences on the ways traditional media (such as print and television broadcast news) report news. In this chapter, we adopt the inter-media agenda-setting framework, i.e. the concept that mainstream media and alternative media influence each other in deciding what makes up the key content of their respective media during the campaign period leading up to Polling Day on 7 May 2011. We first present current studies pertaining to agenda-setting effects of media, in particular those on inter-media agenda setting. This study is timely in view of how new media platforms are creating more opportunities for political challengers and citizens to contribute to the public discourse in Singapore. Following that, we discuss our sampling methodology and method of study, the times series analysis (TSA), before presenting our findings and the implications of our research.

Agenda-setting in a Mixed Media Ecology

Agenda-setting theory posits that the news media can influence issues deemed important by the general public (McCombs and Shaw, 1972). The media's ability to enhance issue saliency among the audience simply by increasing the frequency of coverage of a specific event came to be known as "basic agenda-setting". Defining agenda setting as "the ability of the news media to define the significant issues of the day", Iyengar and Simon (1993, p. 366) found that increases in the level of media coverage of events in the Persian Gulf were associated with increases in the proportion of respondents naming the Gulf crisis as the United States' (U.S.) most paramount problem.

In addition, earlier work does not take into account the increasingly rich media ecology of today and how the growing plethora of media outlets affects one another and how this new situation challenges the agenda-setting theory. Recent inter-media agenda-setting studies have uncovered several interesting developments in an increasingly complex media ecosystem which suggest that the dominance of any particular media, established traditional media vis-à-vis emerging new media based on user-generated platforms, remains inconclusive. In the United States, several studies found that major newspapers such as *The New York Times* shaped the agenda for other newspapers and television networks (Reese and Danielan, 1991; Trumbo, 1995). In discussions on legislative topics, traditional news media set the agenda for political blogs (Lanosga, 2008). However, in a separate study that compared online media (websites belonging to presidential candidates) and offline media (traditional media) during the 2000 U.S. presidential campaign, it was found that the campaign agenda of candidates' websites shaped the news agenda of traditional news media (Ku, Kaid, and Pfau, 2003).

The proliferation of blogs, social networking sites, and microblogs enables members of the public to bypass traditional constraints such as costs and censorship, and empowers them to contribute to public discourse pertaining to politics and society, thereby providing alternative perspectives and creating news (Jenkins, 2006). Through easy-to-use and accessible publishing tools, consumers of information are now producers as well, becoming what Bruns (2008) termed "produsers". Furthermore, networking among users leads to the formation of communities that act in concert to provide perspectives and information countering hegemonic discourse publicised in traditional media, bringing to attention issues that may have been omitted or downplayed in mainstream press. Technological features such as hyperlinks enhance the ease with which online citizens engage in collaboration. In the case of blogs, users experience high interactivity with their readers and other bloggers due to densely connected hyperlinks among blogs, and between blogs and other sites such as web pages and forums (Gil de Zuniga, Puig-I-Abril, and Rojas, 2009). A study of bloggers in the U.S. found comment functions, blogrolls and hyperlinks to be important enablers that increased political discourse and participation in American blog sites (McKenna and Pole, 2004).

In Singapore, Soon and Cho (2011) found that the online network comprising political parties, non-governmental and civil society organisations, news media, discussion forums, and political bloggers followed a power law distribution. This means that a minority of the online population receives the majority of links. Their findings echoed observations by Shirky (2005) in his analysis of LiveJournal blogs and Yahoo! Groups mailing lists. A closer scrutiny of the Singapore sites that held central positions in the number of links they received were political blogs. These key bloggers were well-known personalities as in the cases of Yawning Bread, From a Singaporean Angle, and mrbrown, largely due to their ability to strike a chord with the ordinary citizen (Davie, 2008; De Clearq, 2006; Neo, 2008). Furthermore, within the network, the cluster of political bloggers is a well-connected one as all the nodes are connected to one another directly or indirectly, pointing to the existence of an online community of Singapore bloggers in the cyberspace. Besides demonstrating a close affinity to one another through structural linkages, political blogs empowered ordinary citizens and enabled a "politics of resistance and representation" during the 2006 General Election (Ibrahim, 2009, p. 174). Ibrahim posits that anonymous web sites and blogs, which were less subjected to direct regulatory control, "expanded the sphere of commentary to accommodate topics and discussions deemed too sensitive or taboo by the authorities" (p. 186), and cited examples of how blogs demonstrated the potential of influencing news coverage in traditional mainstream press.

A study that incorporated YouTube and Google News in an analysis of inter-media agenda setting in the U.S. pertaining to Proposition 8 (an amendment which bans same-sex marriage in California) established that social media and online news were strong predictors of coverage on Proposition 8 in traditional news papers (Sayre *et al.*, 2010). However, a recent study that analysed inter-media agenda setting between Singapore's traditional media (*The Straits Times* and *Today*) and political blogs found that traditional media and blogs not only covered similar stories, traditional media were dominant in setting the agenda (Ng, 2010). These divergent results could be a reflection of the very different media ecology in different societies. To understand the effects and significance of inter-media agenda setting in Singapore, the next section discusses in brief the regulatory framework that governs traditional media and up-to-date developments pertaining media use in the nation-state.

Expanding Political Discourse in Singapore

Since Singapore's independence traditional media such as print and broadcast media were deployed by the government for the purposes of nurturing and promoting the city-state, and the government's control of the media to cultivate and disseminate hegemonic views and values was justified on the grounds of building social cohesion among its citizens from diverse ethnic, racial, and religious back-grounds. A system of laws, comprising the Broadcasting Act, the Newspaper and Printing Presses Act, and Undesirable Publications Act, governs traditional media (George, 2012). Furthermore, government control of mass media and the ban on satellite dishes have helped, the government has argued, to maintain both political and social stability, critical factors that are purported to have created Singapore's economic success.

When the use of Internet was introduced to Singapore, its regulation came under the jurisdiction of the Media Development Authority (MDA) and regulation was purported to be essential. MDA argued that regulations such as the Internet Code of Practice and the Class Licence Scheme were not aimed at preventing political bodies from setting up websites but at promoting accountability. However, unlike with traditional media, the inherent characteristics of the Internet and the economic benefits associated with widespread adoption of the technology made it difficult for the government to regulate new media in the same way (George, 2003). Thus, the government's attempt to strike a balance between "illiberal political interventions with market-oriented strategies for economic growth" (p. 247), coupled with the sheer volume of rapidly-transmissible content, led to loopholes that were exploited by marginalised groups and individuals.

In recent years, the growing use of new media for self-expression and the sharing of opinions have spurred the government to recognise new media's potential to change the political landscape. New media such as blogs and social networking sites are gaining popularity, as revealed in a 2008 survey by Infocomm Development Authority of Singapore. Out of a population of 4.5 million people in 2007, 11% created their content (for example, create and maintain their own blogs and broadcast self-produced videos via YouTube and Google Video) and 70% communicated via social networks, blogs, instant messaging, e-mails, and peer-to-peer platforms (Infocomm Development Authority of Singapore, Annual Survey on Infocomm Usage — Households and by Individuals, 2009). Kluver (2007) analysed the political relevance of new media technologies such as blogs, podcasts and instant messaging systems to the 2005 Presidential election and concluded that the Internet was broadening the scope of civic discussion in Singapore as it enabled the public to engage in issues of political and social significance in alternative platforms. Singaporeans have also taken to their blogs, social networking sites, and online videos to raise awareness and garner support for specific causes (Tan, 2008), lending greater credence to scholars' arguments that new media technologies are redefining political and civic discourse in Singapore.

Research Aims

A research agenda that incorporates both traditional and new media in addressing the impact on election coverage is timely, especially in light of the fast-growing adoption of new media among Singaporeans and alternative news and perspectives offered online. The ease and low cost of participation and the provision of a safer place against censorship in the form of online platforms have led to the proliferation of online-based and issue-centred groups such as Repeal 377A (concerning the law criminalising male homosexual intercourse), Singapore Anti-Mandatory Death Penalty and Free Burma, some of which have been quick to leverage social networking sites to build communities of supporters (Soon, 2011). This study aims to reconcile the divergent conclusions on inter-media agenda setting between traditional and new media. Our research agenda takes into consideration the evolution of news producers and includes new media users. Our overarching aim is to examine the interaction between online mainstream media (hereafter, online MSM) and various other types of online and social media. Contextualised against the General Election 2011, the following questions guide our data collection and analysis: What inter-media agenda setting can be observed during the General Elections? Is online MSM setting the agenda for other online media, or the other way round?

The next section discusses how the data were collected and organised into a form that facilitates time-series Granger causality analysis. It contrasts the statistical and everyday meanings of "causality", gives a basic idea of how it works, and presents a literature review of the Granger causality test, especially in its application to agenda setting later.

Research Method

To answer the above research questions, we measured the volume of online media activity by sampling close to 1,200 relevant online media sites. These included (1) websites belonging to MSM such as *The Straits Times* and Channel News Asia, (2) alternative online media, including news sites, blogs, and forums, (3) Facebook, and (4) Twitter (there existed 650 streams with more than 50 tweets). These four streams were archived between 1 February to 16 May 2011. The research problem under investigation is whether the four streams of online media influenced one another in election-related discussions. The sites included in the sample comprised the following:

MSM websites

http://www.straitstimes.com/
http://www.channelnewsasia.com/singapore
http://www.todayonline.com/

Alternative online media

Blog aggregators

http://www.singapore-window.org/
http://www.singazine.com/
http://singaporedaily.net/

Group blogs/sites

http://maruah.org/
http://www.theonlinecitizen.com/
http://www.temasekreview.com/

General Election-oriented sites

http://easyapps.sg/sgep/
http://www.singapore-elections.com/
http://singaporeelection.blogspot.com/

Discussion forums

http://forums.hardwarezone.com.sg/forumdisplay.php?f=16
http://sgforums.com/forums/10
http://groups.google.com/group/soc.culture.singapore/topics?pli=1

Political blogs/semi-political blogs

http://yawningbread.wordpress.com/
http://leelilian.blogspot.com/
http://www.mrbrown.com/

Party websites

http://www.pap.org.sg/
http://www.youngpap.org.sg/
http://www.wp.org.sg/

Facebook

http://m.Facebook.com/theonlinecitizen?v=feed&refid=0
http://m.Facebook.com/ngejay?v=feed&refid=0
http://m.Facebook.com/pages/Lee-Kuan-Yew/26407441459

Twitter

http://www.Twitter.com/mrbrown
http://www.Twitter.com/tocsg
http://www.Twitter.com/ChannelNewsAsia

The selection of sites to be included in the web archives was determined by their relevance to GE2011. While it ought to have been objectively based on domain knowledge, some judgment was required in certain cases.[1] We used two approaches, seed-based and keyword-based harvests, in this project. In a seed-based harvest, a set of starting URLs was designated as seed sites from which the web pages were collected, through exhaustively and recursively traversing the hyperlinks embedded in web pages that satisfied certain scoping rules. This approach typically covered websites such as party and blogger websites. In a keyword-based harvest, a set of keywords was applied to search engines from which the top hits (namely, URLs) within a threshold were fetched and the corresponding web pages archived as part of the collection. The search engines that were used in this project included Google News, Google Blog, YouTube, and Twitter Search. Relevant content were collected through web pages that shared the same domain name and were published by authors who were judged to have been publishing articles related to the themes and events of concern. Additionally, if the content of the web pages contained certain election-related keywords, such as "Singapore election" or "Singapore General Election", it too was archived.

The search tasks were supported by a Web Archiving Information System consisting of software agents, a web crawler, and an interface to search engines so that we could specify the seeds and keywords that automatically harvested the relevant materials, as well as schedule the harvest frequency. As the volume of new material rose towards Polling Day, the frequency of harvesting was also increased and conducted daily during the period from 27 April to 7 May. More than 1.8 million online posts on 48 issues from websites belonging to the four streams of online media were collected. The selection of these 48 issues is explained in the section on agenda setting. Of these posts, about half, or close to 890,000, were used for our analysis. Those not chosen had time stamps outside the election period or with IP addresses that were not included in the domains listed above.

The number of news stories, blog posts, and comments were recorded for each day within the sample period. For each of the 48 issues of interest, four times series of daily counts were produced, corresponding to the four categories of media. One particular approach in TSA that is considered suitable for this type of investigation is testing for Granger causality.

The Granger causality test is intuitively simple. Take the two sets of time series data on hand, one concerning MSM and one the new media. Determine the correlation for the two sets for the same time. Now if one assumes that MSM "causes" new media, then when one shifts the MSM data so that an earlier data point is now correlated to a later new media data point, the correlation should be higher. For example, if the data were by the month, then if, say, the January MSM data were correlated with, say, the March new media data, the correlation would increase; on the other hand, correlating the January new media data with the March MSM data would cause the correlation to decrease.

The main difference between Granger's application of the notion of "causality" and a commonplace understanding of that term lies in the fact that the former is based on meeting prescribed statistical standards. Granger causality between time series A and B is said to occur when the time series A statistically predicts B better than B's history can predict B. The commonplace notion of causality may be regarded as technically less precise than Granger causality as the former and does not usually specify a statistical relationship between the time series A and B. At the same, the commonplace notion could also be broader. For instance, if three time series variables X, Y, and Z were known to have been generated by X giving rise to Y, which in turn gave rise to Z, we would not usually say that Y is the cause of Z in the commonplace notion of causality, but we would say that Y is the cause of Z in the Granger causality sense. Thus Granger causality may depart from more intuitive notions such as "originating from". Despite the limitations of the concept of Granger causality, confining it to an explicit statistical requirement enables us to operationalise what would otherwise have been a rather complicated process of argumentation.

For agenda setting in particular, tests of Granger causality have been applied in various ways, including the analysis of hypotheses about the effects of media framing on the dynamics of racial policy preferences in the U.S. (Kellstedt, 2000), development of a framework for media-public influence (Uscinski, 2009), and demonstration of media-media influence involving YouTube (Sayre *et al.*, 2010).

Findings and Discussion

To analyse the time series relationships, we monitored the frequency of online publications and postings referring to the list of 48 topics of online discussion. The 48 topics are divided into five categories as follows: 14 topics under Major Election Issues, 14 topics under Group Representation Constituencies or GRCs (note: there are in fact 15 GRCs, but West Coast GRC was excluded due to a lack of records), seven political parties, 11 topics with the prominent and controversial opposition candidate "Tan Jee Say" as part of the search term, and finally, the two topics "Nicole Seah" (the immensely popular opposition candidate) and "Tin Pei Ling" (a controversial ruling party candidate) which arose only after the campaigning had gotten under way.

We monitored the frequencies of online postings and publications for these issues in four types of online media, namely online MSM, Facebook, Twitter, and all other forms of online alternative media (such as political blogs, semi-political blogs, discussion forums). Table 1 summarises key statistics. As mentioned earlier, major election issues, political parties and GRCs are categories of search terms. In contrast, "Nicole Seah" and "Tin Pei Ling" are specific search terms. This accounts for why there were more records for category search terms. The table shows that each day within the almost three-and-a-half month period, online discussions referring to the political parties by name averaged 225 traditional media publications, 1,870 Facebook postings, 2,012 tweets and 257 publications/postings in other online forms. The standard deviations are very large and exceeded the mean in all four cases. One reason for the large dispersion was that the publications, posts, and tweets started out very low in February, before climbing exponentially as polling date neared. The activity declined rapidly after Polling Day.

As depicted in Figures 1 to 6, the volume of Facebook postings and tweets far outnumbered the frequency counts of the remaining two media types with one exception. The exception is with "Tan Jee Say" related search terms, where Facebook postings and tweets were way below the other media type in frequency. Despite the difference, Figure 4 does not show any increase in "cross-overs" of the frequencies for Facebook and Twitter, compared with those of online MSM and online alternative media.

Table 1.   Summary statistics

Search term(s)/ category	Statistic	Online MSM	FB	Twitter	Online alternative media
Major election issues	Total Records	22056	79157	71229	35024
	Avg, Daily Count	210.06	753.88	678.37	333.56
	Standard Dev, Daily Count	437.74	1437.48	1588.38	432.47
Political parties	Total Records	23614	196374	211244	27012
	Avg, Daily Count	224.90	1870.23	2011.85	257.26
	Standard Dev, Daily Count	450.84	4388.80	5913.25	377.97
GRCs	Total Records	22288	79253	43095	13676
	Avg, Daily Count	212.27	754.79	410.43	130.25
	Standard Dev, Daily Count	394.96	1964.10	1814.20	245.40
"Tan Jee Say" AND major election issue	Total Records	8418	798	105	6253
	Avg, Daily Count	80.17	7.60	1.00	59.55
	Standard Dev, Daily Count	217.93	26.61	3.53	123.17
"Nicole Seah"	Total Records	1674	11178	5742	1980
	Avg, Daily Count	15.94	106.46	54.69	18.86
	Standard Dev, Daily Count	28.92	239.65	151.00	36.56
"Tin Pei Ling"	Total Records	585	16522	10393	2208
	Avg, Daily Count	5.57	157.35	98.98	21.03
	Standard Dev, Daily Count	13.99	541.10	400.22	31.86

Table 2 reports the tests for Granger causality. Under the null hypothesis of non-causality, the test statistic is distributed as chi-square with degrees of freedom equal to the number of lags of the postulated causal influence being omitted. We used seven lags, corresponding to the daily periodicity of our data. As such the statistics would be significant for a test conducted at the 0.5% level of significance if they exceed the chi-square critical value of 21.955. The values of Table 2 far exceed that, implying that there is significant evidence of Granger causality. This means that

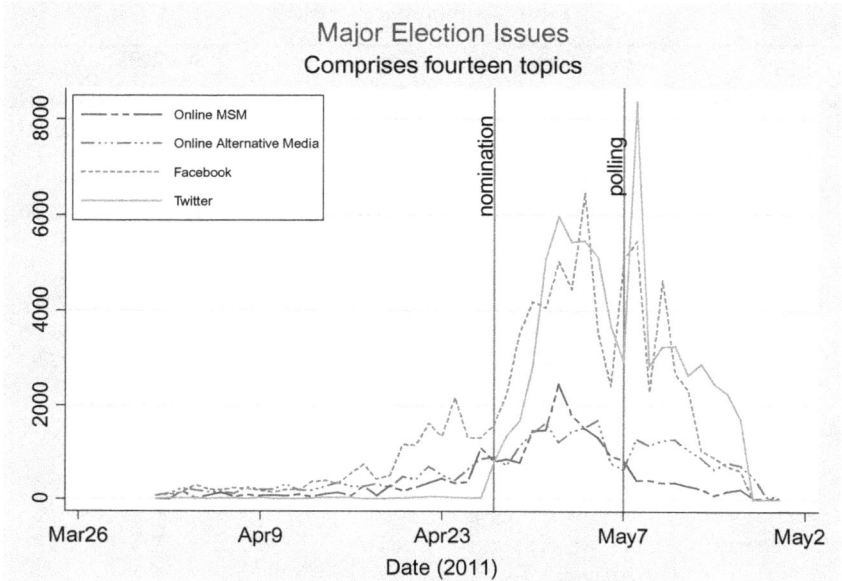

Figure 1: Frequency of fourteen major election issues in online media

the various categories of online media exert an influence on one another. The actual rate of occurrence of false positives, however, is much higher than the nominal 0.1% (see footnote accompanying Table 2). Nonetheless, the evidence is overwhelming at the selected level of significance. The uniformity and strength of this result is quite different from those reported in studies of election-related media influence surveyed earlier, such as Sayre *et al.* (2010). One possible reason is that, rather than approach the problem from a conventional agenda-setting perspective, we did not determine the "agenda" of the different groups of online media through a preliminary poll. Instead, we employed a list of topics that were devised mainly on the basis of convention, and that had been discerned from offline and online discourse during the election period.

In order to derive further understanding of relative strength of the relationships in the results of Table 2, we computed the correlations between the rankings (based on the relative volume

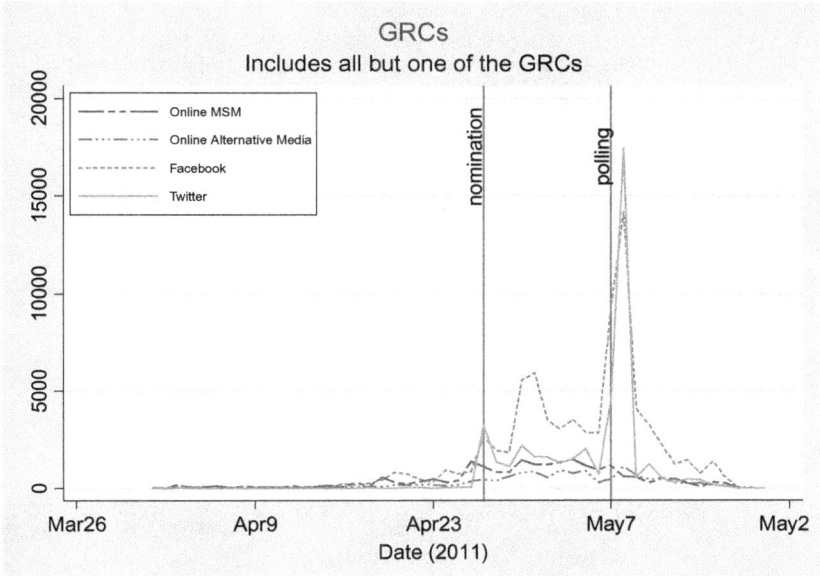

Figure 2: Frequency of GRC presence in online media

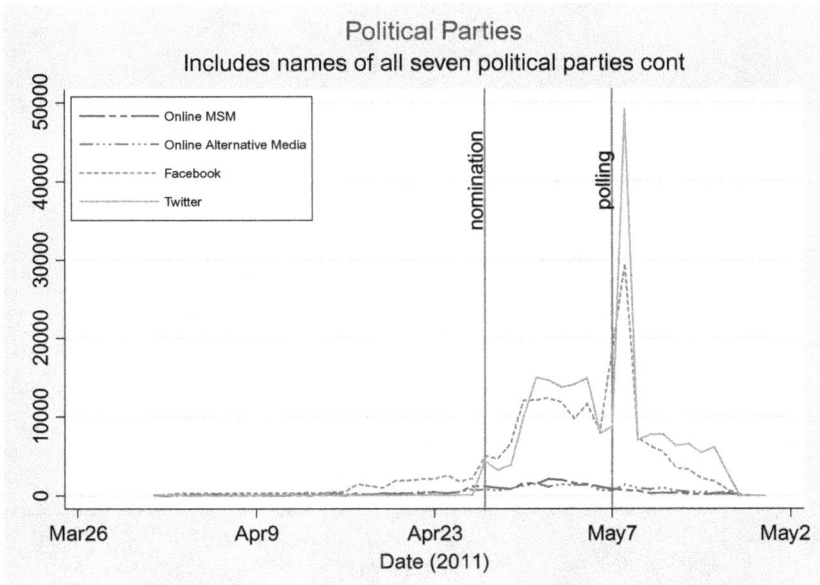

Figure 3: Frequency of political party presence in online media

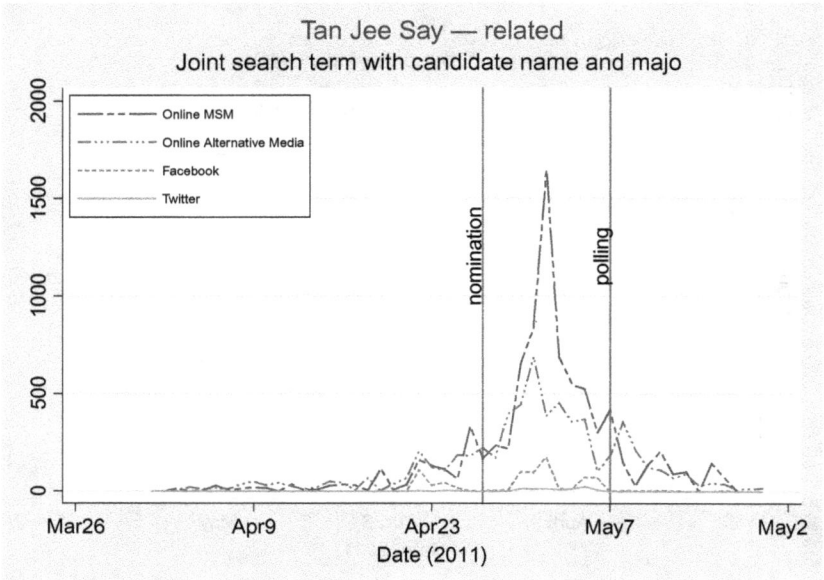

Figure 4:   Frequency of Tan Jee Say's name in online media

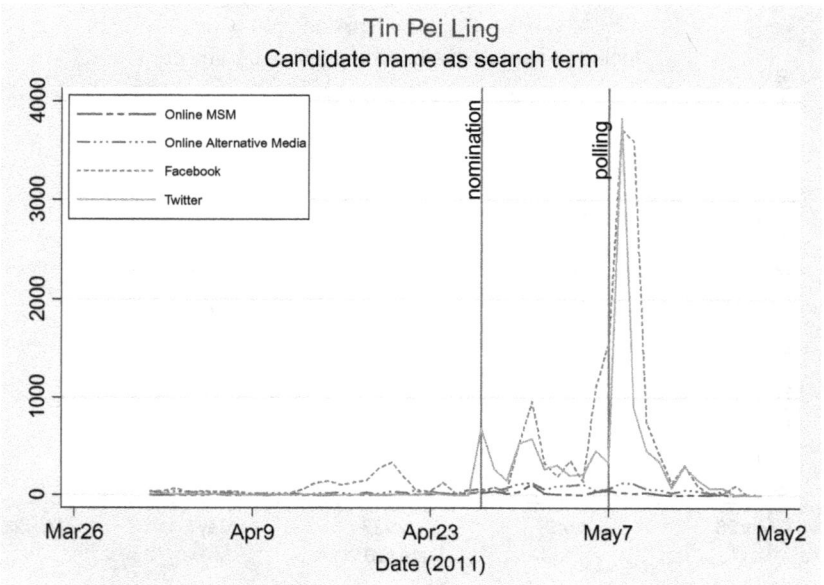

Figure 5:   Frequency of Tin Pei Ling's name in online media

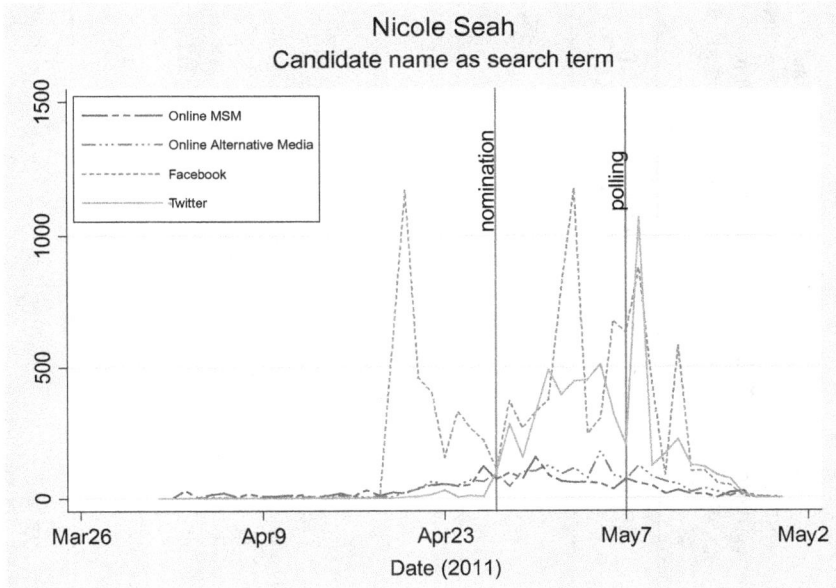

Figure 6:   Frequency of Nicole Seah's name in online media

of publications) of issues by the four different media for the cases of the categories of Major election issues, Political parties, GRCs, and "Tan Jee Say"-related issues. These statistics, akin to the "inter-correlations" derived by McCombs and Shaw (1972), are reported in Table 3. These correlations are generally weakest for Twitter with the other three forms of media. On the other hand, they are generally strong between Facebook and the others. Since both are new forms of social media, and both display similar orders of frequency counts (refer to the Figures, for example), the contrast between them is noteworthy. One possible reason is that Twitter was still relatively new to Singapore's online community, compared to Facebook.

Another way of investigating the results of Table 2 more closely is to consider the specific issues within those broad categories of issues. The tests of Granger causality for the 48 specific issues came up mostly significant. This means that there is bidirectional causality in almost all the issues for all the possible pairs of media types. There

Table 2. Tests of bivariate Granger causality

The reported values are calculated values of statistics for testing the impact of the influencing media (indicated in the second row of the table) on the dependent media (indicated in the first row). Large values present evidence in favour of Granger causality. For example, for media reports related to Major Election Issues, the reported figure of 61.858 is the value of the statistic for testing that Online Alternative Media (OA) have been significant in influencing Online MSM (OM). All of the values reported in the table are in excess of the nominal critical value at the 0.1% level.

Dependent:	Online MSM (OM)			Facebook			Twitter			Online Alternative Media (OA)		
Influence Search Term(s)/Category	OA	FB	TW	OM	ONM	TW	TM	OA	FB	OM	FB	TW
Major Election Issues	61.858	114.18	49.606	304.02	89.271	99.434	396.84	200.14	196.89	98.212	67.555	97.696
GRCs	74.039	35.14	61.291	195.42	1172.2	838.65	101.58	950.96	632.73	184.5	437.61	329.32
Political Parties	61.804	92.203	79.594	104.58	79.333	675.2	117.09	140.12	947.67	67.601	153.6	118.76
Tan Jee Say with Major Issues	632.82	65.321	267.23	52.687	168.9	65.758	444.57	695.76	234.56	110.7	75.818	243.53
Nicole Seah	64.424	47.771	96.142	34.465	32.205	33.258	262.4	436.62	260.88	185.75	174.1	212.78
Tin Pei Ling	56.573	186.33	236.61	1032.1	80.003	841.29	334.49	72.17	20.284	30.727	35.281	31.44

Note: The hypothesis is the presence of Granger causality. Chi-square statistics are for tests in a multivariate VAR. All chi-square values are significant (nominal level of significance 0.1%, actual level of significance 6.95%).

Table 3. Inter-correlations

The correlations are restricted to the range −1 to 1. The nearer values are to 1, the more closely two series track each other's movement through time. Values nearer to zero indicate less co-movement. For example, on Major Election issues, the number of reports on Facebook and Online Alternative Media are highly related, and more closely so than for any other pair of media.

	Online MSM	Facebook	Twitter	Online Alternative Media
Major Election issues				
Online MSM	1			
Facebook	0.710	1		
Twitter	0.336	0.543	1	
Online Alternative Media	0.648	0.903	0.495	1
Political parties				
Online MSM	1			
Facebook	1.000	1		
Twitter	0.750	0.750	1	
Online Alternative Media	0.964	0.964	0.857	1
GRCs				
Online MSM	1			
Facebook	0.481	1		
Twitter	0.371	0.780	1	
Online Alternative Media	0.371	0.903	0.758	1
"Tan Jee Say"-related				
Online MSM	1			
Facebook	0.200	1		
Twitter	0.106	0.745	1	
Online Alternative Media	0	0.382	0.428	1

were only four issues in which some of the Granger causality tests resulted in a failure to reject at the 5% level. These are the issues "CPF", "Healthcare", "Income inequality", and "People's Action Party". Table 4 reports the test results of these cases. In the case of "CPF", for instance, this would mean that online alternative media took the agenda-setting initiative over online MSM.

Table 4. Tests of bivariate Granger non-causality for selected specific issues

Dependent: Influence / Search Term(s)/Category	Online MSM (OM)			Facebook (FB)			Twitter (TW)			Online Alternative Media (OA)		
	OA	FB	TW	OM	OA	TW	OM	OA	FB	OM	FB	TW
CPF	19.222	31.407	610.65	63.457	34.204	48.041	104.14	62.275	36.067	**9.8519**	25.703	16.392
Healthcare	17.269	51.007	98.148	192.05	**5.318**	76.034	307.74	19.808	203.3	13.215	16.316	42.657
Income Inequality	38.686	**11.498**	82.631	89.833	31.911	**11.879**	99.244	11.201	33.016	54.327	45.849	43.118
People's Action Party	**8.2183**	71.129	68.411	77.158	**11.676**	471.54	110.2	14.539	454.35	75.785	101.88	85.233

Note: Chi-square statistics are for tests in a multivariate VAR. Except for the figures in bold which not significant, all other figures are significant at the 5% level.

Table 5. Information flows among online traditional mainstream media, other new media, Twitter, and Facebook

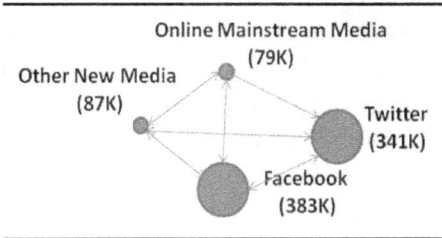

In summary, the study found that the overall agenda-setting effect occurred in both directions between online MSM and online alternative media. Table 5 summarises and demonstrates the information flows (indicated by the directed edges) are bidirectional despite the different volumes (indicated by size of the nodes) among the four types of media. However, at the specific issue type and using classical inter-correlation test, Twitter was shown to be less reflective of the other media types. These statistics are supportive of the realisation of a growing trend in Singapore to adopt Facebook and Twitter as prominent channels of communication and civic engagement.

Conclusion

Our study aimed at providing a first-cut study on inter-media agenda setting with regard to a Singapore election and we focused on how different media channels, online MSM, and online alternative media interact with one another in setting the agenda for election-related topics. The significant bidirectionality between traditional media and new media supports existing theorisations and studies concerning how new media are becoming increasingly influential in setting topics for discussion as traditional media are becoming more sensitised and attuned to what are being disseminated and shared online within alternative media. Whilst previous studies conducted in the U.S. arrived at conflicting conclusions pertaining to inter-media agenda setting, our study established through TSA that MSM and new media are highly sensitive to one another in coverage of election issues. Our findings are contrary to Ng's (2010) study which showed that traditional media set the agenda for new media. This could be due to two reasons — the time lapse between Ng's study and ours, during which new media's stature as alternative news provider has risen to greater prominence; and the exponential increase in online activity during election period due to more fervent posting and sharing of news.

Besides challenging existing studies and establishing that new media are becoming a contender for traditional media in setting the agenda, our study suggests that users of blogs, Facebook and Twitter are also taking their cues from news and issues of the day that are covered in the mainstream press. In addition, the bidirectionality that is observed between MSM and these three media also indicate that traditional news providers are possibly turning to new media for topics hotly discussed in cyberspace. Clearly, new media users in Singapore, akin to their counterparts in other parts of the world, are assuming the roles of consumers and producers of information. In addition to filling a gap in existing scholarship on inter-media agenda setting which is predominantly Western-centric, we argue that our findings must be interpreted in the context of Singapore's political economy. As George (2006) and Kluver (2007) have maintained, Internet technologies have provided a way for members of the public to participate in political and civic discourse. Through blogs, social networking sites, and microblogs, citizens are now able to perform more active roles in information sharing and publishing instead of passively consuming information and news that are disseminated by traditional sources.

One limitation of this study resides in how the agenda or issues were selected. Similar to the approach adopted in many agenda-setting studies, we chose a comprehensive set of issues to study: the election agenda, the parties, the candidates, the constituencies, and the candidate cum agenda pair, which have been covered in the agenda-setting research to date. For the election agenda, a similarly comprehensive approach is adopted to identify both the obtrusive, of which the public tends to have direct experiences, and the unobtrusive issues, of which the public tends not to have direct experience: the societal/social issues, for example, education and national service, the economic issues, for example, cost of living and rising HDB prices, and the political system issues, for example, freedom of speech and First World Parliament. We acknowledge that this could be a potential limitation in that human judgement made on the selection of issues and topics could have been primed by discourse present in both traditional media and new media. The source of issue or topic could have biased the directionality of inter-media agenda setting. However, this is mitigated by the fact that bidirectionality is observed across different types of media in spite of the potentially different sources of origin.

In our study, our focus is on the overall trend of agenda setting between the traditional mainstream and new media in the context of a Singapore election. We did not investigate the public agenda, which can only be done through survey or public opinion poll, neither the political adoption of the public. Future work could also assess agenda-setting effects of different media by comparing the effects of issue coverage in various media and salience associated with those issues by the public, along the lines of Uscinski (2009). Another direction for further research will be to conduct social network analysis of the different media as represented by their websites. This line of investigation will generate insights into who the central actors are and how they may influence and shape public discourse.

References

Bruns, A. *Blogs, Wikipedia, Second Life, and Beyond: From Production to Produsage* (New York: Peter Lang, 2008).

Davie, S. "The blog father". *The Straits Times*, 3 September 2008. Retrieved 1 August 2009 from Factiva database.

Flew, T. *New Media: An Introduction* (Melbourne: Oxford University Press, 2005).

Gil de Zuniga, H., E. Puig-I-Abril, and H. Rojas. "Weblogs, Traditional Sources Online and Political Participation: An Assessment of How the Internet is Changing the Political Environment", *New Media and Society*, 11(4), (2009): 553–74.

George, C. "The Internet and the Narrowing Tailoring Dilemma for "Asian" Democracies", *The Communication Review*, 6 (2003): 247–68.

George, C. *Contentious Journalism and the Internet: Towards Democratic Discourse in Malaysia and Singapore* (Singapore: Singapore University Press, 2006).

George, C. *Freedom from the Press* (Singapore: NUS Press, 2012).

George, C. "Alternative Media: New Era in Ties". *The Straits Times*, 25 June 2011, p. A32.

Granger, C.W.J. "Investigating Causal Relations by Econometric Models and Cross-spectral Methods", *Econometrica*, 37 (1969): 424–38.

Ibrahim, Y. "Textual and Symbolic Resistance: Re-mediating Politics Through the Blogosphere in Singapore". In *International Blogging*, Russell, A. and N. Echchaibi (eds.) (New York: Peter Lang Publishing, 2009).

Infocomm Development Authority of Singapore (2009). Infocomm Usage — Households and Individuals for 2008, 2009. Available at http://www.ida.gov.sg/Publications/20070822125451.aspx#usage Hse3 (accessed 1 September 2009).

Iyengar, S. and A. Simon. "News Coverage of the Gulf Crisis and Public Opinion: A Study of Agenda-setting, Priming, and Framing", *Communication Research* 20(3) (1993): 365–83.

Jenkins, H. *Fans, Bloggers and Gamers: Exploring Participatory Culture* (New York: New York University Press, 2006).

Kellstedt, P.M. "Media Framing and the Dynamics of Racial Policy Preferences", *American Journal of Political Science*, 44(2), (2000): 245–60.

Kluver, R. "The Internet and the Expansion of Political Discussion in Singapore Elections". Paper presented at the International Communication Association Conference, San Francisco, California, May 2007.

Ku, G., L.L. Kaid, and M. Pfau. "The Impact of Web Site Campaigning on Traditional News Media and Public Information Processing", *Journalism and Mass Communication Quarterly*, 80(3), (2003): 528–47.

Lanosga, G. "Blogs and Big Media: A Comparative Study of Agendas". *Conference Papers, International Communication Association* (2008): 1–25.

McCombs, M. and D.L. Shaw. "The Agenda-setting Function of Mass Media", *Public Opinion Quarterly*, 36(2), (1972): 176–87.

McKenna, L. and A. Pole. "Do blogs matter? Weblogs in American politics". Paper presented at the American Political Science Association's Annual Meeting, Chicago, IL, September 2004.

Neo, C.C. "Singapore-kini as an Alternative?" *Today*, 25 April 2008 (Retrieved 1 August 2009 from Factiva database).

Ng, A.Y.K. "The Relationship Between Blogs and Newspapers in Singapore: An Intermedia Agenda-setting Study". Masters thesis, National University of Singapore, 2010.

Ng, T.Y. "Facebook trolls can be the most valuable fans". *The Straits Times*, 17 May 2011, p. A2.

Reese, S. and L. Danielian. "Intermedia Influence and the Drug Issue: Converging on Cocaine." In *Agenda-setting: Readings on Media, Public Opinion, and Policymaking*, pp. 237–49, Protess, D. and M. Maxwell (eds.) (Hillsdale, NJ: Lawrence Earlbaum Associates, 1991).

Sani, M.A.M. "The Emergence of New Politics in Malaysia: From Consociational to Deliberative Democracy", *Taiwan Journal of Democracy*, 5(2), (2009): 97–125.

Sayre, B., L. Bode, D. Shah, D. Wilcox, and C. Shah. "Agenda Setting in a Digital Age: Tracking Attention to California Proposition 8 in Social Media, Online News and Conventional News". *Policy and Internet*, 2(2), (2010): 7–32.

Shirky, C. "Power Laws, Weblogs and Inequality". In *Extreme Democracy*, Lebkowsky, J. and M. Ratcliffe. Lulu.com, 2005.

Soon, C. "OMGs! Offline-based Movement Organizations, Online-based Movement Organizations and Implications for Network Mobilization and Issue Framing". Paper presented at Asia's Civil Spheres: New Media urban Public Space, Social Movements, Asia Research Institute Roundtable, 29–30 September 2011, Singapore.

Soon, C. and H. Cho. "Flows of Relations and Communication Among Singapore Political Bloggers and Organizations: The Networked Public Sphere Approach", *Journal of Information Technology and Politics*, 8, (2011): 93–109.

Tan, W. "Rise of Online Activists". *The Straits Times*, 9 August 2008, p. B11.

Trumbo, C. "Longitudinal Modeling of Public Issues: An Application of the Agenda-setting Process to the Issue of Global Warming", *Journalism and Mass Communication Monographs*, 152, (1995): 57.

Uscinski, J.E. "When Does the Public's Issue Agenda Affect the Media's Issue Agenda (and Vice-Versa)? Developing a Framework for Media-Public Influence", *Social Science Quarterly*, 90(4), (2009): 796–815.

Winner, L. "The Internet and Dreams of Democratic Renewal". In *The Civic Web: Online Politics and Democratic Values*, D.M. Anderson and M. Cornfield (eds.) (Lanham: Rowman & Littlefield, 2003).

6

DIFFERENT BUT NOT THAT DIFFERENT: NEW MEDIA'S IMPACT ON YOUNG VOTERS' POLITICAL PARTICIPATION

Trisha T.C. Lin and Alice Y.H. Hong

Abstract

To examine the impact of new media and youth on the 2011 Singapore General Election, this post-election national telephone survey interviewed 447 young Singaporeans aged 21 to 35. Young Singaporeans, on the one hand, engaged more in this election due to the prevalent use of new media; on the other hand, with higher dissatisfaction over media control and cynical attitude towards the government, almost 50% of them still trusted old media and a higher percentage of them supported the ruling party instead of the opposition. The results show that the youth who were aware of media content control still spent more time on mainstream media than new media, and perceived the former as more important and trustworthy sources of election information. Data analysis reveals that media use was significantly correlated to youth's perceived importance of media on voting decisions. Mass media still had more influence on youth's voting decisions, but the impact of new media on young citizens' votes was greater than on older counterparts. The study also finds that more mature, less-educated, and female respondents tended to support the ruling party more.

The 2011 Singapore General Election (GE2011) has been regarded as a watershed in Singapore's election history by various political parties, as well as by Prime Minister Lee Hsien Loong. He attributed the 6 percentage point swing against the ruling People's Action Party (PAP) and its loss of the five-seat Aljunied constituency to two main factors: the increasing number of critical and outspoken young voters and the prevalent use of new media (Leong, 2011). One quarter of the 2.21 million voters in GE2011 were youth, which we define as those aged between 21 and 34 (Singapore Elections Department, 2011). New media, especially the Internet, provide crucial channels for Singaporeans to express and read political opinions not found in mainstream media due to censorship (Lin and Lim, 2010). Young Singaporeans tend to be more tech savvy than older citizens, which leads to the question of the impact of new media on youth's political participation and voting behaviour.

There are two dominant models of perceived youth engagement in politics: active and engaged, or passive and disengaged (Bennett, 2008; Delli Carpini, 2000). The engaged youth model postulates that the young generation becomes more connected via virtual communities and social media, which empowers them to express ideas and opinions across platforms. In contrast, the disengaged youth model argues that online political participation is sporadic, and parallels the decline in offline political participation and voting. To examine if the youth were more or less engaged politically in GE2011, our study analyses the data from a nation-wide survey carried out after the election. The 2,000 voters surveyed by telephone include 447 youth aged between 21 to 34 years old. Our study aims to uncover the political participation, attitudes, voting behaviour, and media communication patterns among youth in this election. It also investigates how young citizens' use of and attitudes towards media are correlated with their voting behaviour and political traits.

Digital Youth Political Participation and Elections

Advocates of the engaged youth model emphasise that despite declining trust in public discourses, new media empower the young generation to express socio-political perspectives and to participate in online civic action via peer networks or virtual communities (Bennett *et al.*, 2006). Many studies have shown that the new media had critical impact on the youth since the 2008 United States (U.S.) Presidential Election. New media was American youth's first choice for seeking or sharing election information (Wu, 2009) and for keenly creating political content (Stelter, 2008). The Pew Survey showed young voters were crucial in helping propel Obama's 2012 re-election (Pew Research Center, 2012). However, some argue that although new media offer possibilities for civic participation and online political debates, they lead to fragmentation of socio-political views (Bennett, 2008). Proponents of the disengaged youth model see declining political participation and voting, distrust of the press, and indifference in political discussions even before the rise of the Internet. In their view, young people's "zealotic" new media engagement is not necessarily translated into civic engagement (Bennett *et al.*, 2006).

According to Coleman (2008), there is a cross-national genera-tional shift in the post-industrial democracies, with people transi-tioning from engaged *dutiful citizens* (DC) to disengaged *actualising citizens* (AC). Dutiful citizens who are more engaged in democracies feel obliged to participate in politics and to vote, to be informed via the media, and to be part of civil society. Actualising citizens who are more disengaged in democracies feel less need for government intervention and less meaning in voting, mistrust the media, as well as favour loosely networked activism to address political issues. In many nations, youth are among those most excluded from the public discourses of government, policy arenas and elections, and hence are AC (Bennett, 2008). They feel that politics is distant, irrelevant, and inauthentic, and tend not to participate or vote.

The evidence is mixed on whether information and communi-cation technology (ICT) savvy Singapore youth can be regarded as engaged DC or disengaged AC in politics and elections. On the one hand, Singapore's political parties have seen a healthy increase in youth involvement before the country prepared for the GE2011 (Lim, 2010). Compared with older counterparts, the youth engage in politics more actively and consume more political content primarily through online channels (Tan, Chung and Zhang, 2011). On the other hand, before GE2011, a *New Paper* survey found that about 40% of Singapore young respondents would not vote in the election if it was not compulsory by law (Tay, 2011a). It also found that the younger the respondents, the more likely they were to say they would not vote.

Due to inconclusive evidence about young Singaporeans' political engagement and disengagement, we raise the following research questions:

Q1. To what extent did young voters participate in politics during GE2011?

Young AC trust the government less and show a more cynical attitude towards the current administration. According to Hong (2009), politically cynical people tend to show distrust of the political system, including officials and institutions. To find out how youth perceive government control and the extent of their trust in politicians, this study also asks:

Q2. To what extent were young voters politically cynical?

Old and New Media in Singapore Politics and Elections

Since the election in 2001, Singapore has introduced a series of regulations concerning new media, politics, and elections. Under the class license, political websites are automatically licensed, but are also required to be registered with the regulator, the Media Development Authority (MDA), if asked to do so. Several websites, like the now-defunct Sintercom, were asked to register by the MDA and identify the editorial team to ensure that they provided "responsible" online political information.

The 2006 election was the first to see extensive use of the Internet on politics due to the proliferation of online political and election content (Rahim, 2006; Gomez, 2008). Political party websites incorporated interactive features and multimedia content. Opposition politicians used online media to bypass mass media to reach out to the public. Blogging emerged as a critical medium for alternative voices on election issues (Lin and Lim, 2010). Some well-known political blogs even influenced the way mainstream media reported the election (Gomez, 2008).

Just before GE2011, more changes were made to regulations governing new media use in elections. In 2010, online election advertising laws were liberalised, including legalising non-political websites to engage in political discussions (Shanmugam, 2010). In 2011, regulations were amended to allow new forms of online election campaigning (George, 2011).

Singapore politicians have become more Internet-savvy. Some political parties extensively used social media as a campaign tool. Since April 2011, politicians also used social media to humanise themselves and established Facebook pages to express issues and respond to people's queries (Lai, 2011). GE2011 has been marked by an increasing amount of political participation on Facebook, the third favourite online source for GE2011 information (Wee, 2011). Even Prime Minister Lee Hsien Loong used the PAP's Facebook account to participate in an interactive online chat and discussed election-related issues with voters before GE2011. More than half of the Members of Parliament (MP) had Facebook accounts to interact with citizens (Hussain, 2011). The opposition parties in GE2011 used the new media to increase their visibility online (Lim, 2010). Netizens actively posted election-related writings and videos, clearly showing that the online platform with looser content regulation had become a popular virtual space for free exchange and sharing of political information.

Recently, highly vocal youth have become active in using new media to engage in political debates (Tay, 2011a). *The New Paper's* survey finds that youth still regarded traditional media as reliable sources of political information, but used online information as supplementary sources (Tay, 2011b). The frequency of media use and perceived media importance are key factors which affect political attitudes of youth (Pinkleton and Austin, 2002). Whether traditional or new media are perceived to be credible by youth is also worth investigating. In order to examine the usage and perceptions of media communication in relation to youth's political behaviour and voting, this study asks:

Q3. How often did young voters use old and new media in GE2011?

Q4. How important did young voters perceive old and new media as information sources about GE2011?

Q5. How trustworthy did young voters perceive old and new media as information sources about GE2011?

Q6. Were the perceptions of new media (i.e. perceived importance, perceived credibility) correlated to youth voting behaviour?

Research finds that when individuals are biased against traditional media, they turn to the Internet for alternative information aligned to their beliefs (Weeks and Southwell, 2010). The Singapore government tailors media laws to maintain national security or social harmony (Rodan, 2003), which leads to criticisms of biased traditional media controlled by content regulation and licensing (Gomez, 2008). With looser content regulation, new media provide a free virtual space for Singaporeans to express alternative voices and read political information usually neglected by mainstream media (Lin and Lim, 2010). It has been argued that content control over mainstream media served as a stimulus for Singaporeans to rely more on political websites and blogs. Indeed, Singaporeans who value alternative perspectives and freedom of speech actively use online political information or engage in discussions (Hong, Lin, and Ang, 2010). Prior studies have found that demographic variables, such as age, socioeconomic status, and educational background, affected individual political inclination and attitudes (Pinkleton and Austin, 2002). This study aims to investigate the relation between youth perceptions of government's media control and voting behaviour. Hence, we propose the following research questions:

Q7. How did young voters perceive government control of old and new media? How did that relate to youth voting behaviour in GE2011?

Q8. Did demographic variables (age, gender and education) affect youth voting behaviour in GE2011?

Method

Besides investigating the research questions, this study also examines whether new media communication (perceived media importance, credibility, and control) and the demographic variables are correlated to the voting behaviour of youth. Our independent variables include old and new media use, perceived media importance, perceived media credibility, media control, and demographic variables (i.e. age, gender, educational level), while dependent variables are political participation, cynical attitude towards the government, and voting behaviour (i.e. who the respondents voted for and which channels influenced them most). This study further compares the results of the youth respondents with the results of the total sample in this GE2011 survey in order to find how the young citizens differ from average Singaporeans in their media use and political participation in this election.

Findings

Q1: To What Extent did Young Voters Participate in Politics, Election, and Voting in GE2011?

The results show that 21 to 34 year old respondents were not keen in participating in offline political activities. Even though 30% of them attended one or more political rallies in GE2011, only 3.6% volunteered to help political parties and 7.5% wrote to newspapers, the government, or an MP in the past six months (Figure 1). In terms of online political participation, we find 28.2% of them wrote on blogs, Facebook or Twitter about the election, and 20.2% forwarded or shared online election content by e-mails, Facebook or Twitter.

Asked which party they voted for, 15.9% of respondents answered "opposition parties"; 26.2% of them answered "PAP"; 14.3% reported "not voting"; and a high percentage of respondents (43.6%) refused to answer (Figure 2).

Q2: To What Extent did Young Voters Hold Cynical Attitudes Towards the Government?

The study shows that young Singaporeans tend to be politically cynical as more than half the respondents (50.2%) agreed that there were too many rules against political participation in Singapore, and

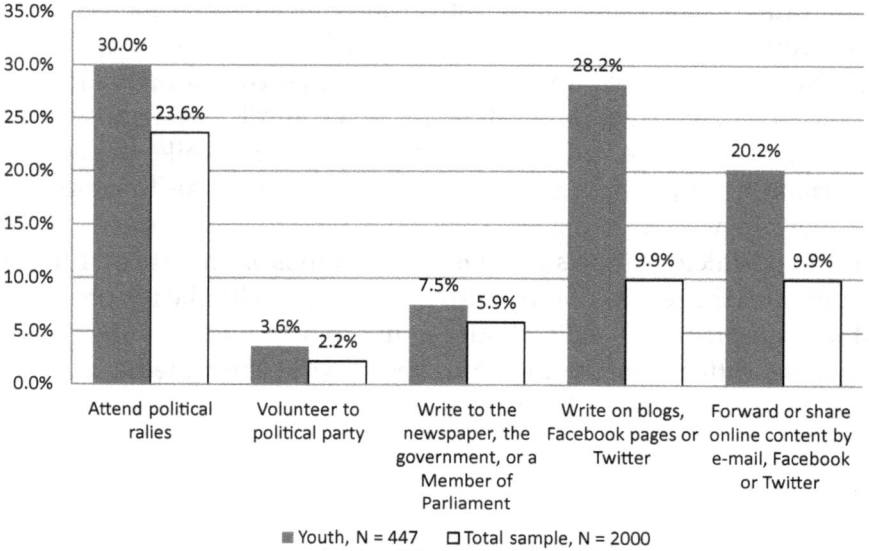

Figure 1: Young citizens' political participation in GE2011

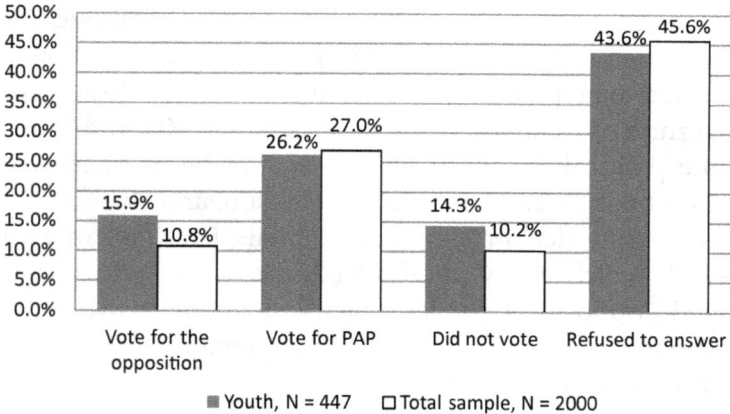

Figure 2: Young citizens' self-reported voting behaviour

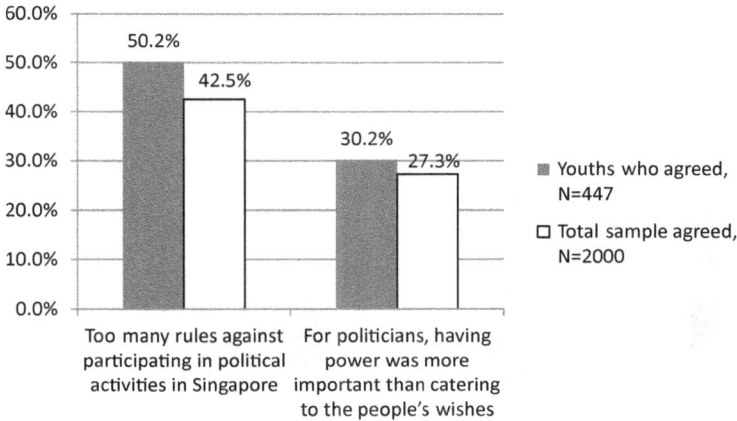

Figure 3: Young citizens' cynical attitude towards the government

30.2% believed that politicians were more interested in power than in serving the public (Figure 3).

Q3: How Often did the Young Voters Use the New Media and Old Media in the 2011 Singapore General Election?

Asked how long they usually used various media to read, listen, or watch GE2011 news, TV, mainstream media-affiliated websites, and newspapers appeared as their top three choices (Figure 4). The study finds that 30.6% of young respondents spent 30 minutes and 9.6% spent 60 minutes a day watching election news on TV; 14.1% spent 30 minutes and 8.5% spent 60 minutes daily reading online websites of Singapore's mainstream media, and 18.8% spent 30 minutes and 6.5% spent 60 minutes a day reading election news on newspapers. Also, 7.6% of them spent 30 minutes reading election news on Facebook, while 7.8% spent 60 minutes daily. In addition, 7.2% spent 30 minutes and 4.5% spent 60 minutes a day reading Internet-only alternative online media (local blogs or news sites such as The Online Citizen, Yawning Bread and Temasek Review). Only 4.3% of youth spent 30 minutes and 2.7% spent 60 minutes daily listening to election news on radio.

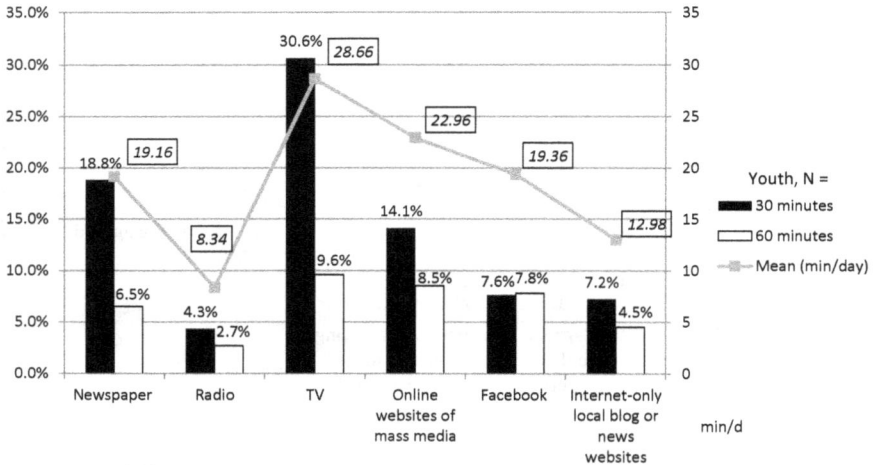

Figure 4:   Young citizens' use of old and new media

We find on average that young people spent the most amount of time watching TV to obtain election news during the period of the general election (28.66 min/day), followed by reading mass media affiliated websites (22.96 min/day), reading newspapers (19.16 min/day), learning about election information on Facebook (18.36 min/day), reading Internet-only local blogs or news websites (12.98 min/day), and listening to radio (8.34 min/day). In short, young citizens tend to spend more time using online media than all traditional media except watching TV.

Q4: How Important did Youth Perceive New and Old Media as Information Sources About GE2011?

With respect to perceived media importance, 62.9% of young respondents in this study reported "important" or "very important" when considering using TV and their websites as sources of information about GE2011 (Figure 5). A marginally lower percentage, 51%, considered Singapore newspapers and their websites as important information sources, while 40.3% of them viewed political party websites as "important" or "very important" to them. Facebook and microblogs (i.e. Twitter, Weibo and Plurk) were perceived as important media by 36.2% and 29.2% respondents respectively.

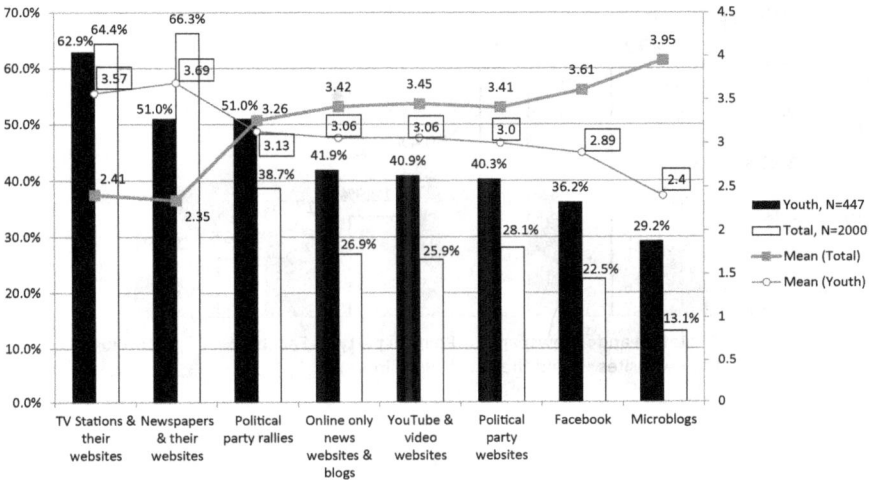

Figure 5: Young citizens' perceived importance of media

Note: 1–5 Likert scale was applied to means: 1 represents "unimportant;" 5 represents "very important."

Mean scores show that newspapers and their websites were perceived by youth as the most important information source about GE2011, and this is closely followed by TV and their websites. Other information sources such as attending political party election rallies, online-only news websites and blogs, YouTube and other video websites, and political party websites were perceived as more important than Facebook and microblogs.

Q5: How Trustworthy did Youth Perceive Old and New Media as Information Sources About GE2011?

When respondents were asked how trustworthy TV stations and their websites were perceived as sources of information about the election, 47.2% of them answered "trustworthy" or "very trustworthy", and 47% of them considered newspapers and their websites as credible. Almost a third (30.4%) reported that political party websites were trustworthy, while 17.7% and 10.5% of the respondents trusted Facebook and microblogs respectively (Figure 6).

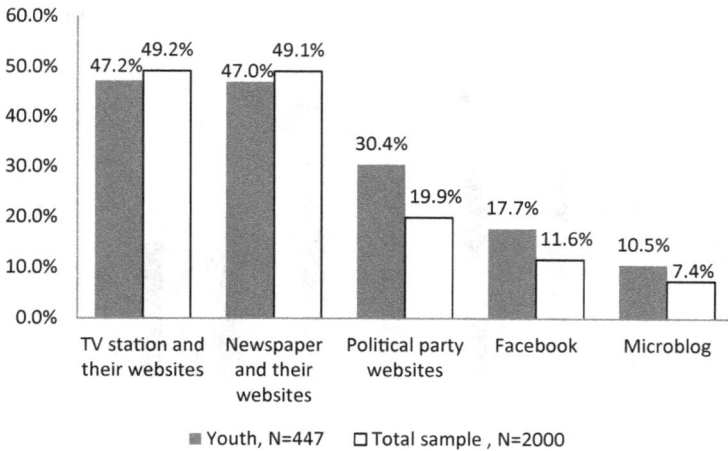

Figure 6: Youth citizens' perceptions of media credibility

Q6: Were the Perceptions of New Media (i.e. Perceived Importance, Perceived Credibility) Correlated to Youth's Voting Behaviour?

Among the respondents who reported voting for the opposition party, 54.8% of them perceived new media (for example Facebook, microblogs, YouTube, online-only news websites and blogs, mobile phone SMSs) as important sources of information about GE2011, and 52.5% of them believed that new media were trustworthy information sources about GE2011 (Figure 7). More than half of the respondents who reported voting for opposition parties considered new media to be important (54.8%) and trustworthy (52.5%). Among those who reported voting for the PAP, only 39.8% of them believed new media were important and 38.6% believed new media were trustworthy.

Q7: How did Young Voters Perceive Government's Control on Old and New Media? How was Perceived Government Media Control Related to Youth's Self-Reported Voting Behaviour in GE2011?

With respect to media control, 64.9% of respondents agreed that there was too much government control over mass media content

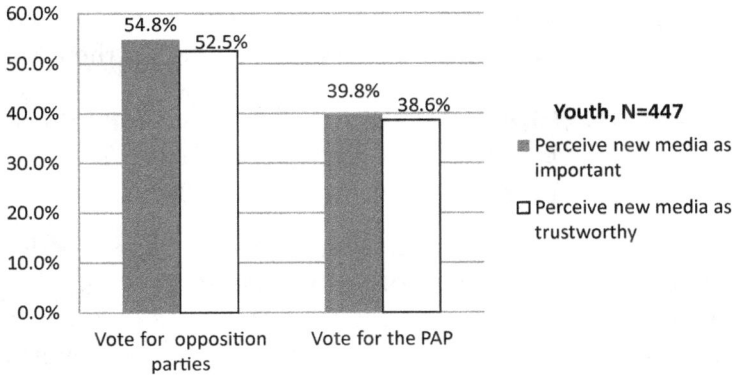

Figure 7: Young citizens' media perceptions and voting

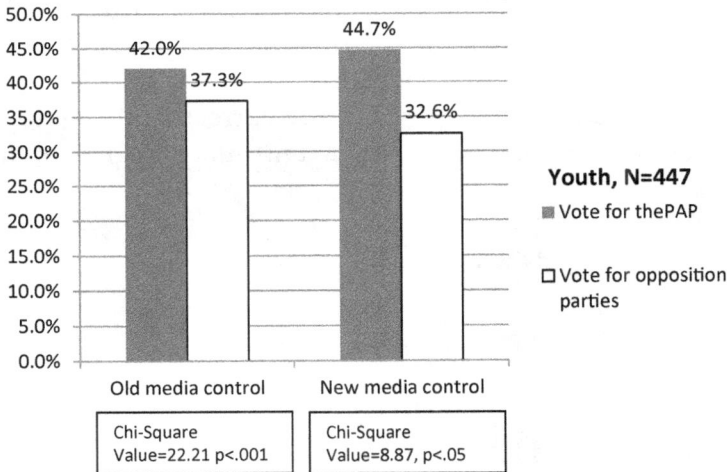

Figure 8: Perceived media control and voting

and 49.9% believed that there were too many restrictions on writing about politics and government on blogs, Facebook, and Twitter. Of those who agreed that there was too much government control over mainstream media, 37.3% of them reported voting for the opposition and 42% reported voting for the PAP (Figure 8). Among the respondents who agreed that there were too many restrictions on online political discussions, 32.6% of them reported voting for the opposition parties and 44.7% reported voting for the PAP.

Q8: Did Demographic Variables (Age, Gender and Education) Have any Connection with Youth's Self-Reported Voting Behaviour in GE2011?

We also find significant relationships between age, gender, and education and self-reported voting behaviour. Young males were less likely to say they voted for the PAP (20.2%) than for the opposition parties (28.6%). On the other hand, young females were more likely to say they voted for the PAP (23.1%) than for the opposition parties (10.3%) (Figure 9). In the 21 to 24 age group, 25.7% of respondents said they voted for the PAP and 18.8% for the opposition parties. In the age group of 25 to 29, 23.1% said they voted for the PAP and 17.5% voted for opposition parties, while 31% of the respondents aged between 30 to 34 said they voted for the PAP and 8.8% of them voted for opposition parties.

The education level is significantly correlated to the reported voting behaviour. Of those with a university degree or higher

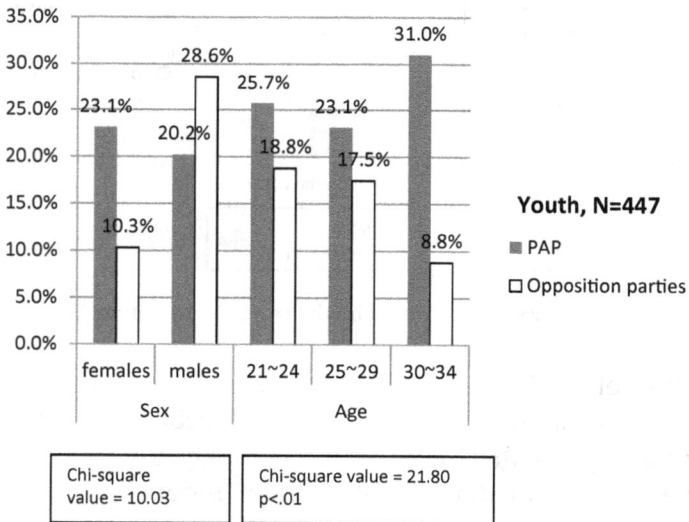

Figure 9: Sex, age and voting

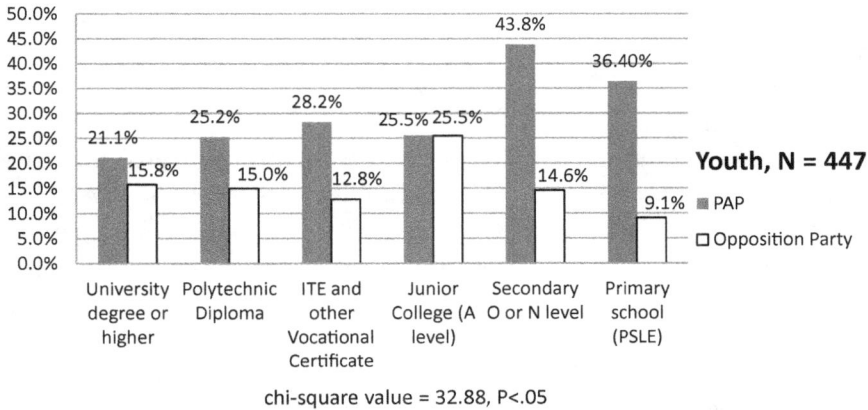

chi-square value = 32.88, P<.05

Figure 10: Education and voting

qualification, 21.1% said they voted for the PAP and 15.8% of them said they voted for opposition parties (Figure 10). Besides, 43.8% of the young people whose education level was Secondary O or N level reported they voted for the PAP and 14.6% of them reported they voted for the opposition parties. Respondents with junior college (A level) qualifications show strongest reported support for opposition parties.

Discussion

Similar to findings in most countries, Singapore's young voters did not participate in traditional offline political activities as actively as they engaged online. Some 30% of them attended one or more political rallies in GE2011, an increase over the previous elections in 2006 and 6.4 percentage points higher than the results of the whole sample population shown in the overall GE2011 survey. Only 3.6% of them volunteered to assist political parties and 7.5% wrote to media or the government about the election and politics. The youth did not show significant differences in offline political participation when compared to the whole population. In contrast to the results of the total sample in the GE2011 survey, youth engaged more in online political participation: 28.2% of the respondents wrote on their blogs,

Facebook or Twitter about this election (much higher than 9.3% for the whole sample), and 20.2% forwarded or shared online election content via e-mails, Facebook or tweets (much higher than 9.9% of the whole sample).

Young citizens showed themselves to be more cynical than the average Singapore voter: compared with the total sample, 7.7% more young respondents viewed political participation in Singapore as over-regulated and 2.9% more young respondents distrusted politicians. On their voting decisions, 14.3% said they did not vote, slightly higher than 10.8% of the whole sample. Among the 42.1% of youth who revealed they voted for PAP or the opposition, 37.8% said they voted for the opposition (much higher than 26.8% of the total sample who indicated voting for the opposition). That is, young citizens were more likely to say they voted for the opposition than the whole population even though the results showed 10.3 percentage points more of the youth who said they voted for the PAP than the opposition parties. Their voting behaviour reflected the degree of their political cynicism and distrust in government and politics.

Surprisingly, this study shows that young respondents aged 21–34 still spent more time on TV (29 min/day) and newspapers (19 min/day) to obtain news about GE2011 and perceived these media as more important and credible information sources, similar to the general Singapore public. In contrast to their use of traditional media, young citizens spent less time reading Facebook (18 min/day) or Internet-only local blogs or news websites (13 min/day) to obtain election information. The analysis indicates that media use was significantly correlated to people's perceived importance of media on voting decisions. As the youth used mass media more often, they tended to think they had greater impact on their voting decisions in GE2011 than new media. However, when compared with the whole population, as the young generation spent more than double the amount of time on Facebook, Internet-only blogs/websites, as well as consumed considerably more political and election news online, youths' voting behaviour was more affected by new media compared to the total population.

In addition, even though they were aware of the government's content control on mainstream media, a higher percentage of youth still considered offline media and their affiliated websites as more important and trustworthy than alternative online media, similar to the responses from the total sample. In contrast with the total sample, youth placed much more significance on new media, especially online only news websites and blogs (41.9%) as important or very important sources of election information followed by YouTube and video sites (40.9%) and party websites (40.3%). Also, 13.7% and 16.1% more young respondents considered Facebook and microblogs as important media for GE2011 than the total sample. Youth showed the highest trust in TV, newspapers and their affiliated websites as well as political party websites, consistent with the results from the total sample's responses. However, their trust in Facebook (17.7%) and microblogs (10.5%) were 6.1% and 3.1% percentage points higher than the whole population. These figures indicate that the cynical youth perceived more importance and trustworthiness in new media's political functions than their older counterparts, even though they were not dramatically different in their media use and their trust in government controlled mass media's political information.

More young respondents (64.9%) believed there was too much government control over mass media content than over new media (i.e. blogs, Facebook, and Twitter) (49.9%). Moreover, those who said they voted for the opposition were more likely to consider new media as important and trustworthy compared to those who said they voted for the ruling party. Among youth, 54.8% of self-reported opposition voters perceived new media (i.e. Facebook, microblogs, YouTube, alternative news websites, blogs, and SMSs) as crucial channels for disseminating election information. Furthermore, 52.5% regarded political information from new media as trustworthy, compared to slightly less than 40% for the self-reported PAP supporters.

Both perceptions about control of new and old media control influenced youth's voting decisions. Of the youth who saw too much government control over mainstream media, 37.3% said they voted for opposition parties and 42% for the PAP. Among the youth who said there were too many restrictions on new media, 32.6% voted for opposition parties and 44.7% for the PAP.

Moreover, the survey finds that the older and less-educated tended to support the ruling party. Among the youth who revealed their voting decisions, young males voted for the opposition party 18.3% more than young females, while female voters supported the PAP by just 2.9% more than young males.

Conclusion

In Singapore, public discussions of politics are considered a sensitive matter and political participation is less encouraged and less active than in other countries. This study finds young Singaporeans are more engaged politically in GE2011, especially online, than their older counterparts. Compared to older voters, they perceived new media as more important and trustworthy and tended to express their preference for voting opposition. However, despite their dissatisfaction over media control and a cynical attitude towards the government, almost half of young citizens still trusted the mass media and said they voted for the ruling party. In terms of political participation in GE2011, young citizens' media use for politics and election was different from their older counterparts, but not revolutionarily distinctive.

The seemingly conflicting findings reflect the contradictory mindsets of Singaporean youth's attitudes towards politics and mass media. Like the majority of Singaporeans, they agree that the ruling party brings Singapore stability and prosperity, but they long for more freedom. On the one hand, being aware of content control in mass media, the youth trust traditional media for its gatekeeping mechanism, information credibility, and journalistic professionalism. On the other hand, they, more than other populations, value the importance of new media for providing unfiltered and alternative political information and perspectives. Nevertheless, Singaporean youth tended to be less willing to vote if voting were not compulsory (Tay, 2011a), to show less trust in government, politicians, and mainstream media, and to prefer to use online platforms to address their political concerns. However, as the young voters became actively participatory in GE2011, particularly online, they cannot be categorised as the typical disengaged AC. More importantly, the youth appeared to be more AC-typed in GE2011 than Singaporean voters as a whole. Therefore, Singapore's case fits Coleman's (2008) cross-national generational shift from DC to AC, but the youth with some characteristics of AC used online media to engage in GE2011 actively. The dyalic model of AC and DC requires contextualised adjustments.

In this wired society, new media are expected to gain momentum in political communication, as the growing digital-savvy population will increasingly seek political information and engage in politics across platforms. It is more difficult to reach the youth generation by mass media (Bennett, 2008). Their increasing new media consumption and engagement do not translate directly into engaged political participation. Improved civil curriculum which incorporates the appropriate use of new technologies and social media for political purposes will boost youth's interest and trust in politics and teach them to behave responsibly in the virtual world. Besides, the government should make good use of social media and mobile platforms as effective tools to reconnect with youth-built networks and improve communication with empowered digital natives. It is crucial for the politicians and political parties to develop sophisticated new media strategies for open dialogue with young citizens and assign specialists to facilitate their political discussions and activities on alternative media.

Due to the high non-response rate, this election survey cannot reflect the silent majority's perceptions. Future investigations of relevant issues will further clarify the relationships between youth's media use and political participation and voting.

References

Bennett, L.W., Bers, M., Coleman, S., Earl, S., Foot, K., Levire, P., ... Xenos, M. "MacArthur Online Discussions on Civic Engagement", 2006. Available at http://spotlight.macfound.org/resources/

Civic_Engagement-Online_Discussions'06.pdf (accessed 30 August 2011).

Bennett, L.W. "Changing Citizenship in the Digital Age". In *Civic Life Online: Learning How Digital Media Can Engage Youth*, Lance W.B. (ed.) (New York: MacArthur Foundation, 2008).

Coleman, S. "From Big Brother to Big Brother: Two Factors of Interactive Engagement". In *Young Citizens and New Media: Learning and Democratic Engagement*, Dahlgren, P. (ed.) (New York: Routledge, 2008).

Delli Carpini, M. "Gen Com: Youth, Civic Engagement, and the New Information Environment", *Political Communication*, 17, (2000): 341–49.

George, C. "Internet Politics: Shouting Down the PAP". In *Voting in Change*, Tan, K.Y.L. and T. Lee (eds.) (Singapore: Ethos Books, 2011).

Gomez, J. "Democracy and Elections: The Impact of Online Politics in Singapore", September 2008. Available at http://www.academia.edu/Democracy_and_Elections_The_Impact_of_Online_Politics_in_Singapore (accessed 30 August 2011).

Hong, Y.-H. "Different Media, Different Impact? Comparing Internet and Traditional Sources on Political Cynicism and Voting Behaviour". Paper presented at International Conference on Emerging Mode of Communication: Technology Enhanced Interaction, Hong Kong Baptist University, 26–27 March 2009.

Hong Y.-H., T.T.-C. Lin and A.P. Hwa. "Political Campaigning in Cyberspace: Innovation Resistance among Internet Users in Singapore". Paper presented at 19th AMIC Annual Meeting, Singapore, June 2010.

Hussain, Z. "Have You 'Poked' Your MP Today?" *The Straits Times, Singapore*, 20 February 2011.

Lai, G. "Social Media 'Humanises Politicians,'" AsiaOne, 7 April 2011. Available at http://news.asiaone.com/News/AsiaOne+News/Singapore/Story/A1Story20110407-272175.html (accessed 4 December 2012).

Leong W.K. "'Distinct Shift' in Political Landscape, Says PM Lee". *Today*, 8 May 2011.

Lim, P. "Singaporean Youth Wanting Bigger Piece of Political Pie". *Jakarta Globe*, 5 September 2010. Available at http://www.thejakartaglobe.com/world/singaporean-youth-wanting-bigger-piece-of-political-pie/394752 (accessed 30 August 2011).

Lin, T.T.-C. and X. Lim. "Content and Presentation of Political Blogs in Singapore". Paper presented at the 8th Annual International Conference on Communication and Mass Media, Athens, Greece, May 2010.

Pew Research Center. Young Voters Supported Obama Less, but May Have Mattered More November 26, 2012. Available at http://www.pbs.org/newshour/bb/politics/july-dec12/youth_11-26.html (accessed 1 February 2013).

Pinkleton, B.E. and E.W. Austin. "Exploring Relationships among Media Use Frequency, Perceived Media Importance, and Media Satisfaction in Political Disaffection and Efficacy", *Mass Communication & Society*, 5, (2002): 141–63.

Rahim, F.A. "Bloggers, Podcasts Online may be Subjected to Parliamentary Elections Act", Channel News Asia, 19 February 2006. Available at http://www.lkyspp.nus.edu.sg/ips/docs/media/yr2006/CNA_Bloggers,%20podcasts%20online%20may%20be%20subject%20to%20Parliamentary%20Elections%20Act_190206.pdf (accessed 30 August 2011).

Rodan, G. "Embracing Electronic Media but Suppressing Civil Society: Authoritarian Consolidation in Singapore", *The Pacific Review* (2003). Available at http://www.informaworld.com/smpp/title~content=t713707111 (accessed 30 August 2011).

Shanmugam, K. Second Reading Speech: Parliamentary Elections (Amendment) Bill 2010, October 2010. Available at http://www.elections.gov.sg/mediarelease/Second_Reading_by_Law_Minister_K_Shanmugam_on_the_Parliamentary_Elections_Amendment_Bill.pdf (accessed 30 August 2011).

Singapore Elections Department. Total Votes Cast for General Election 2011, May 2011. Available at http://www.elections.gov.sg/pressrelease%5CParE2011%5C2011_05_11%20Press%20release%20on%20total%20voter%20turnout.pdf (accessed 30 August 2011).

Stelter, B. "Finding Political News Online, the Young Pass It On". *The New York Times*, 27 March 2008. Available at http://www.nytimes.com/2008/03/27/us/politics/27voters.html (accessed 30 August 2011).

Tan, T.H., C. Siyoung and Z. Weiyu. "Apathetic? Not Singaporean Youth". *The Straits Times* (Singapore), 27 May 2011.

Tay S. "Would You Vote if it's Not Compulsory?" *The New Paper* (Singapore), 30 March 2011a.

Tay S. "Newspaper still most trusted". *The New Paper* (Singapore), 6 April 2011b.

Wu, J. "Facebook Politics: An Exploratory Study of American Youth's Political Engagement during the 2008 Presidential Election". Paper presented at International Communication Association, 2009 Annual Meeting, May 2009.

Wee, W. "Facebook Chat with Singapore Prime Minister Lee Set for Tonight," *Techinasia*, 4 May 4, 2011. Available at http://www.techinasia.com/facebook-chat-singapore-prime-minister-lee/ (accessed 3 December 2012).

Weeks, B. and B. Southwell. "The Symbiosis of News Coverage and Aggregate Online Search Behavior: Obama, Rumors, and Presidential Politics Mass media and society". *Mass Media and Society*, 13(4), (August 2010): 341–60.

7

THE LEAP FROM THE VIRTUAL TO THE REAL: FACEBOOK USE AND POLITICAL PARTICIPATION

Marko M. Skoric

Abstract

This study examines the relationship between the use of mobile phones and social network sites (SNS), and the online and offline political participation during the 2011 Singapore General Election. Based on a national survey of Singapore citizens, it was found that using mobile phones to express opinions, discuss issues, and share news was positively related to both online and offline participation during the elections. Generic Facebook use and membership in political groups also predicted online engagement, while only the frequency of Facebook political groups use had a weak positive relationship with traditional, offline participation.

The proliferation of mobile phones and social media within the last decade has undoubtedly reinvigorated the debate about the impact of information and communication technologies (ICTs) on political life. As a way of contributing to this ongoing conversation, this study examines the use of SNS such as Facebook as well as the use of mobile phones during the 2011 Singapore General Election. The focus is both on traditional, offline political activities such as volunteering to help a political party, as well as on those activities that happen online such as posting comments and discussing politics on forums. Although the evidence supporting a positive impact on participation is not equivocal, the current near ubiquity of mobile phones and increasing popularity of SNS necessitates a closer look into this issue. Until relatively recently, mobile phones and SNS offered rather distinct technological advantages to their users. However, the widespread adoption of smartphones has brought greater complexity to this issue, leading potentially to greater convergence of user practices and behaviours in the domain of politics.

In recent years, some journalists and pundits have portrayed social media as playing a key role in social unrest and political demonstrations, praising their democratic potential (for example, Grossman, 2009; Shane, 2011). Others have rejected these views, suggesting that social media are neither a necessary nor sufficient condition for democratisation (Gladwells, 2010; Morozov, 2011). In the context of established democracies, studies show that social and mobile media can be effectively used to reach and mobilise voters. In the 2008 Presidential Election in the United States (U.S.), Barack Obama's team used the Internet and mobile phones extensively to provide information about his rallies and policies to the voters (Stirland, 2008). Research also supports the link between specific uses of mobile phones and SNS, and civic and political engagement beyond the context of elections (Campbell and Kwak, 2010; Valenzuela, Park, and Kee, 2009). Given the increasingly competitive nature of the elections in Singapore, it is important to evaluate the implications of different uses of new technologies for political participation, particularly in the case of mobile and social media, which are currently the mostly widely used digital platforms in the country.

Literature Review

Mobile Phones and Social Media as Sources of Political Information

Recent research suggests that new media platforms, including mobile phones and social media, have played a largely positive role in promoting civic and political engagement in the U.S. and elsewhere (for example, Campbell and Kwak, 2010; Skoric and Kwan, 2011; Valenzuela, Park, and Kee, 2009; Zhang *et al.*, 2010).

Among other functions, social and mobile media provide low-cost, easily accessible platforms for dissemination and consumption of political information, which is of prime importance during the election campaigns. Indeed, more than half a century ago it was suggested that political information had three functions, namely activation, reinforcement, and conversion, all of which are vital during elections (Lazarsfeld, Berelson, and Gaudet, 1944). In this context, the use of media for surveilling the political environment is crucial in equipping individuals with the necessary information to reflect and deliberate on political matters (Shah *et al.*, 2005). Informational uses of communication technologies are related to political expression in online domains and political expressions online are, in turn, related to offline or traditional civic and political participation (Rojas and Puig-i-Abril, 2009). Both mobile phones and SNS can potentially play important roles in the dissemination of political information. More specifically, informational use of the mobile phone has been found to be a positive predictor of civic and political involvement (Campbell and Kwak, 2010). Social network sites like Facebook represent hybrid sources of political information as they provide information from both traditional media and from interpersonal networks (Hanson *et al.*, 2010). For example, it has been found that college students use Facebook as a platform to promote other online sources (Fernandes *et al.*, 2010). Real-time updates on social media such as videos of election rallies on YouTube, news links that appear on Twitter or politically related status updates on Facebook provide a connection within online social networks. Social network sites could, therefore, reach out to users who are disinterested in politics, providing them with political information when they least expect it. This gives them an advantage over political sites, since visitors to political sites are already highly involved or interested in politics (Utz, 2009).

There have also been criticisms of social media as a source of political information. A study on the use of online media for political purposes among college students did not find a relationship between attention to social media, political self-efficacy (the belief that one can influence the political system), and involvement (Kushin and Yamamoto, 2010). The researchers suggest several reasons for this, including the lack of awareness of social media sources of political information, the exposure to cynical or highly partisan content which could inhibit involvement, and sheer information overload that made it difficult to extract relevant information. There is also evidence of "astroturfing" practices on social media platforms, namely individuals and organisations using numerous yet centrally-controlled Twitter accounts to create an impression of widespread support for political candidates and parties (Ratkiewicz *et al.*, 2011).

Mobile Phone and Social Media as Platforms for Civic and Political Organisation

Above and beyond the role of informing voters about campaign issues and policies, mobile phones and social media represent the means of political mobilisation and organisation. For example, some features of Facebook such as low cost, high speed and direct targeting of specific recipients, promote rapid information exchange and efficient political mobilisation. Indeed, specific uses of SNS like being a member of a political group on Facebook have been found to be associated with political and civic participation (Valenzuela, Park, and Kee, 2009). Although the everyday use of Facebook is not associated with participation, joining a political Facebook group allows users to receive mobilising information which they might not receive from other channels (Valenzuela *et al.*, 2009). In the context of Singapore, Facebook has been used for mobilising citizens and organising offline protests (for example, Skoric *et al.*, 2011). Even generic, non-political use of Facebook has a weak positive relationship with both online and traditional political participation among youth (Skoric and Kwan, 2011).

The use of mobile technology and the Internet in Obama's campaign aimed at recruiting volunteers for traditional political activities (Silberman, 2009) shows an important link between online and offline political involvement. Many features of mobile phones, combined with the power of social networks, allow for great improvements in dissemination of event information, micro-coordination of offline activities, sharing of pictures and video from political rallies, and on-site reporting for news media. Many of these technological affordances were put to use in the aftermath of the Iranian presidential elections in 2009 when supporters of the presidential candidate, Mir-Hossein Mousavi, were mobilised to show their support on the streets with the use of mobile technology (Cook, 2010). The supporters also sent out thousands of Twitter messages with photos and videos, updating their online networks with information from the offline protest (Barnett, 2009).

Mobile Phone and Social Media as Forums for Expression and Connection

Campbell and Kwak (2012) argue that a key ingredient to a knowledgeable and active citizenship is talking about politics, including talking about it over a mobile phone with family members and friends. Indeed, discussing politics has been found to lead to other forms of participation (Gastil, Deess, and Weiser, 2002; Lenart, 1994; Kwak *et al.*, 2005). Engaging in political discussions has also been found to help citizens understand political issues better (Kwak *et al.*, 2005). The use of mobile phones and social media leads to much improved connectivity, offering alternative channels of communication and potentially facilitating greater political participation among users.

The use of mobile phones for discussing politics and public affairs with one's close networks has been found to be positively associated with political participation and openness (Campbell and Kwak, 2012). Talking with others about politics and current affairs could increase openness to dissonant perspectives. While there are concerns of social insularity (Habuchi, 2005, pp. 165–82; Ling, 2008), which could result from frequent mobile communication with one's close social networks, discussing political issues with a heterogeneous group of people could in fact open one's mind to different views. This is why the convergence between mobile phones and SNS could be potentially beneficial for political engagement, as SNS bring a different social dimension to mobile communications, namely one of bridging cross-cutting ties between diverse individuals (Ellison, Steinfield, and Lampe, 2007).

In addition to providing horizontal communication between citizens, mobile phones and social media also connect candidates with their voters. This form of interaction cuts through the usual red tape that plagues most of the interactions with government officials. Candidates who make the effort to interact with users on SNS are perceived more favourably by citizens (Utz, 2009). Obama's success in the election could, therefore, be due partly to his effective use of forums on SNS to build relationships with his supporters (Cook, 2010).

Campbell and Kwak (2012) found that discussing politics with others with similar views leads to mobilisation. This pattern of interacting with like-minded people could be found during elections when SNS groups are formed to support a party or a candidate. Facebook groups formed during the last U.S. Presidential Election to support different candidates were places where citizens spent most of their time praising their preferred candidates and criticising the opponents (Fernandes *et al.*, 2010). Taken together with the findings of Campbell and Kwak (2012), it can be argued that being a member of such Facebook groups could work to enhance one's involvement in the campaign activities of the preferred candidate, but without actually increasing political understanding or tolerance.

Lastly, mobile phones are tools that could penetrate private spaces (Hermanns, 2008), and allow expressions of views and opinions which would otherwise be censored in mainstream media. Hermanns (2008) quotes the example of North Korea, in which mobile phones have become a channel for political expression in the tightly-controlled political regime.

Political Campaigning in Singapore

While the expression of political opinions is not strictly controlled in Singapore, the nation has been said to have an underdeveloped and constrained civil society (Soh and Yuen, 2006). In the past, studies found Singaporeans to be indifferent about politics (Rodan, 1998). However, the climate of indifference was reversed in the most recent

2011 General Election (GE2011). The popularity of Facebook and Twitter has brought greater visibility to online political discourse. Adding to the momentum, the Singapore government more fully embraced a "soft touch" approach to Internet regulation in the years prior to the GE2011. Indeed, online media were allowed more leeway to challenge the ruling party or the government. While traditional media outlets are subjected to political controls, online media such as blogs were allowed to adopt an adversarial position towards the ruling party and the government (George and Raman, 2008). This is partly due to the government's inability to actively control and censor online content without significantly compromising its position as a financial, educational, and informational hub of Southeast Asia.

As a consequence of this policy, Singaporeans have actively used social media to engage, including promoting environmental awareness or the welfare of domestic helpers. Blogs, bulletin-board systems (BBS), Facebook and Twitter have all increased the visibility of political opinions, and have been used to promote offline participation as well (Skoric *et al.*, 2011). Most recently, in response to the public uproar about insensitive racial remarks about Indians, citizens started the "Curry Sunday" movement to defend racial harmony and celebrate Singaporean identity.

This increase in online political activity is also partly due to the recent policy amendments, including the amendments to the Parliamentary and Presidential Elections Act introduced in 2010. With these changes, political parties and candidates were able to use a wider range of online platforms for their electoral campaigns. Notably, while Singaporeans were criticised for being indifferent and politically apathetic in the past, the recent elections saw the "political awakening of the average Singaporean" (Hoe, 2011), manifested by the outpouring of dissatisfaction with the ruling party in numerous online fora.

The heightened level of enthusiasm for political expression in the recent GE in Singapore was not surprising as online expression is positively related to situational political involvement. Situational political involvement could be understood as a degree of interest in social situations such as the election outcome (Kushin and Yamamoto, 2010). With increased channels for expression, the citizens were able to voice their concerns and feel a greater stake in the outcome of the election. These expressions represent an important aspect of online political involvement. This is because participation in online social environments is associated with greater understanding of, and connection to, fellow users (Brown, Broderick, and Lee, 2007). This sense of connectedness with others is important as social media use could potentially mitigate political cynicism (Hanson *et al.*, 2010). Therefore, some level of online social interaction could be beneficial to facilitating greater political involvement. The recent "political awakening" could well be related to this increased sense of connectedness amongst voters, who were able to connect through various social media platforms and voice their satisfaction with government policies.

Given the above, the aim of this study is to answer the following research questions:

1. How are different patterns of mobile phone use related to offline and online political participation?
2. Is everyday Facebook use related to offline and online participation? Is the membership in Facebook groups about politics and public affairs related to offline and online participation?

Method

Participants

A post-election computer-assisted telephone interviewing (CATI) survey was conducted a few weeks after the elections on a total of 2,000 Singapore citizens, aged 21 to 88. More detailed information on the survey methodology is provided in Appendix 1.

Survey Questions

The post-election survey contained a range of questions assessing the citizens' use of mobile phones and social media, as well as their political participation in online and offline domains.

For examining the participants' generic use of Facebook, we utilised an adapted version of the Facebook intensity scale by Ellison, Steinfield, and Lampe (2007); the participants were asked to indicate their level of agreement and disagreement with the following statements: Facebook is part of my everyday activity; Facebook has become part of my daily routine; I feel out of touch when I haven't logged onto Facebook for a while; I feel I am part of the Facebook community; and I would be sorry if Facebook shut down. In addition, the participants were also asked to indicate how many Facebook groups related to politics/public affairs they were members of, and how often they read and wrote on their discussion boards/walls.

The survey also contained questions assessing different kinds of uses of the mobile phone, by asking the participants to indicate the number of days in a typical week they used a mobile phone to do a number of things such as: go online to share content that is entertaining; browse the web just for fun; go online to share content about hobbies or personal interests; and go online to upload content that is mostly just for fun (entertainment uses); call friends or family; and use text/instant messages to interact with friends or family (family contact); go online to express my opinions about issues; go online to share news items; and use text/instant messages to discuss political matters (informational/expressive uses).

To assess traditional/offline and online/mobile political participation during the elections, two different scales were used. For traditional/offline participation, the participants were asked to indicate how often they did each of the following in the previous six months: I volunteered to help in a political party; I attended a meeting of discussion or dialogue organised by the Residents' Committee, Community Centre, or the Government; and I wrote to the newspapers, the government, or a Member of Parliament. For measures of online participation, the participants were asked how often they engaged in the following activities during the elections: I wrote on my blog, my Facebook page or Twitter account about the election or matters related to the election; I wrote or commented on other people's blogs, Facebook page, or responded to a tweet on the election or matters related to the election; I took part in online political or social issues forums to discuss issues related to the election; I forwarded or shared online content on the election or matters related to the election to other people by e-mail, Facebook or Twitter; I forwarded SMSes about the election or matters related to the election on my mobile phone; and I wrote SMSes to people I know about the election or matters related to the election. These questions assessed specific election-related activities that citizens engaged in online and/or using their mobile phones. Lastly, the participants were asked a set of standard demographic questions and also to indicate their interest in political issues (scale of 1–5).

Findings

According to the results of the survey, 46.7% of Singaporeans had a Facebook profile, while 18% of Facebook users reported being members of at least one political or public affairs group. Furthermore, 90.7% of respondents reported having a mobile phone.

Tables 1 and 2 present basic statistics on Facebook and mobile phone usage. For Facebook, Table 1 shows the percentage agreement

Table 1. Intensity of Facebook use ($N = 933$)

	Percentage (%)				
Items	Strongly agree	Agree	Neutral	Disagree	Strongly disagree
1. Facebook is part of my everyday activity.	18.9	35.0	9.8	31.1	5.0
2. Facebook has become part of my daily routine.	16.9	30.9	8.6	38.2	5.1
3. I feel out of touch when I haven't logged onto Facebook for a while.	9.8	20.9	10.3	51.1	7.5
4. I feel I am part of the Facebook community.	6.9	28.2	12.2	46.1	6.0
5. I would be sorry if Facebook shut down.	10.9	27.2	10.6	42.8	7.8

Table 2. Frequency of different mobile phone usage ($N = 1,814$)

	Percentage (%)		
Items	**0**	**1–6**	**7**
1. How many days in a typical week do you use mobile phone to go online to share content that is entertaining?	82.0	10.8	6.7
2. How many days in a typical week do you use mobile phone to browse the web just for fun?	69.3	14.0	16.0
3. How many days in a typical week do you use mobile phone to go online to share content about hobbies or personal interests?	84.9	9.9	4.6
4. How many days in a typical week do you use mobile phone to go online to upload content that is mostly just for fun?	83.4	12.1	3.9
5. How many days in a typical week do you use mobile phone to call friends or family?	6.9	26.6	64.4
6. How many days in a typical week do you use mobile phone text/instant messages to interact with friends or family?	20.6	19.4	58.7
7. How many days in a typical week do you use mobile phone to go online to express your opinions about issues?	86.5	9.0	3.5
8. How many days in a typical week do you use mobile phone to go online to share news items?	85.8	10.3	3.0
9. How many days in a typical week do you use mobile phone text/instant messages to discuss political matters?	93.3	5.2	1.2

with the statements about the intensity of Facebook use. For mobile phones, Table 2 shows how frequently people used their mobile phones for different purposes.

Basic statistics for both offline and online/mobile forms of participation are presented in Tables 3 and 4. From the results it is evident that a large majority of Singaporeans did not engage in offline participation, as only between 2.8 per cent and 6.6 per cent of citizens reported taking part in one of the offline political activities. Similarly, online participation numbers were low, although slightly higher than the offline ones, possibly indicative of lower barriers to entry for online engagement.

Table 3. Offline political participation ($N = 2,000$)

	Percentage (%)	
Items	No	Yes
1. Did you volunteer to help in a political party in the past 6 months?	97.3	2.8
2. Did you attend a meeting of discussion or dialogue organised by the Residents' Committee, Community Centre, or the Government in the past 6 months?	95.0	5.1
3. Did you write to the newspaper, the government, or a member of Parliament in past 6 months?	93.5	6.6

Table 4. Online political participation via social media and mobile phone ($N = 2,000$)

	Percentage (%)	
Items	No	Yes
1. Did you write on your blog, Facebook page or Twitter account about the election or matters related to the election during the election?	89.0	10.0
2. Did you write or comment on other people s blog, Facebook page, or responded to a tweet on the election or matters related to the election during the election?	86.0	13.0
3. Did you take part in online political or social issues forums to discuss issues related to the election during the election?	95.5	3.8
4. Did you forward or share online content on the election or matters related to the election to other people by email, Facebook or Twitter during the election?	89.1	10.0
5. Did you forward SMSes about the election or matters related to the election on your mobile phone during the election?	93.9	5.4
6. Did you write SMSes to people you know about the election or matters related to the election during the election?	92.7	6.7

Multivariate Analyses

To provide answers to the research questions, hierarchical linear regressions were utilised, which allowed us to find out the relationship between various variables called predictors (for example, age,

Table 5. Predicting different forms of political participation from demographic, political interest and mobile phone use variables ($N = 1{,}814$, all participants)

	Traditional/offline participation β	Online/mobile participation β
Demographics		
Age	−0.21**	−0.10*
Gender	−0.05	0.00
Family income	0.03	−0.02
Father's education	0.10	−0.01
Mother's education	0.02	−0.02
R^2 change (%)	7.1	2.4
Interest in politics		
Interest in political issues	0.09	0.28**
R^2 change (%)	1.4	9.9
Mobile phone use		
Entertainment	−0.03	−0.04
Family	−0.03	0.03
Informational/expressive	0.23**	0.34**
R^2 change (%)	4.5	10
Total R^2 (%)	13.0	22.3

$p < 0.10$, *$p < 0.05$, **$p < 0.01$.

gender, income, or Facebook and mobile phone uses) and the main (criterion) variables of interest (in this case traditional/offline participation and online/mobile participation). The technique allowed us to find out whether Facebook and mobile phone use had relationships with different forms of participation after taking into consideration other demographic variables. The results are presented in Tables 5 and 6.

Table 5 shows that for mobile phone use, only informational/expressive uses of the mobile phone had a positive relationship with both traditional and online/mobile participation. In addition, interest in politics was a significant predictor of online/mobile participation, while this relationship was only of marginal significance in the case of traditional participation. Interestingly, age was also a significant predictor of both traditional and online/mobile

Table 6. Predicting different forms of political participation from demographic, political interest and Facebook use variables ($N = 933$, Facebook users only)

	Traditional/offline participation B	Online/mobile participation β
Demographics		
Age	−0.14**	−0.05
Gender	0.06	−0.06
Family income	0.07	0.03
Father's education	0.18*	−0.11
Mother's education	0.00	0.01
R^2 change (%)	8.1	1.9
Interest in politics		
Interest in political issues	−0.01	0.17*
R^2 change (%)	0.1	9.4
Facebook use-generic		
Facebook use intensity	0.06	0.20**
R^2 change (%)	0.3	6.8
Facebook use-political		
Political group member	0.04	0.43**
Frequency of pol. group use	0.13*	0.11*
R^2 change (%)	1.6	17.1
Total R^2 (%)	10.2	35.1

*$p < 0.05$, **$p < 0.01$.

participation, with younger citizens being more likely to take part in election-related activities.

Table 6 shows that the generic use of Facebook had no relationship with traditional participation, while the relationship with online/mobile participation was positive. Furthermore, the findings show that while both the membership in Facebook political groups as well as the frequency of their use were positive predictors of online/mobile participation, only the frequency of political group use positively predicted offline participation.

For both mobile phone and Facebook use, a similar pattern of findings emerged. For traditional offline participation, only very specific uses (i.e. political, informational) of these platforms were significant but weak predictors of participation, whereas online/mobile participation was related to the generic use of Facebook and more strongly associated with Facebook political group membership and use.

Discussion

The findings reveal that using a mobile phone to express opinions and discuss issues related to politics is positively related to both traditional/offline and online participation during the elections. The results also indicate that while the generic use of Facebook is not related to the measure of traditional political participation, the frequency of Facebook political group use had a positive relationship with it. Generic use of Facebook also had a positive relationship with online/mobile participation, as did the membership in Facebook political groups and intensity of their use.

In general, the results are largely in line with the previous research done in the U.S. (for example, Valenzuela, Park, and Kee, 2009; Campbell and Kwak, 2010) and Singapore (Skoric and Kwan, 2011). During the election, only certain uses of social and mobile platforms are related to the increased likelihood of offline participation. More specifically, using mobile phones to express opinions, share news, and discuss issues is associated with greater likelihood of participation in traditional, election-related activities. No such relationship is found for other types of mobile use, including seeking entertainment or connecting with family and friends. This is somewhat unexpected as Campbell and Kwak's (2012) U.S. study reported a positive association between mobile communication with one's close social circle and political participation. Still, their measures of mobile use were designed to specifically measure discussion of politics and public affairs, while this study captured a more generic mobile contact with friends and family. It should be noted that such communication was not found to suppress participation either, as it is sometimes assumed. Everyday use of Facebook also has no relationship with offline participation, nor does simply being a member of a political Facebook group — only a weak relationship is found between frequency of use of such groups and offline participation. These findings differ slightly from Valenzuela, Park, and Kee (2009) who found that the membership in political Facebook groups predicted participation among a sample of U.S. college students. Given that this study (1) includes a much broader demographic profile, and (2) that the data was collected four years after Valenzuela, Park, and Kee (2009), some minor shifts in patterns of results are to be expected.

Not surprisingly, social and mobile media use is more strongly associated with other, online forms of participation during the elections. These activities, including posting comments online, discussing elections on forums, and forwarding political content over social and mobile media, require less effort and involve considerably lower personal risks for the participants. Under the conditions of such lower barriers to entry to election-related participation, even the generic, everyday use of Facebook can play a positive role, as observed in our study. The findings also demonstrate that membership in Facebook groups focused on politics and public affairs is a robust predictor of online participation as was the frequency of their use, although to a lesser extent. Similar to offline participation, expressive and informational uses of mobile phones are related to greater likelihood of participating in online political activities, confirming the findings from previous research conducted in the U.S.

Conclusion

In summary, this study demonstrates that during the 2011 Singapore General Election, the use of mobile phones and SNS played a predominantly positive role in promoting active participation in political life, both online and offline. It is no surprise that the use of new media platforms was more strongly associated with online participation than with traditional forms of engagement, although the findings show that specific uses of these platforms can also play a positive role in offline participation. Overall, there is a reason to be cautiously optimistic about the future role of social and mobile media in the political process in Singapore. Although their role in traditional election-related activities seems limited, social and mobile media provide important opportunities and venues for online participation. This form of participation is also likely to be more common than the traditional activities, especially among the younger generations of newly enfranchised Singaporean citizens. Indeed, the most common forms of political participation during the 2008 Presidential Elections in the U.S. among undergraduate students were those low in resource intensity, such as watching a political debate, while political actions that required more commitment, such as volunteering, were less common (Vitak, Zube, Smock *et al.*, 2011). Interestingly, in the case of Singapore, younger people are more likely to take part in both traditional and online activities. In the coming years, it will be important to examine whether these new forms of political participation can lead to tangible political outcomes, or whether they simply represent "low effort, low yield" substitutes for genuine political engagement.

References

Barnett, R. "Up to 200,000 Tweets About Iran Sent An Hour". *Sky News*, 18 June 2009. Available at http://news.sky.com/home/world-news/article/15311513 (accessed 26 August 2011).

Brown, J., A.J. Broderick, and N. Lee. "Word of Mouth Communication Within Online Communities: Conceptualizing the Online Social Network", *Journal of Interactive Marketing*, 21(3), (2007): 2–20.

Campbell, S.W. and N. Kwak. "Political Involvement in 'Mobilized' Society: The Interactive Relationships among Mobile Communication, Network Characteristics, and Political Participation", *Journal of Communication*, 61(6), (2012): 1005–24.

Campbell, S.W. and N. Kwak. "Mobile Communication and Civic Life: Linking Patterns of Use to Civic and Political Engagement", *Journal of Communication*, 60(3), (2010): 536–55.

Cook, C. "Mobile Marketing and Political Activities", *International Journal of Mobile Marketing*, 5(1), (2010): 154–63.

Coleman, J.S. "Social Capital in the Creation of Human Capital", *American Journal of Sociology*, 94, (1988): 95–120.

Ellison, N., C. Steinfield and C. Lampe. "The Benefits of Facebook 'Friends:' Social Capital and College Students' Use of Online Social Network Sites", *Journal of Computer-Mediated Communication*, 12(4), (2007): 1143–68.

Fernandes, J., M. Giurcanu, K.W. Bowers, and J.C. Neely. "The Writing on the Wall: A Content Analysis of College Students' Facebook Groups for the 2008 Presidential Election", *Mass Communication and Society*, 13, (2010): 653–75.

Gastil, J., E.P. Deess, and P. Weiser. "Civic Awakening in the Jury Room: A Test of the Connection between Jury Deliberation and Political Participation", *Journal of Politics*, 64(2), (2002): 585–95.

George, C. and R. Raman. "When Big Media Meet 'We' Media in Singapore", *Australian Journalism Review*, 30(2), (2008): 61–73.

Gladwell, M. "Small Change: Why the Revolution Will Not be Tweeted", *The New Yorker*, 4 October 2011. Available at http://www.newyorker.com/reporting/2010/10/04/101004fa_fact_gladwell (accessed 17 October 2011).

Grossman, L. "Iran Protests: Twitter, the Medium of the Movement". *Time*, 17 June 2009. Available at http://www.time.com/time/world/article/0,8599,1905125,00.html (accessed 17 March 2011).

Habuchi, I. "Accelerating Reflexivity". In *Personal, Portable, Pedestrian: Mobile Phones in Japanese Life*, Ito, M. D. Okabe and M. Matsuda (eds.) (Cambridge, MA: MIT Press, 2005).

Hanson, G., P.M. Haridakis, A.W. Cunningham, R. Sharma and J.D. Ponder. "The 2008 Presidential Campaign: Political Cynicism in the Age of Facebook, MySpace, and YouTube", *Mass Communication and Society*, 13, (2010): 584–607.

Hermanns, H. "Mobile Democracy: Mobile Phones as Democratic Tools", *Politics*, 28(2) (2008): 74–82.

Hoe, Y.N. "The Impact of New Media on GE 2011". *Channelnewsasia*, 13 May 2011. Available at http://www.channelnewsasia.com/stories/singaporelocalnews/view/1128681/1/.html (accessed 17 August 2011).

Kushin, M.J. and M. Yamamoto. "Did Social Media Really Matter? College Students' Use of Online Media and Political Decision Making in the 2008 Election", *Mass Communication and Society*, 13(5) (2010): 608–30.

Kwak, N., A. Williams, X. Wang, and H. Lee. "Talking Politics and Engaging Politics: An Examination of the Interactive Relationships Between Structural Features of Political Talk and Discussion Engagement", *Communication Research*, 32(1) (2005): 87–111.

Lazarsfeld, P.F., B. Berelson, and H. Gaudet. *The People's Choice: How the Voter Makes Up His Mind in a Presidential Campaign* (New York: Duell, 1944).

Lenart, S. *Shaping Political Attitudes: The Impact of Interpersonal Communication and Mass Media* (Thousand Oaks, CA: Sage, 1994).

Ling, R. *New Tech, New Ties: How Mobile Communication is Reshaping Social Cohesion* (Cambridge, MA: MIT Press, 2008).

Morozov, E. *The Net Delusion: The Dark Side of Internet Freedom* (New York: Public Affairs, 2011).

Ratkiewicz, J., M. Conover, M. Meiss, B. Gonçalves, A. Flammini and F. Menczer. "Detecting and Tracking Political Abuse in Social Media". *Proceedings of the 5th International Conference on Weblogs and Social Media*, Association for Advancement of Artificial Intelligence (AAAI), 2010 (Palo Alto: The AAAI Press, 2011).

Rodan, G. "The Internet and Political Control in Singapore", *Political Science Quarterly*, 11(1), (1998): 63–89.

Rojas, H. and E. Puig-i-Abril. "Mobilizers Mobilized: Information, Expression, Mobilization and Participation in the Digital Age", *Journal of Computer-Mediated Communication*, 14, (2009): 902–92.

Shah, D.V., J. Cho, W.P. Eveland, Jr., and N. Kwak. "Information and Expression in a Digital Age: Modeling Internet Effects on Civic Participation", *Communication Research*, 32, (2005): 531–65.

Shane, S. "Spotlight Again Falls on Web Tools and Change". *The New York Times*, 29 January 2011. Available at http://www.nytimes.com/2011/01/30/weekinreview/30shane.html?_r=1&ref=egypt (accessed 28 February 2011).

Silberman, M. Obama and the New Media Campaign Tools of 2012, 20 April 2009. Available at http://webofchange.com/blog/obama-and-the-new-media-campaign-tools-of-2012 (accessed 20 August 2011).

Skoric, M.M. and G.C.E. Kwan. "Do Facebook and Video Games Promote Political Participation Among Youth? Evidence from Singapore", *eJournal of eDemocracy and Open Government (JeDEM)*, 3(1) (2011): 70–79.

Skoric, M.M., N.D. Poor, Y. Liao, and S.W.H. Tang. "Online Organization of an Offline Protest: From Social to Traditional Media and Back". *Proceedings of the Hawaii International Conference on System Sciences*. Washington, D.C.: IEEE Computer Society, 2011. doi:10.1109/HICSS.2011.330

Soh, E. and B. Yuen. "Government-Aided Participation in Planning Singapore", *Cities*, 23(1), (2006): 30–43.

Stirland, S. "Obama's Secret Weapons: Internet, Databases and Psychology", 29 October 2008. Available at http://www.wired.com/threatlevel/2008/10/obamas-secret-w (accessed 14 October 2011).

Utz, S. "The (Potential) Bene?ts of Campaigning Via Social Network Sites", *Journal of Computer-Mediated Communication*, 14(2), (2009): 221–43.

Valenzuela, S., N. Park, and K.F. Kee. "Is There Social Capital in a Social Network Site?: Facebook Use and College Students' Life Satisfaction, Trust, and Participation", *Journal of Computer-Mediated Communication*, 14, (2009): 875–901.

Vitak, J., P. Zube, A. Smock, C.T. Carr, N. Ellison, and C. Lampe. "It's Complicated: Facebook Users' Political Participation in the 2008 Election", *Cyberpsychology, Behavior, and Social Networking*, 14(3), (2011): 107–14.

Zhang, W., T.J. Johnson, T. Seltzer, and S.L. Bichard. "The Revolution Will be Networked. The Influence of Social Networking Sites on Political Attitudes and Behavior", *Social Science Computer Review*, 28(1), (2010): 75–92.

8

DAVID VS GOLIATH: TWITTER'S ROLE IN EQUALISING BIG-PARTY DOMINANCE

Xu Xiaoge

Abstract

Will Twitter level the electoral playing field for opposition parties as predicted by equalisation theory or merely reinforce politics according to normalisation theorists? After comparing the contesting political parties on Twitter during the 2011 Singapore General Election, this study found that Twitter had a more equalisation effect than the normalisation effect. In other words, the new media did have the effect of empowering the opposition parties although that effect did not appear to affect the final election outcome.

Although constrained to 140 characters per message, Twitter is not constrained at all in serving as an information provider. As for disseminating information from its sender, Twitter allows its users to follow, to be followed, to mention, to be mentioned, to reply, to be replied, to retweet, and to be retweeted. Through short bursts of information, a Twitter user can convey a sense of being connected to his or her followers. Besides these functions, Twitter further allows its users to hyperlink to content from other sources, be it a website, a social networking site or a blog. These functions of Twitter have been used to great effect to persuade and mobilise people in events such as the German federal election (Tumasjan *et al.*, 2010), the 2009 post-election demonstrations in Iran (Zhou *et al.*, 2010), and the 2010 midterm United States (U.S.) election (Jackson, Lilleker, and Schweitzer, 2010).

The General Election of 2011 (GE 2011) in Singapore saw the first use of Twitter in an election. Although Twitter had a penetration rate of only 6.66% of the resident population (StatCounter, 2011), this study found that the hashtagged topic #sgelections alone during the 12-day campaign period from the nomination day (27 April 2011) to the post-polling day (8 May 2011) generated 77,957 election-related tweets or an average daily of 6,496 tweets.

During the 12-day campaign period, six contesting parties published 2,436 tweets or on average 203 tweets daily, according to the search results of this study. For opposition parties in Singapore, Twitter and other social media provided them an unprecedented opportunity to make their voices heard and to win the hearts and minds of the electorate, as mainstream media remain tightly controlled by the People's Action Party (PAP) government. For the ruling party, on the other hand, it also promises a great opportunity for them to extend their offline dominance online. Whether used by the ruling or opposition parties, Twitter has great potential to contribute to electoral democracy (Bimber and Davis, 2003; Gibson *et al.*, 2003; Margolis and Resnick, 2000, cited in Gomez and Muhamad, 2010).

Twitter and Elections

The role of Twitter in elections has been well documented in previous studies. With the convergence of mass media and socially networked communication, the public sphere has shifted from the institutional realm to the new communication space (Castells, 2007) characterised by social network sites available on mobile and regular Web, such as Facebook, blogs, microblogs, and YouTube. Social networks play a crucial role in the spread of information on social network sites (Lerman and Ghosh, 2010). Social media have become viral in presence, penetration and influence as a political communication tool in election campaigns, as shown in the 2004 U.S. presidential election being described as "a critical turning point" (Xenos and Moy, 2007, p. 704).

In the 2009 German federal election, Tumasjan *et al.* (2010) found that Twitter was used extensively for political deliberation and that the mere number of party mentions accurately reflected the election result. They also found that positive or negative sentiment associated with tweets about a politician corresponded closely to voters' political preferences.

In their investigation of the 2009 post-election protests in Iran, Zhou *et al.* (2010) found that Twitter and its large community of users played an important role in disseminating news, images, and videos worldwide and in documenting the events. Their results indicate that the probability of a retweet — reflecting the likelihood that a tweet may go viral — was highly content dependent.

In examining a number of features that might affect retweetability of tweets, Suh *et al.* (2010) found that amongst content features, URLs and hashtags, the number of followers and followees (people who are being followed) as well as the age of the account seem to affect retweetability while, interestingly, the number of past tweets does not predict retweetability of a user's tweet.

As a convention within Twitter, retweeting constitutes a conversational practice in different styles and for diverse reasons (Boyd, Golder, and Lotan, 2010).

Ifukor (2010) argued that citizens' access to social media electronically empowers the electorate to be actively involved in democratic governance, encouraging more public discussions about politics. And the research results point to a dialectical relationship between social media discourse and the process of political empowerment.

Election tweets can be used to inform, critique, explain, praise, promote, criticise, curse, monitor, call for voting for the ruling party, or call for voting for opposition parties. Tweets can also play an important role in coordinating different types of political campaign media.

Although previous studies have examined forms and functions of Twitter in elections, they have not investigated the role of Twitter in enabling the ruling party to maintain online dominance in elections. According to normalisation theorists, "new media reinforces 'politics as usual' instead of creating a more equitable political culture" (Gomez and Muhamad, 2010, p. 2). As part of new media, will Twitter play such a role in elections? Similarly, earlier studies have not examined the role of Twitter in allowing opposition parties to reduce the dominance of the ruling party. According to an equalisation theory, the Internet and social media "can equalise the electoral playing field among political parties" (Gomez and Muhamad, 2010, p. 2).

Research Questions and Methods

This study aims to answer the question whether Twitter's effect in the 2011 Singapore General Election was normalising or equalising. Therefore, the research questions in this study are as follows:

1. Did Twitter equalise the electoral playing field for the contesting opposition parties?
2. Did Twitter normalise the electoral playing field for the ruling party?

To address the two research questions, this study drew on the ideas of conceptualising equalisation and normalisation from earlier studies. Equalisation was conceptualised as "equal information access to the voters", "a much cheaper and easier mode of marketing", "low cost, interactive" (Bimber and Davis, 2003; Kamarack, 1999, p. 14), "a better chance of inter-party competition with the major parties on the Internet than they do in traditional media and thus can reach larger audience" (Margolis, Resnick and Levy, 2003, p. 58). Normalisation was conceptualised as transferring the major parties' dominance on traditional media onto the Web and new media (Margolis and Resnick, 2003; Norris, 2003; Ward and Vedel, 2006; Small, 2008).

Guided by earlier studies' conceptualisations of normalisation and equalisation, this study proposed to operationalise Twitter's normalising and equalising effects in these 12 different Twitter components identified by earlier studies: (1) tweeting, (2) being tweeted, (3) mentioning, (4) being mentioned, (5) replying, (6) being replied, (7) retweeting, (8) being retweeted, (9) vote for tweeting,

(10) vote for being tweeted, (11) tweeting links, and (12) tweeting hot topics. Explanations of those components are provided in later sections.

Selecting Political Parties on Twitter

Seven parties contested in GE2011: the ruling party PAP and six opposition parties: Workers' Party (WP), Singapore Democratic Party (SDP), National Solidarity Party (NSP), The Reform Party (RP), Singapore People's Party (SPP), and Singapore Democratic Alliance (SDA).

Among the opposition parties, SPP and SDA did not have active Twitter accounts at the time of the election period. So only PAP, WP, SDP, NSP, and RP were selected for analysis.

Selecting Tweets Under Scrutiny

Although constrained by the same amount of characters allowed in each tweet, contesting political parties had unconstrained space in tweeting, being tweeted and being retweeted. To collect tweets, this study used the tweet collector Palanteer, developed by a team of researchers at School of Information Systems, Singapore Management University. Palanteer allows users to search for socio-political Twitter data generated by a set of Twitter users in Singapore. Its features include (1) keyword search for tweets, (2) tweet retrieval, (3) identification of popular keywords that have been used to search for tweets, and (4) identification of popular tweets that have been been retweeted and replied to.

1. *Political parties tweeting*: Daily political party tweets were collected each day by keying in the following political party Twitter accounts: (1) @PAPSingapore, (2) @wpsg, (3) @nsp_sg, (4) @there-formparty, and (5) @YourSDP in the search field of Palanteer.
2. *Political parties being tweeted*: Using the same procedure in collecting political party tweets, this study collected tweets on political parties and news media by keying in the following keywords: (1) PAP, (2) WP, (3) SDP, (4) NSP, and (5) RP in the search field of Palanteer.

3. *Political parties being mentioned*: A mention "is any Twitter update that contains @username anywhere in the body of the Tweet" (Twitter, n.d.). The same procedure was used in collecting mentions of the contesting political parties by keying the following keywords: (1) PAP, (2) WP, (3) SDP, (4) NSP, and (5) RP in the search field of Palanteer.

4. *Political parties being replied*: "A reply is any update posted by clicking the "Reply" button on another Tweet" (Twitter, n.d.). Also the same procedure was used in collecting replies to the contesting political parties by keying the following keywords: (1) PAP, (2) WP, (3) SDP, (4) NSP, and (5) RP in the search field of Palanteer.

5. *Political parties being retweeted*: Being retweeted refers to tweets starting with RT, which indicates retweets. To retweet is to share tweets you have received with all of your followers. And the same procedure was used in collecting retweets on the contesting political parties by keying the following keywords: (1) PAP, (2) WP, (3) SDP, (4) NSP, and (5) RP in the search field of Palanteer.

6. *Call-for-vote tweets and retweets*: Tweets or retweets in which a call for votes such as "vote for PAP" or "vote for WP" was contained were collected from Nomination Day to Polling Day by keying in the Twitter user names of all the five selected contesting political parties in the search field of Palanteer.

7. *Links and Hot Topics Tweeted*: Links or shortened URLs (that is web addresses) in tweets provide further information on the topic being tweeted. Among all the tweets, the number of links contained in each tweet was compared among the contesting parties. All hot topics tweeted, such as housing, Goods and Services Tax (GST), healthcare, cost of living, Central Provident Fund (CPF), public transport, ministerial salary, foreign talent, and ageing population, were selected and compared among the contesting parties.

Processing Collected Tweets

All the collected tweets were processed through a program written for this study. First, the program identifies the key components in each tweet, namely who is the poster (the person who post the message), what is the comment or content of the tweet itself, the date and time posted, who it mentions (using @username in the middle of a message), whether it is a reply to someone (using @username to start a message), whether it is a retweet (RT@username), whether it has a link to other content, and what is the topic (denoted by "#"). Second, the program counts the number of occurrences of single words, pairs of words, and a group of three words (these are called unigrams, bigrams and trigrams). A table is created giving every word that appears in all the tweets and the number of times it appears. Similar tables are created for bigrams and trigrams. In the case of bigrams,

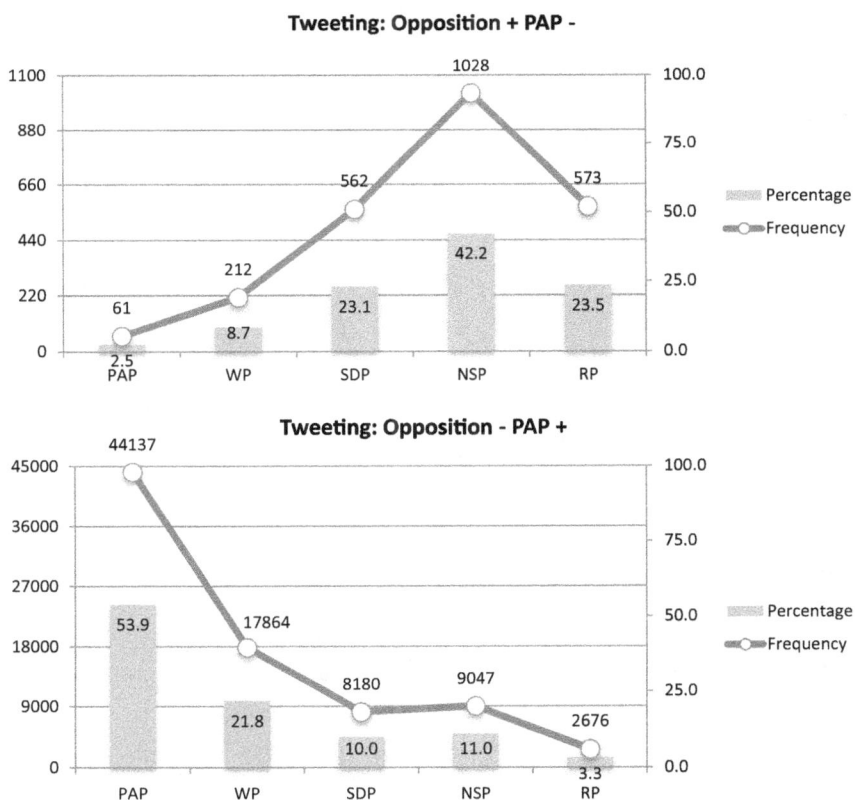

Figure 1: Tweeting and being tweeted

every pair of two words that appears in tweets is used to create a similar table of their frequencies. For trigrams, every occurrence of three consecutive words that appear in all the tweets is counted.

Findings

1. Tweeting and being tweeted: Opposition parties versus ruling party

During the election period, all the contesting opposition parties tweeted more than the ruling party. Measured in terms of the number of tweets, Twitter seemed to play a part in the efforts of the opposition parties to equalise the electoral playing field. The opposition parties, however, were tweeted about far less than the ruling party (see Figure 1).

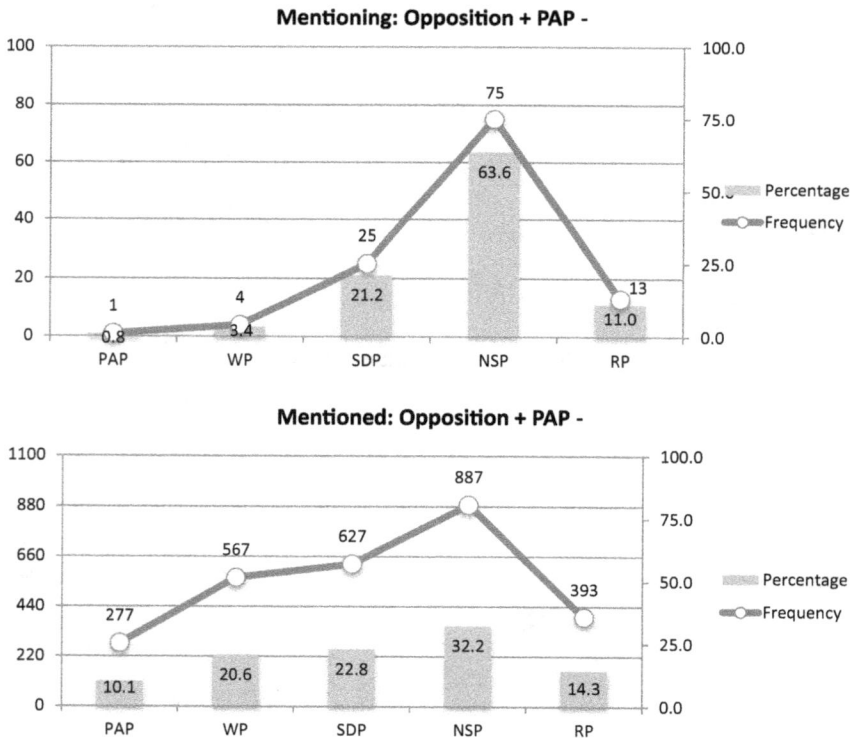

Figure 2:   Mentioning and being mentioned

2. *Mentioning and being mentioned: Opposition parties versus ruling party*

As shown in Figure 2, the results suggested that the opposition parties collectively or respectively had far more mentions and at the same time were far more mentioned than the ruling party.

3. *Replying and being replied: Opposition parties versus ruling party*

Among the contesting parties on Twitter, NSP had far more replies than other contesting parties while RP had just slightly more replies than the ruling party. Both WP and SDP did not reply at all during the election period to tweets. In the case of being replied in tweets, all the opposition parties were ahead of the ruling party (see Figure 3).

4. *Retweeting and being retweeted: Opposition parties versus ruling party*

Another mixed situation, where the opposition political parties differed, was in retweeting voters' tweets by the parties. The NSP

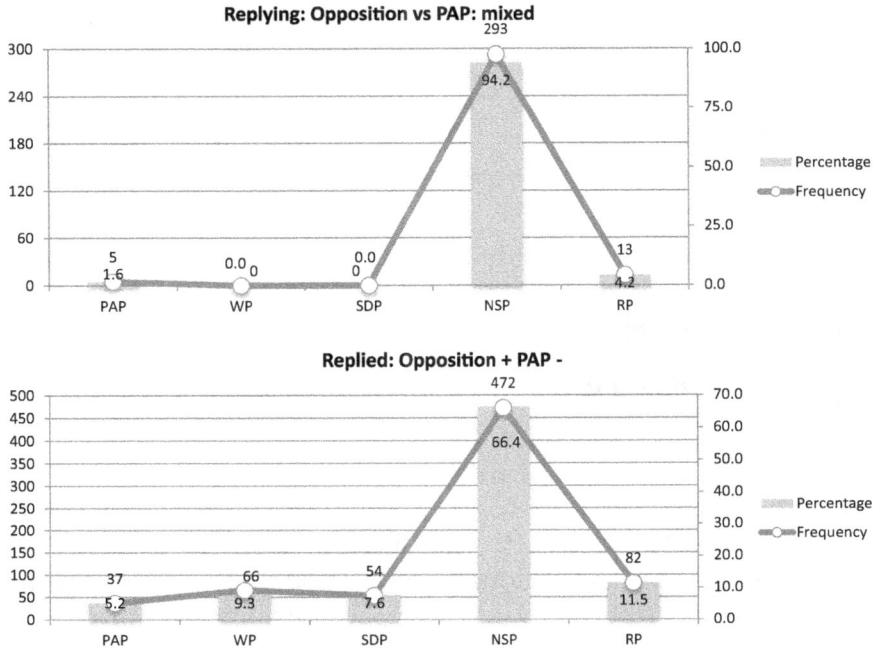

Figure 3: Replying and being replied

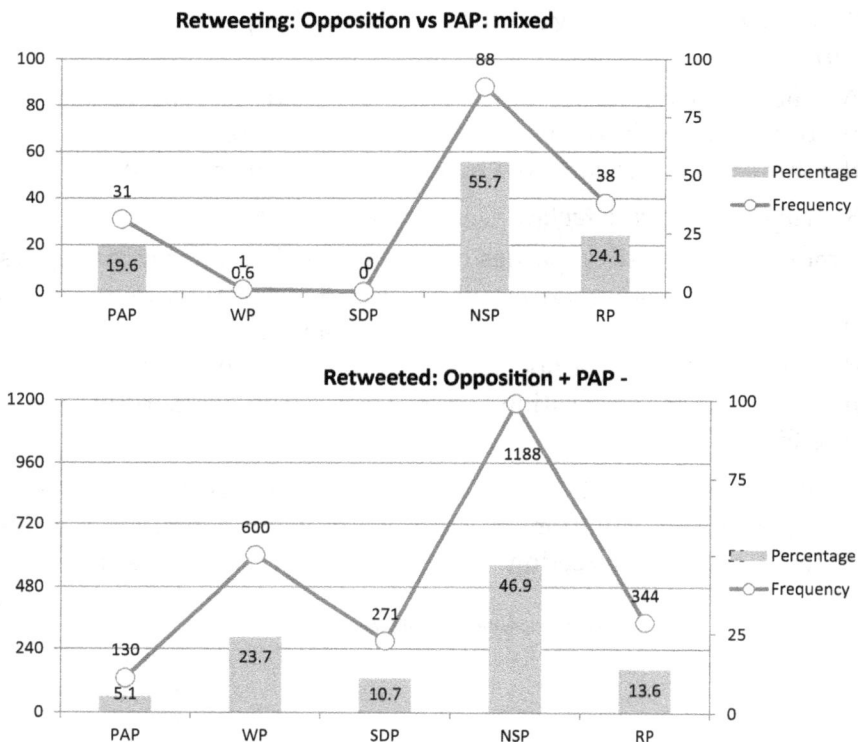

Figure 4:   Retweeting and being retweeted

and RP (but not the WP and SDP) retweeted more than the ruling party. But the opposition parties were all retweeted far more than the ruling party (Figure 4).

5. *Vote-for tweeting and being tweeted: Opposition parties versus ruling party*

Although the opposition parties tweeted far more vote-for messages than the ruling party, there were far fewer tweets from voters urging others to vote for the opposition parties than for the PAP. This suggests that even though Twitter could play a part in the normalisation efforts of the opposition parties in vote-for tweets, its role was rather limited when vote-for tweets by voters are taken into account (Figure 5).

Vote-for Tweeting: Opposition + PAP -

Vote-For Tweeted: Opposition - PAP +

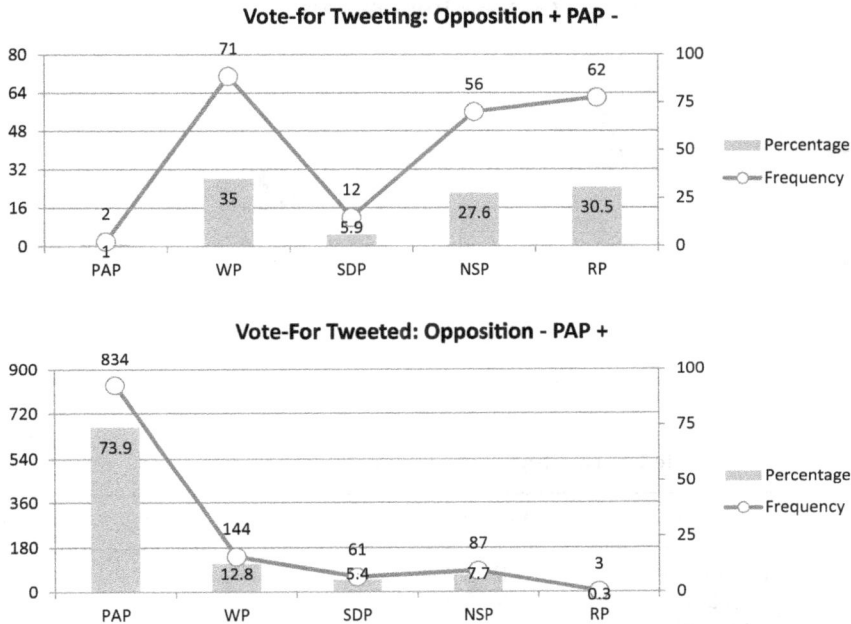

Figure 5:   Vote-for tweeting and being tweeted

6. *Links and hot topics tweeted: Opposition parties versus ruling party*

Measured by the percentage of the total number of links tweeted by the political parties, all the opposition parties provided more links in their tweets than the ruling party (Figure 6). Equalisation efforts of the opposition parties seemed to take place in tweeting links. In addition, while topics such as housing, GST, healthcare, cost of living, CPF, public transport, ministerial salary, foreign talent, and ageing population were tweeted by members of the electorate, they were hardly tweeted by political parties. Although opposition parties marginally tweeted slightly more than the ruling party, all the parties did not follow up on the popular election-related topics in their tweets.

Putting together the results of measuring 12 components of Twitter, this study found that Twitter did equalise the electoral playing field for the contesting opposition parties since they outperformed the ruling party in seven components (tweeting, mentioning,

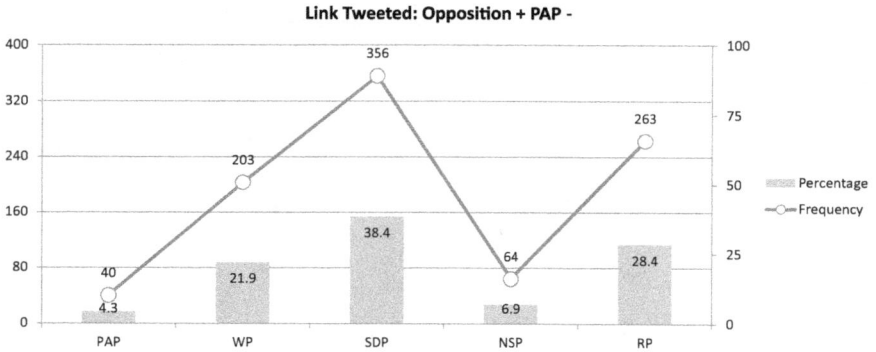

Figure 6: Links tweeted

Table 1. Tweeting election: Equalised or normalised?

Indicator	Overall	PAP	WP	SDP	NSP	RP
Tweeting	E	−	+	+	+	+
Tweeted	N	+	−	−	−	−
Mentioning	E	−	+	+	+	+
Mentioned	E	−	+	+	+	+
Replying	Mixed	−	−	−	+	+
Replied	E	−	+	+	+	+
Retweeting	Mixed	−/+	−	−	+	+
Retweeted	E	−	+	+	+	+
Vote **for** tweeting	E	−	+	+	+	+
Vote for tweeted	N	+	−	−	−	−
Link tweeted	E	−	+	+	+	+
Hot topics tweeted	Neither	−	−	−	−	−

Note: E = Equalise, N = Normalise, + = more, − = less.

mentioned, replied, retweeted, vote for tweeting, and link tweeted) while the ruling party normalised the electoral playing field by winning over the opposition parties in only two components (tweeted about and tweeted about with a vote-for message) (Table 1).

Discussion

The results of the comparison of tweeting showed that the opposition parties, who had limited access to highly-controlled mainstream media, were more eager to use Twitter to tweet about the General Election than the ruling party. Despite the dominance by the opposition parties in tweeting, the ruling party dominated in being tweeted about. When it comes to mentioning and being mentioned, however, the opposition parties dominated. The opposition parties dominated in the category of being replied to in the tweets. Another mixed situation existed in retweeting among the contesting parties. When it comes to being retweeted by others, however, the opposition parties dominated this component of Twitter. In vote-for tweeting, understandably, the opposition parties dominated while the domination went to the ruling party when it came to vote for being tweeted. In tweeting links, in other words, providing hyperlinks in tweets to give additional information, the opposition parties tweeted more. In tweeting on hot topics such as housing, GST, healthcare, cost of living, CPF, public transport, ministerial salary, foreign talent, and ageing population, which were popularly tweeted by individual Twitter users, neither the ruling party nor the opposition parties dominated.

Putting together the findings of measuring the 12 components of Twitter, this study found that there were more instances of equalisation than normalisation. The opposition parties equalised the electoral playing field in seven out of the 12 components while the ruling party normalised it in only two components. Overall, therefore, it would be possible to conclude that Twitter had a more equalisation effect than the normalisation effect. In other words, Twitter did have the effect of empowering the opposition parties. The effect, however, did not appear to translate to affecting the final outcome reflected by the number of votes. This could be the function of the relatively small number of Twitter users in the country.

As shown in the results of this study, the ruling party did not fully utilise Twitter so as to normalise the Twittersphere or to reinforce its political dominance on Twitter as it did in the offline news media. The opposition parties, however, seemed to be more aggressive in their equalisation efforts. The impact of their equalisation efforts, however, were limited as the opposition parties did not fully leverage Twitter as an alternative to enhance and enlarge their campaign efforts and effects.

After winning the election, Singapore Prime Minister Lee Hsien Loong urged his PAP party to strengthen its online presence and to use new media more effectively instead of just using Facebook and Twitter, calling for "being on the same wavelength as the netizens and resonating with the Internet generation" (Ramesh, 8 September 2011).

References

Bimber, B. and D. Richard. *The Internet in U.S. Election* (New York: Oxford University Press, 2003).

Boyd, D., G. Scott and L. Gilad. "Tweet, Tweet, Retweet: Conversational Aspects of Retweeting on Twitter". Paper Presented at the HICSS-43, IEEE, Kauai, HI, 2010.

Castells, M. (ed.) *The Network Society: A Cross-cultural Perspective* (Northampton, MA: Edgar Elgar, 2004).

Gibson, R. K., M. Margolis, D. Resnick, and S. Ward. "Election Campaigning on the WWW in the US and the UK: A Comparative Analysis", *Party Politics*, 9(1) (2003): 47–76.

Gomez, J. and R. Muhamad. "New Media and Electoral Democracy: Online Opposition in Malaysia and Singapore". Paper presented at Malaysia and Singapore Workshop: Media, Law, Social Commentary, Politics, The University of Melbourne, Australia, 2010.

Ifukor, P. " 'Elections' or 'Selections'? Blogging and Twittering the Nigerian 2007 General Elections", *Bulletin of Science, Technology & Society*, 30(6), (2010): 398–414.

Jackson, N., D. Lilleker, and E. Schweitzer. "Towards a Non-hierarchical Campaign? Testing for Interactivity as a Tool of Election Campaigning in France, the US, Germany and the UK". Paper presented at the IAMCR Conference 2010: Communication and Citizenship, Braga, Portugal, July 2010.

Kamarack, E.C. "Campaigning on the Internet in the elections of 1998". In *Governance.com: Democracy in the Information Age*, Kamarack, E.C., and J.S. Nye, Jr. Hollis (eds.) (NH: Hollis Publishing, 1999).

Lerman, K. and R. Ghosh. "Information Contagion: An Empirical Study of the Spread of News on Digg and Twitter Social Networks". Paper presented at the Fourth International AAAI Conference on Weblogs and Social Media, Washington, DC, 2010.

Margolis, M., D. Resnick, and J. Levy. "Major Parties Dominate, Minor Parties Struggle? US Elections and the Internet". In *Political Parties and the Internet: Net Gain?* Gibson, R., P. Nixon, and S. Ward (eds.) (London: Routledge, 2003).

Margolis, M. and Resnick, D. *Politics as Usual: The Cyberspace Revolution* (Thousand Oaks, CA: SAGE Publications, 2000).

Norris, P. "Preaching to the Converted? Pluralism, Participation and Party Websites", *Party Politics*, 9, (2003): 21–45.

Palanteer. "About Us". (n.d.). Available at http://palanteer.sis.smu.edu.sg/about.php (accessed 9 September 2011).

Ramesh, S. "PAP needs to reflect on General Election: PM Lee". Channel News Asia, Singapore News. Available at http://www.channelnews-asia.com/stories/singaporelocalnews/view/1151857/1/.html (accessed 9 September 2011).

Small, T.A. "Equal Access, Unequal Success — Major and Minor Canadian Parties on the Net", *Party Politics*, 14(1), (2008): 51–70.

StatCounter (2011). "Top 7 Social Media in Singapore from April to May, 2012". Available at http://gs.statcounter.com/#social_media-SG-monthly-201104-201105 (accessed 22 July 2012).

Suh, B., L. Hong, P. Pirolli, and Chi E.H. "Want to be Retweeted? Large Scale Analytics on Factors Impacting Retweet in Twitter Network". Paper presented at the IEEE International Conference on Social Computing, 2010.

Tumasjan, A., T.O. Sprenger, P.G. Sandner, and I.M. Welpe. "Predicting Elections with Twitter: What 140 Characters Reveal about Political Sentiment". Paper presented at the Fourth International AAAI Conference on Weblogs and Social Media, 2010.

Ward, S. and T. Vedel. "Introduction: The Potential of the Internet Revisited", *Parliamentary Affairs*, 59(2), (2006): 210–25.

Xenos, M.A. and P. Moy. "Direct and Differential Effects of the Internet on Political and Civic Engagement", *Journal of Communication*, 57 (2007): 704–18.

Zhou, Z., R. Bandari, J. Kong, H. Qian and V. Roychowdhury. "Information Resonance on Twitter: Watching Iran". Paper presented at the 1st Workshop on Social Media Analytics (SOMA '10), July 2010.

9

LIFTING THE VEIL OF IGNORANCE: INTERNET'S IMPACT ON KNOWLEDGE GAP

Debbie Goh

Abstract

The digital divide creates new knowledge gaps and this may disproportionately benefit the elites who possess more resources and can more effectively use the Internet to gain political knowledge. This study examines the
relationship between Internet use and political knowledge of opposition
parties in Singapore. The findings indicate that people who did not use
the Internet for political information during the 2011 General Election
were indeed less knowledgeable about opposition politics. Those who
consumed mainstream media could only gain limited political knowledge
of opposition parties. Contrary to criticism that political discourse on
the Internet is inaccurate and untrustworthy, this study shows that the
Internet was a reliable and effective source in helping citizens to be more
knowledgeable about alternative parties, their candidates and their policy
positions on issues. The challenge is to enable and encourage more voters
to access alternative political sites.

The information society is premised on the idea that power and
control lie in the hands of those with knowledge (Galbraith, 1972;
Porat, 1977). Because the Internet facilitates political discussion
and online activism, and enables rapid news and information
dissemination to mass audiences at lower cost and greater ease than
traditional media, it provides a platform for opposition movements

and minor or fringe parties to challenge autocratic regimes and level the political playing field (Norris, 2001). This also benefits citizens as multiple sources of information enhance their understanding of alternative electoral choices, and their evaluation of those in authority and the possible consequences of their votes (Norris, 2001). Cyber-optimists thus hold high hopes that the Internet can facilitate democracy, empowerment, and equality by breaking barriers to political knowledge (UNDP, 2001).

Concerns of digital divide effects, however, make political observers and scholars ambivalent about the Internet's ability to reinforce democracy. The digital divide often refers to the gap in opportunities to access information and communication technologies (OECD, 2001). Besides physical and infrastructural reasons, the divide also exists because of ineffective use of the Internet to fully participate in social, economic, and political activities (Selwyn, 2004; Servaes, 2003; Van Dijk, 2005; Warschauer, 2002). Scholars worry that the digital divide creates an information elite and new knowledge gaps as those who are more educated and better off are more likely to effectively harness the Internet to gain political knowledge (Bonfadelli, 2002). Such inequalities in knowledge can further lead to exclusion from social resources and inequalities in social power (Bonfadelli, 2002). Norris (2001) too warns of an existing and substantial democratic divide between those who do and do not use multiple political resources available on the Internet for civic engagement. She stresses that Internet politics will disproportionately benefit the elites who possess the authority and resources to re-establish their predominance online, and those who are apathetic and underprivileged risk being further marginalised.

The concerns of these scholars resonate particularly in Singapore, where the Internet could be a vital source of alternative political information. Singapore's government-controlled mainstream media is, as expected, pro-government, supports the ruling People's Action Party (PAP), and is known for not providing sufficient coverage of opposition parties, or for reporting negatively about the opposition (Gomez, 2008; Kavita, Kuo and Lee, 2003; Klüver, 2004). The bias persisted till the 2006 elections (Cenite *et al.*, 2008). The development of the Internet spurred the growth of sociopolitical news sites and blogs and opposition parties' websites that Ho *et al.* (2002) describe as "sites of resistance... to focus attention on issues that were rejected or downplayed by traditional media" (in Gomez, 2008, p. 592).

In the 2011 election, much hope was again placed on the alternative online media as a source of information on opposition parties and alternative political views. Opposition candidates saw the Internet, from blogs to newer social media platforms such as Facebook and Twitter, as an important campaigning tool (Leong, 2011; Ng, Saad and Ismail, 2011; Wong, 2010, 2011). Parties with limited financial and human resources could use the Internet as an affordable means to "get the truth out" to voters by giving them access to party and election information, and to target specific groups of voters, particularly those aged 18 to 35, many of whom were first-time voters.

On the surface, the digital divide hardly seems to be a major problem in Singapore. On one hand, the island-nation is one of the world's most wired and computer-literate countries. In 2010, 84% of Singaporean households had access to at least one computer at home (52% had two or more computers), and 82% had broadband Internet access at home (Infocomm Development Authority of Singapore, 2011). Indeed, voters' use of the Internet for political information during Singapore's 2011 General Election (GE2011) in May had increased. A 2010 survey found that only 13% of Singaporeans read political blogs, but a survey on GE2011 showed that percentage jumping to 21% during the election period (Tan and Mahizhnan, Chapter 1, this volume). The latter survey also found that 30% of voters used Facebook and/or blogs for election information.

On the other hand, the GE2011 survey found that 86% still turned to offline mainstream media for election information. Also, those who used the Internet for political information or were more politically engaged online tended to be male, younger, more educated, and had higher household incomes. This raises questions on the extent of the democratic digital divide in Singapore, and the extent to which the Internet narrows or (in the case where the Internet provides misinformation) exacerbates the political knowledge gap between voters on election matters in general and on opposition party information in particular.

This study thus examines the democratic digital divide among Singapore voters during the 2011 Singapore General Election by determining if a knowledge gap about opposition parties exists between those who turned to opposition party and alternative websites and blogs for election news and those who used mainstream media. It also seeks to establish the factors that correlated with the knowledge gap.

Knowledge Gap and the Digital Divide

Can the mass media close information gaps? It has been argued that as mass media information increases, the higher social economic status (SES) segments of the population — often measured by education status and/or income — are able to acquire information faster than those of lower SES (Tichenor, Donohue, and Olien, 1970). The better-educated have better abilities to use and interpret media information, possess greater prior knowledge of topics, have more relevant social contacts that provide additional information, are more active in seeking out information, and more likely to use media rich in public affairs information (see Bonfadelli, 2002, for detailed review and explanations). This results in a gap in knowledge between these segments, with those of higher SES being more knowledgeable.

Knowledge gap hypothesis is frequently used to test political knowledge, and has been found to be more prevalent for in-depth and difficult topics such as politics (Gaziano, 1983). This draws criticism that the theory has a middle-class bias in favour of the better educated as it assumes topics such as international or foreign affairs, national issues, and public affairs have universal appeal (Bonfadelli, 2002; Ettema and Kline, 1977). Moreover, the gap also varies according to interest in particular issues (Weaver and Drew, 2001). Critics argue that the knowledge gap hypothesis needs to consider people's motivations for acquiring information as well as the functionality of that information (Bonfadelli, 2002; Ettema and Kline, 1977). Such variables underline the importance of examining the digital divide in relation to the knowledge gap hypothesis in political communication. Norris (2001) points out that while the Internet makes it easier for citizens to learn about public affairs and be politically engaged, it does not automatically make them more inclined to do so. Very likely, digital politics would bypass the disengaged and engage those who are already engaged. The engaged are more likely to be people of higher SES. Those with higher education use the Internet for informational and service-oriented purposes, and they learn more from political websites, compared to those with lower education who use the Internet for entertainment (Bonfadelli, 2002; Kim, 2008; Wei and Hindman, 2011). Informational uses are preferable as they increase users' political knowledge and participation while entertainment use weakens them (Lee, Ham, and Thorson, 2009; Wei and Hindman, 2011).

Professional knowledge, economic resources, and computer and media literacy skills are important prerequisites for effectively engaging digital content in an increasingly complex media environment (Lee, Ham, and Thorson, 2008; Lucas and Sylla, 2003; Selwyn, 2004; Servaes, 2003; Warschauer, 2002). Online content is heterogenous and seemingly unlimited, and unlike old media that have journalists to filter and frame information, effective use of the Internet requires users to possess new skills like purposeful searching strategies, assessment of source's credibility, and construction of meaningful frames for interpretations (Bonfadelli, 2002). People with lower income and education are those most likely to face barriers in gaining such digital literacy skills, forming a class of "new illiterates" (Servaes, 2003). The Internet is thus likely to serve and benefit the affluent and well educated who possess prior knowledge, cognitive skills, and technical abilities to engage in online politics (Norris, 2001). Singaporean voters using online political sources during Singapore's recent general election for information and political engagement were more likely to be male, younger, more educated, and have higher income (Tan and Mahizhnan, Chapter 1, this volume). These same variables were found to influence both the digital divide and knowledge gap, suggesting that a knowledge gap in Singapore will also exist along these lines.

Knowledge Gap and Information Consumption

Increased news consumption can mitigate the influence of SES on the knowledge gap. Studies have shown that, after controlling for demographics and SES, different media affects the knowledge gap in different ways depending on a variety of factors. Holbrook (2002) found that televised United States presidential debates reduced the knowledge gap quite dramatically, leading him to conclude that without debates, the knowledge gap would widen. He argued that the televised debates make political information most accessible (in terms of skills needed and literacy level) to low information voters, providing them the best opportunities to learn about candidates and gain ground on high information voters. Norris and Sanders's (2003) experiment with campaign learning across different media (newspapers, television, and party websites) demonstrated that content carried in the medium, rather than the medium itself, was responsible for a knowledge gap. Their study also established that in a First World democracy like Britain, the public remained unaware of many basic issues, that is the majority are "know-nothings" or "know-littles". But when exposed to campaign information, learning occurs, especially so for those who were poorly informed. Weaver and Drew (1993) found that attention to television advertisements and newspaper coverage and not exposure to TV news coverage of the U.S. senate campaign contributed to knowledge about candidates' issue position. They also found that voters who paid more attention to campaign information online during the 2004 U.S. presidential election were more knowledgeable than those who did not (Weaver and Drew, 2006).

These studies suggest that consumption of political information in itself can bridge knowledge gaps, regardless of SES. This is particularly so for political information that people have not previously been exposed to. In Singapore, the pro-ruling party bias in the mainstream media suggests that if voters turn to alternative online sources for information about the opposition, they are likely to be more knowledgeable about them. This may also hold true after accounting for demographic factors and SES. On the other hand, ineffective or lack of use of the Internet for political information may further widen the knowledge gap.

Research Question and Hypotheses

The discussion above suggests relationships between demographics, SES, offline and online mainstream media use, alternative online media use and gaps in knowledge about opposition parties in Singapore. This study focuses on examining knowledge about opposition parties as the gaps are most likely to occur between those who consumed mainstream media, where there is limited and less accurate opposition information, and alternative online media, where opposition information is prolific. It asks the following research questions:

1. What are the factors predicting political knowledge about opposition parties in Singapore?
2. Is there a knowledge gap that contributes to a democratic digital divide in Singapore?

The study also proposes the following hypotheses:

H1. Voters who read alternative online sites such as political blogs and non-mainstream online news sites will be more knowledgeable about opposition parties in Singapore.
H2. Voters who read information on political party websites are more knowledgeable about opposition parties in Singapore.
H3. Voters who are politically engaged online will be more knowledgeable about opposition parties in Singapore.

Method

Sample

Data for this study were derived from a nationwide survey of media use and political activity during the 2011 Singapore General Election (see Appendix 1 in this book on the survey details).

Measurements

Political knowledge of opposition parties

Knowledge gap research on political campaigns typically tests respondents' knowledge on campaign-specific information (Drew and Weaver, 2006; Moore, 1987; Weaver and Drew, 1993; 1995; 2001). These include factual knowledge about candidates and their positions on issues as they indicate information gains during the course of campaigning (Nadeau *et al.*, 2008). This study uses two fact-based questions and two issues-based questions to assess respondents' knowledge about opposition parties and their candidates (see Appendix in this chapter for question wording). The two factual questions asked respondents to identify which opposition parties 11 candidates belonged to. One point was given for each correct answer.

Given that the mainstream media tended to give more prominence to what ruling party candidates were doing and saying during elections, while opposition candidates had more opportunities to promote themselves and state and clarify their positions online, the third and fourth questions focused on two controversial issues during the election that received high prominence and coverage — albeit different treatments — in both the mainstream media and alternative online news sites, blogs, and political party websites.

The first issue pertains to the Singapore Democratic Party candidate Tan Jee Say, a former Principal Private Secretary to Emeritus Senior Minister Goh Chok Tong of the ruling PAP when he was the country's deputy Prime Minister. Tan's candidacy drew much attention because of his former high-ranking position in the government service. The second issue pertains to the opposition Workers' Party (WP) manifesto, *Towards a First World Parliament*. Tan's credentials and his campaign position on the manufacturing sector in Singapore, as well as the WP manifesto, received much flak and criticism from PAP candidates, and these critical views were widely carried in the mainstream press. Less prominent coverage was given to Tan and the WP on their positions. Online, however, information about Tan's credentials and the full paper of his proposal for the manufacturing sector were circulated on alternative news sites and blogs (Loh, 2011) while the WP's defence of its manifesto was disseminated through their party website and alternative online news sites and blogs. Four statements were formulated for each of the two issues: three reflected PAP criticism of Tan and the WP, and the fourth (which is the correct answer) was based on Tan and the WP's own declarations of their positions on the respective issues. One point was also awarded for correctly answering the two questions. The total score for the four questions were then combined into an index for political knowledge of opposition parties.[1]

Media use

A series of questions was asked to determine how respondents were using various forms of media for political information during the elections.

1. *Mainstream media use:* Respondents were asked to indicate, in 5-minute intervals, how many minutes they spent daily reading newspapers (mean = 24.7 minutes) listening to radio (mean = 12.7 minutes), watching television (mean = 32.2 minutes), and reading websites of mainstream media (mean = 12.4 minutes) for election news. These items were summed to create an index measuring combined mainstream media use (mean = 82.0 minutes).

2. *Foreign news sites:* Foreign news outfits such as Reuters, Yahoo! News and *BBC* also reported on the Singapore elections. For control purposes, respondents were also asked to indicate the number of minutes spent on foreign news sites (mean = 3.7 minutes).

3. *Alternative online media:* Two items measuring the number of minutes respondents spent learning about the elections on Facebook (mean = 7.8 minutes) or Singapore blogs and Internet-only news sites (mean = 6.3 minutes) were combined to create an index for alternative online media use (mean = 14.2 minutes).

---

[1]Cronbach's $\alpha = 0.87$.

4. *Party websites and Facebook pages:* A series of questions asked how often respondents visited each of the eight active political parties' websites or Facebook pages during the two weeks of election campaigning (from 0 = Never to 5 = Daily). An overwhelming majority of respondents did not visit the websites, while those who did visited only one to three times. Hence, the items were recoded (0 = Never, 1 = visited in the last two weeks) and then combined to create an 8-point index measuring number of political party websites and Facebook pages visited in the last two weeks (mean = 0.74 sites visited).

Online political engagement

According to Norris (2001), political engagement online goes beyond reading news. It involves obtaining information on political issues across multiple news sources, forwarding news to peers and discussing issues in online forums. Four questions asked respondents how often (0 = Never to 4 = 10 times or more) they wrote about the election on their own (mean = 0.20) or other people's (mean = 0.25) blogs, Facebook pages or Twitter account, forwarded or shared election information through email, Facebook or Twitter (mean = 0.19), and discussed the election in an online forum (mean = 0.07). These were combined to create a scale measuring online political engagement.

Results

The first research question asks how consumption of different media relates to political knowledge on opposition parties in Singapore. Table 1 shows the results for the hierarchical multiple regression that was used to test and control for the possible effects of various types of factors. That is, statistical tests were done in steps to find out the relationship between a series of factors and political knowledge of opposition parties. First, demographic (including SES) factors were used to find out their relationship to political knowledge (regression 1 in Table 1).

Table 1. Hierarchical regression analysis of predictors of political knowledge of opposition parties ($N = 1{,}429$)

Predictor Variables	Regression 1 β	Regression 2 β	Regression 3 β
Demographics and SES			
Gender	0.153**	0.142**	0.140**
Age	0.118**	0.165**	0.169**
Education level	0.310**	0.263**	0.257**
Income	0.208**	0.192**	0.193**
Media use			
Mainstream media		0.103**	0.103**
Foreign media		0.002	−0.002
Alternative online media		0.166**	0.139**
Visit party websites		0.133**	0.122**
Online political engagement			0.064*
R^2	0.190	0.271	0.274
Adjusted R^2	0.190	0.267	0.269
R^2 Change	0.192	0.079	0.003
F Change	84.79**	38.48**	5.28*

*$p < 0.05$, that is there is less than 5% chance that the results happened randomly
**$p < 0.001$, that is there is less than 1% chance that the results happened randomly

Then, tests were carried out to discover the relationship between media use (use of mainstream media, foreign news, alternative media, and political party websites and Facebook pages) and political knowledge, after taking into account the effect of demographics on political knowledge found in the first test (regression 2 in Table 1). Finally, tests were carried out to find the relationship between online political engagement and political knowledge, after factoring in the effect of demographics and media use (regression 3 in Table 1).

The analyses show that all three types of measures — demographics, media use, and online political engagement — had significant influence on political knowledge. Educational level and income are the two strongest predictors of political knowledge.

Use of alternative online media is the third strongest predictor. These are followed by age, visiting party websites, gender, use of mainstream media, and lastly, online political engagement. Thus a short answer to the first research question is that those who had higher education and income, and used alternative online media were the most likely to be more knowledgeable about opposition parties. Those who were male and older, consumed mainstream media and were more politically engaged online were also likely to have better knowledge of opposition parties. The confirmation of the influence of demographic and SES factors, as well as use of online political sources, suggest that these can contribute to differences in political knowledge.

To answer the second research question, statistical tests were also carried out to see whether a knowledge gap is related to the use of different types of media and the intensity of use. Table 2 shows the mean knowledge score of users and non-users of mainstream and alternative media. In general, respondents who did not use either mainstream or alternative media scored the lowest (mean score = 1.82) and were the least knowledgeable about opposition parties, while those who consumed both forms of media were the most knowledgeable (mean score = 8.21). High to intensive users of alternative media were also more knowledgeable than high to intensive users of mainstream media. Those who did not use mainstream media at all but were low to average users of alternative media were more knowledgeable (mean score = 8.15) about opposition parties than high and intensive users of mainstream media who did not use alternative media at all (mean score = 5.76).

Table 2. Mean knowledge scores for mainstream and alternative media users ($N = 1,909$)

Alternative Media	Don't Use	Low to Average Use	High to Intensive Use
Mainstream media			
Don't use	1.82	5.88	6.8
Low to average use	3.95	6.09	8.15
High to intensive use	5.76	7.61	8.21

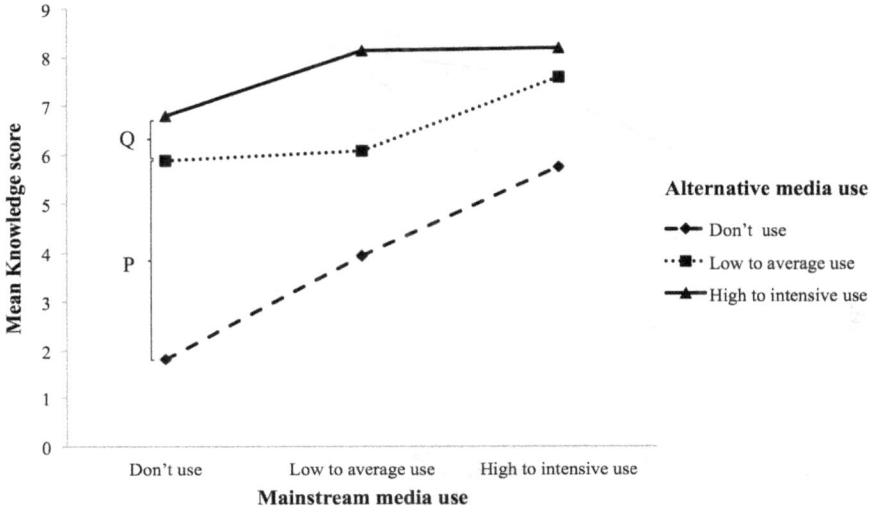

Figure 1: Interaction effect of alternative media use on knowledge score

The analysis further shows an interaction effect between mainstream and alternative media use. That is, the size of the effect of the use of mainstream media on political knowledge of opposition parties depends on the level of use of alternative media, and vice versa. Figures 1 and 2 illustrate this interaction effect. The graphs show that the knowledge scores of users increase when they read both mainstream and alternative media. The differences in scores (presented in the graph as height difference) between each group (non-users, average users, and high users of mainstream media in Figure 1, and non-users, average users, and high users of alternative media in Figure 2) depict the knowledge gap.

For example, in Figure 1, if we just look at the non-users of mainstream media, the gap between those in this group who were non-users of alternative media and average users of alternative media (the height P) is larger than the gap between average users of alternative media and high users of alternative media (the height Q). Also, in Figure 1 the top two lines representing average users of alternative media and high users of alternative media are not as steep as the lowest line representing non-users of alternative media; this shows that the political knowledge of users of alternative media

Debbie Goh

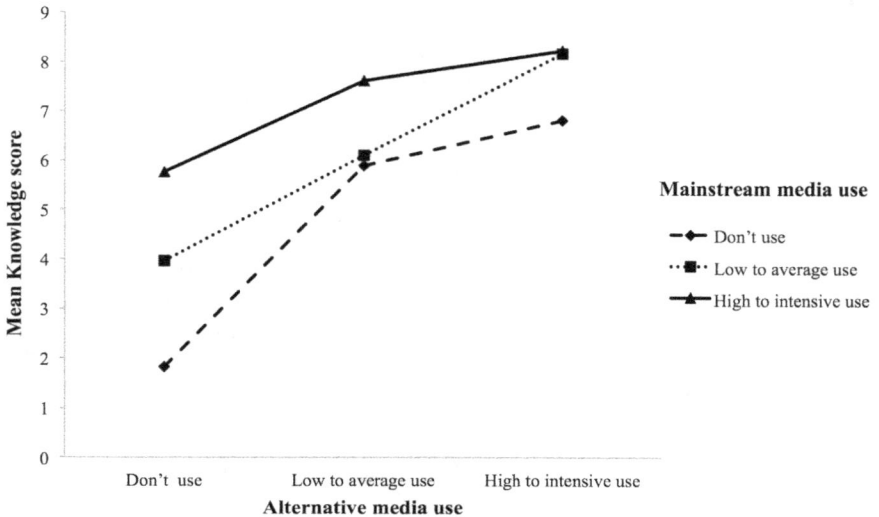

Figure 2:   Interaction effect of mainstream media use on knowledge score

(whether average or high users) was not much affected by their use of mainstream media, whereas the political knowledge of non-users of alternative media was very much affected by how much mainstream media they used. Among average mainstream media users, the gap also widened between the average and high user of alternative media. The gap among alternative media users only narrowed among respondents who were high users of mainstream media. The gap between non-users of alternative media and the rest, however, remained almost unchanged. The flatness of the graph for high users of alternative media also suggests that more intense use of mainstream media did not increase their knowledge. In sum, the graph indicates that while using mainstream media alone will narrow the knowledge gap (they can go from the leftmost point of the lowest line to the rightmost point), the effect is limited (they cannot reach the rightmost point of the top or middle graph, where political knowledge is greater). Those who did not use alternative media were unable to narrow the knowledge gap. Also, intensive use of only mainstream media will help narrow the gap but only partly, supporting existing studies that found limited coverage of opposition parties in the mainstream media. Furthermore, even with intensive use, the knowledge gain was limited.

Figure 2 shows that among those who did not use any alternative media (extreme left side points), the intensity of mainstream media increases political knowledge accordingly — ranging from about 2 to 6 in mean knowledge score. The mean knowledge score for average users of both mainstream and alternative media was just below 6. Those who used alternative media intensely but did not use mainstream media achieved even higher scores exceeding 6. Those who used alternative media intensely and used mainstream media at average or high level achieved almost the same level of knowledge of about 8, the highest score in this graph. In fact, the average users of mainstream media caught up with intense users of mainstream media when their alternative media use increased from average to high (as can been seen from the two upper lines almost meeting on the right side of Figure 2).

Taking both graphs together, high use of both mainstream media and alternative media produced, predictably, the highest level of political knowledge, a score of about 8. High users of mainstream media with no use of alternative media achieved average political knowledge scores of about 5. Average users of mainstream media with no use of alternative media achieved less than average political knowledge with scores of about 4. Non-users of mainstream and alternative media had, predictably again, very low political knowledge with scores of about 2. On the other hand, high users of alternative media with no use of mainstream media achieved better than average political knowledge with scores of about 6. Average users of alternative media with average use of mainstream media also achieved a slightly better than average political knowledge with scores between 5 and 6.

Overall, the knowledge gaps between alternative media users are larger than those of mainstream media users, indicating that there are greater differences among those who went online for alternative political information and those who did not. Furthermore, intensive users of alternative media were unable to gain more knowledge with intensive use of mainstream media, but mainstream media users were still gaining knowledge with intensified use of alternative media: this strongly suggests that going online had a disproportional impact on helping them gain political knowledge than reading mainstream media. The analysis supports the first hypothesis: that voters who read alternative online sites such as political blogs and non-mainstream online news sites were more knowledgeable about opposition parties in Singapore. These findings support the widely held belief that mainstream media did not provide adequate coverage of the opposition. It could also be that alternative media provided disproportionately higher coverage for the opposition. Thus these findings should be viewed as a reflection of the inherent bias the different media streams have.

Respondents who visited party websites during the election period also scored higher (mean score = 7.65) than those who didn't (mean score = 4.66). Those who were politically engaged online were also more knowledgeable (mean score = 7.51) compared to those who weren't (mean score = 4.86). These findings support hypotheses 2 and 3: that voters who went to party websites for election information and who were politically engaged online were more knowledgeable about opposition parties in Singapore. They also strongly indicate that a knowledge gap exists between users and non-users of online political resources, contributing to a democratic digital divide in Singapore.

Discussion

This study sets out to determine whether use of the Internet for political information would influence Singaporeans' political knowledge about opposition parties that could create a democratic divide among Singaporeans. In Singapore, mainstream mass media's newsroom practice of giving prominence to the ruling party, the PAP, clearly is in place. Moreover, the mainstream media is known to adhere closely to its role as the government's partner in national development, giving more coverage of PAP candidates and their issue positions that is often more positive (Cenite, 2008).

Opposition parties therefore viewed the Internet as a platform for balancing the scope and depth of political information. As Internet penetration and usage in Singapore is high, there is often little doubt that the digital divide in terms of physical access has almost been overcome, and that Singaporeans can easily engage in political activities online. While the number of alternative political news sites and blogs has grown in Singapore (Lee and Kan, 2009), little is known about Singaporeans' political activities online and the effect of such use on their political knowledge.

The findings indicate that people who did not access alternative online sources or political websites or were not politically engaged online were indeed less knowledgeable about opposition politics. Those who consumed only mainstream media could only gain limited political knowledge of opposition parties. While it is beyond the scope of this study to conclude that the Internet alone increased political knowledge, the analysis showed that alternative media use had the strongest influence among all media types on political knowledge. The findings thus strongly suggest that the Internet had been an effective tool in helping people become more informed about opposition parties and their positions on issues. Even among those most motivated and interested in the election (the high users), the data showed that knowledge gain was greatest for those who used alternative websites.

An implication of this finding is that the Internet can be used to enhance more diverse political knowledge. Contrary to criticism that political discourse on the Internet is inaccurate and untrustworthy, this study shows that the Internet can positively influence citizens' political knowledge about alternative parties, their candidates, and policy positions on issues. The challenge is to enable and encourage more voters to access alternative political sites. Despite Singapore's world-class telecommunication infrastructure, a democratic digital divide still exists along socioeconomic lines. Education and income are the strongest predictors of political knowledge. Demographic variables of gender and age (in favour of men and young people) are also significant predictors of knowledge about opposition parties in Singapore. This finding is unsurprising given that those who employed the Internet for election information tended to be men, were younger, had higher income, and were more educated (Tan and Mahizhnan, Chapter 1, this volume).

Physical access to the Internet may no longer be an impediment to Singaporeans but other barriers still need to be removed before more will become politically engaged online. Political parties and candidates keen to draw voters online need to consider that social and cultural issues discourage or present barriers to women, older voters, and voters with lower income or lower education. This may include developing content and language that are accessible and appealing to these voters. Parties would do well to also consider when these voters will be able to be engaged online. Perhaps with these in place, Singaporeans can look forward to an election where there will be diverse and equitable participation not just in terms of political parties but also voters themselves.

Appendix: Questions Measuring Opposition Party Knowledge

1. Did you know each of the following candidates contesting in Aljunied GRC? Choose Yes, No or Don't know

   (1) Vivian Balakrishnan
   (2) Low Thia Kiang
   (3) Kenneth Jeyaretnam
   (4) Sylvia Lim
   (5) Vincent Wijeysingha
   (6) Chen Show Mao
   (7) Chee Soon Juan
   (8) Muhammad Faisal
   (9) Abdul Manap
   (10) Pritam Singh
   (11) Hazel Poa

2. Which party is Mr Chiam See Tong from?

   (1) Workers' Party
   (2) Singapore Democratic Party

(3) Singapore People's Party
(4) Singapore Democratic Alliance
(5) Don't know

3. Which one of the following statements best describes Singapore Democratic Party candidate Tan Jee Say? Please pick one of the statements.

(1) He did not make the cut to be a Permanent Secretary
(2) He wants to close down factories and abandon the manufacturing sector
(3) He believes incentives for Singapore factories should stop
(4) He said opposition will provide a "rojak government with rojak policies"
(5) Don't know

4. Which one of the following statements best describes the Workers' Party's manifesto, "Towards A First World Parliament".

(1) The Workers' Party wants to rock Singapore's foundation
(2) The Workers' Party in Parliament can support and advise the driver, making sure he can complete the journey
(3) The Workers' Party will eventually take over the government
(4) The Workers' Party wants Aljunied citizens to look at the big picture and sacrifice for true democracy
(5) Don't know

References

Bonfadelli, H. "The Internet and Knowledge Gaps: A Theoretical and Empirical Investigation", *European Journal of Communication*, 17(1), (March 2002): 65–84.

Cenite, M., S.Y. Chong, T.J. Han, L.Q. Lim, and X.L. Tan. "Perpetual Development Journalism? Balance and Framing in 2006 Singapore Election Coverage", *Asian Journal of Communication*, 18(3), (2008): 280–95.

Drew, D. and D. Weaver. "Voter Learning in the 2004 Presidential Election: Did the Media Matter?", *Journalism and Mass Communication Quarterly*, 83(1), (Spring 2006): 25–42.

Ettema, J.S. and F.G. Kline. "Deficits, Differences, and Ceilings: Contingent Conditions for Understanding the Knowledge Gap", *Communication Research*, 2(4), (1977): 179–202.

Galbraith, J.K. *The New Industrial State* (Harmondsworth: Penguin, 1972).

Gaziano, C. "The Knowledge Gap: An Analytical Review of Media Effects", *Communication Research*, 10(4), (1983): 447–86.

Gomez, J. *Internet Politics: Surveillance and Intimidation in Singapore* (Singapore: Think Centre, 2002).

Gomez, J. "Online Opposition in Singapore: Communications Outreach Without Electoral Gain", *Journal of Contemporary Asia*, 38(4), (November 2008): 591–612.

Ho, K.C., Z. Baber and K. Habibul. "Sites of Resistance: Alternative Websites and State-Society Relations." *British Journal of Sociology*, 53(1), (2008): 127–148.

Holbrook, T.M. "Presidential Campaigns and the Knowledge Gap", *Political Communication*, 19, (2002): 437–54.

Infocomm Development Authority of Singapore. *Annual Survey on Infocomm Usage in Households for 2010*, (Singapore: IDA, 2011).

Kavita, K., E.C. Kuo, and S. Lee. "Where is the Opposition? Media Coverage, Political Interest and Voting Behaviour in Singapore's 2001 election". Paper presented at the annual meeting of the International Communication Association, San Diego, California, 2003.

Kim, Sei-Hill. "Testing the Knowledge Gap Hypothesis in South Korea: Traditional News Media, The Internet, and Political Learning", *International Journal of Public Opinion Research*, 20(2), (Summer 2008): 193–210.

Klüver, R. "Political Culture and Information Technology in the 2001 Singapore General Election", *Political Communication*, 21(4), (October 2004): 435–58.

Lee, J., C.D. Ham, and E. Thorson. "Knowledge Gap in the Media-Saturated '08 Presidential Election". Paper presented at the annual meeting of the International Communication Association, Chicago, Illinois, 2009.

Lee, Terence and Cornelius Kan. "Blogospheric Pressures in Singapore: Internet Discourses and the 2006 General Election", *Continuum: Journal of Media and Cultural Studies*, 23(6), (2009): 871–86.

Leong, W.K. "Opposition Parties Raise their Internet Profiles". *Today*, 22 April 2011.

Loh, Andrew. "Tan Jee Say's paper on New Economy". *The Online Citizen Blog*, 24 April 2011. Available at http://www.theonlinecitizen.com/

2011/04/tan-jee-says-paper-on-new-economy-reproduced-here-in-full/.

Lucas, H. and R. Sylla. "The Global Impact of the Internet: Widening the Economic Gap between Wealthy and Poor Nations", *Prometheus*, 21(1), (2003): 3–22.

Moore, David W. "Political Campaigns and the Knowledge-Gap Hypothesis", *Public Opinion Quarterly*, 51(2), (Summer 1987): 186–200.

Nadeau, Richard, Neil Nevitte, Elisabeth Gidengil, and Andre Blais. "Election Campaigns as Information Campaigns: Who Learns What and Does it Matter?", *Political Communication*, 25(3), (July 2008): 229–48.

Ng, E., I. Saad, and S. Ismail. "A Game-Changer for the Polls?" *Today*, 15 March 2011.

Norris, P. *Digital Divide: Civic Engagement, Information Poverty, and the Internet Worldwide* (Cambridge, UK: Cambridge University Press, 2001).

Norris, P. and D. Sanders. "Message or Medium? Campaign Learning During the 2001 British General Election", *Political Communication*, 20(3), (2003): 233–62.

OECD. *Understanding the Digital Divide*. 2001. Available at http://www.oecd.org/dataoecd/38/57/1888451.pdf (accessed on 29 April 2004).

Porat, M. *The Information Economy, Vol. 1* (Washington, D.C.: U.S. Department of Commerce, 1977).

Selwyn, N. "Reconsidering Political and Popular Understandings of the Digital Divide", *New Media & Society*, 6(3), (2004): 341–62.

Servaes, J. "Digital Citizenship and Information Inequalities: Challenges for the Future". In *The European Information Society: A Reality Check*, Servaes, J. (ed.), pp. 231–38 (Bristol: ECCR Book Series, 2003).

Tichenor, P.J., G.A. Donohue, and C.N. Olien. "Mass Media Flow and Differential Growth in Knowledge", *Public Opinion Quarterly*, 34, (1970): 159–70.

United Nations Development Program (UNDP). *Human Development Report 2001: Making New Technologies Work for Human Development* (New York, UNDP, 2001).

Van Dijk, J. *The Deepening Divide: Inequality in the Information Society* (Thousand Oaks, CA: Sage Publications, 2005).

Warschauer, M. "Reconceptualizing the Digital Divide", *First Monday*, 7(7), (2002). Available at http://firstmonday.org/issues/issue7_7/warschauer/index.html (accessed 1 January 2008).

Weaver, D. and D. Drew. "Voter Learning in the 1990 Off-Year Election: Did the Media Matter?", *Journalism Quarterly*, 70(2), (1993): 356–68.

Weaver, D. and D. Drew. "Voter Learning in the 1992 Presidential Election: Did the "Nontraditional" Media and Debates Matter?", *Journalism Quarterly*, 72(1), (1995): 7–17.

Weaver, D. and D. Drew. "Voter Learning and Interest in the 2000 Presidential Election: Did the Media Matter?", *Journalism and Mass Communication Quarterly*, 78(4), (2001): 787–98.

Wei, L. and D. Hindman. "Does the Digital Divide Matter More? Comparing the Effects of New Media and Old Media Use on the Education-Based Knowledge Gap", *Mass Communication & Society*, 14, (2011): 216–35.

Wong, T. "The Battle for Eyeballs is On". *The Straits Times*, 4 December 2010.

Wong, T. "Easing of rules on new media 'inevitable.'" *The Straits Times*, 15 March 2011.

10

SQUARING POLITICAL CIRCLES: COPING WITH CONFLICTING INFORMATION

Natalie Pang

Abstract

The increasing volume of user-generated content via blogs, public forums, and social networks has led to a significant increase in conflicting or contradictory views being generated, and added to the level of complexity in the information that the electorate must process. Yet little is known about the effects of processing such conflicting information. In this study, 60 eligible voters were randomly assigned to two different experimental groups. In the first group, participants were exposed to conflicting views on the issue of foreign labour in Singapore. In contrast, the second group was exposed only to information that presented consistent views. Results show that exposure to conflicting views made participants perceive themselves as more knowledgeable on the issue, more decisive that the issue was significant enough to influence support for a party, and more tolerant towards divergent opinions compared with participants given only consistent information. However, exposure to conflicting views also created doubts about their original views and about the sources of these views. The findings provide a useful lesson on how to raise democratic participation in Singapore, as greater exposure to multifaceted information on multiple media platforms can lead to better informed participants (as self-perceived). Additionally, exposure to a range of information could also lead to greater media literacy, as participants learn to discern how information are constructed, including the contexts and sources that shape the information they encounter.

The quick diffusion of technologies and broadband Internet infrastructure has made Singapore one of the most networked cities in the world (Lee and Kan, 2009). Some 82% of households in Singapore have access to the Internet (IDA, 2011). In 2009 (IDA, 2010) the most common activity when using the Internet was emailing (56%), followed by social networking (30%) and information browsing (24%). The widespread adoption of the Internet in Singapore has led to the flourishing of online content, with a notable growth in the blogosphere, a rise in the number of people with social networking accounts such as Facebook and Twitter, more news from mainstream media going online, and greater online participation in forums and citizen-generated news sites such as the Straits Times Online Mobile Print (STOMP). The enthusiasm for online media has gained notable attention from political leaders, given the ruling party's control of Singapore's mainstream media (Tan, 2010). As Tan (2010) highlighted, mainstream media has been managed traditionally with the goal of being compliant with "national interests". This also implied that citizens who read only mainstream media may not have much opportunity to encounter information contrary to what the mainstream media disseminates. The rise of online media is hence significant as a source of alternative political information.

Alternative online media in Singapore gained political traction with the 2006 election, as citizen bloggers defied the sanctions placed upon them by the Parliamentary Elections (Elections Advertising) Regulations in using blogs for political campaigning (Tan and Mahizhnan, 2008). An amendment in 2010 removed these restrictions on blogs, thereby allowing citizens to participate in political discourse and campaigning online. Consequently, there is also greater diversity in information being generated, increasing the likelihood of encountering conflicting information and perspectives.

One policy in particular, that of allowing the influx of foreign labour into Singapore, has been heavily criticised by the electorate (Venkat, 2011) resulting in a considerable amount of discourse generated in both mainstream and online media on the issue. In Singapore, however, perspectives on the issue are clearly divided by the types of media carrying this information. Consistent with Tan's (2010) point about compliance, Singapore's mainstream media carries perspectives that are mostly supportive of the pro-foreign labour policies of the state. Political and thought leaders in main-stream media argue that foreign labour is critical to sustain a vibrant economy, and helps to create new business opportunities. These benefits collectively contribute to a higher standard of living, they add. The picture is very different when one turns to the alternative online media for information about the issue. In blogs, forums, and social media, critiques and comments reflecting unhappiness with the influx of foreign labour abound. Concerns about the consequences of the foreign labour influx such as overcrowding in public transport, inflated property prices, and competition for jobs were widely carried in alternative online media, contradicting the prevailing views found in mainstream media. In the run-up to the 2011 General Election, it became evident that the topic of foreign labour was going to be a hot issue for political parties and candidates. This led to a substantial volume of information being produced in both mainstream and alternative online media, thus generating the scenario of some voters encountering conflicting information on the issue.

Although Singapore's mainstream media remain tightly con-trolled, there is a high level of trust in the accuracy, quality, and authenticity of content published on these platforms. In the survey conducted by Tan and Mahizhnan (Chapter 1, this volume), it was found that only 21% of respondents read alternative online media for information about the election. Given this scenario, it implies that most of the population in Singapore are encountering consistent information because they read only mainstream media, whereas about 21% may be encountering conflicting information frequently, as perspectives on issues found on alternative online media can vary considerably from the ones published in mainstream media.

To validate this assumption, the study draws on a nationwide representative survey of 2,000 voters to find out the incidence of conflicting information as perceived by the electorate (Appendix 1 in this book). Specifically, one question in the survey asked: "In getting information from the media about the election, did you encounter situations where information conflicted with or contradicted what you read previously?" The results in Figure 1 show 25% said that

**In getting information from the media about the election, did
you encounter situations where information conflicted with
or contradicted what you read previously?**

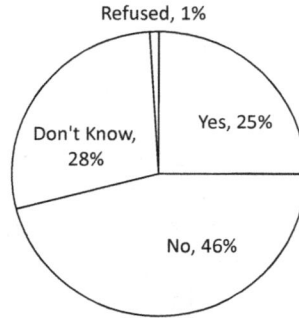

Figure 1: Incidence of conflicting information as perceived by nation-wide post election survey respondents

they encountered conflicting information. The percentage is close to the 21% who use online media. While 46% of survey respondents said no, 28% of survey respondents actually said "don't know". It may be that they did not feel that they had accessed enough alternative media or information to respond with certainty to this question. On the other hand, this could also imply that people in this group were also aware that there was a possibility of conflicting information "out there", even though they may not have encountered it personally.

The study of conflicting information is not new, with work from scholars from disciplines such as philosophy (Cantwell, 1998), communications (Cozzens and Contractor, 1987), and psychology (Kienhues, Stadtler, and Bromme, 2011). Cantwell (1998) observed that when confronted with conflicting information, the means by which rational human agents conjoin different pieces of information, that is, decide on what information to reject, may be determined based on what is known about the information sources. Cozzens and Contractor (1987) found that confronted with conflicting information, scepticism towards mass media tend to occur. In Kienhues *et al.* (2011)'s study where participants encountered conflicting medical information, they advanced in their epistemic beliefs in medicine-related knowledge, that is, exposure to conflicting information made them more informed about medicine and how to acquire medical knowledge.

The study of personal epistemic beliefs began in 1968 (Perry, 1968), where interviews with college students revealed differences in the conceptions and beliefs about knowledge. As students advance in their epistemic beliefs, they move beyond simple representations of knowledge to ask questions about knowledge of certain issues or topics, which include acknowledging their uncertainty, and the need to understand the contexts of how knowledge is constructed and their sources (King and Kitchener, 1994). Voters with access to multiple sources of information will have to assess volumes of information, make decisions about which information is more important and valid than others, and how conflicting information can be resolved (or not). How the individual voter reconciles his own opinions with the information he encounters is shaped by the beliefs he holds about the nature of political knowledge.

With the rise of the Internet as a medium for alternative discourse and information, studies have emerged focusing on the understanding and resolution of conflicting information by users in different subject domains such as health (Eysenbach *et al.*, 2002) and consumer product information (Yin, Han, and Yu, 2008). Few studies, however, have been done on the impacts of conflicting information in the political arena.

In the context of political knowledge, information processing by the electorate may be more complex for those who consume information from both mainstream and alternative media and may therefore encounter conflicting information on issues. However, they may also advance in their epistemic beliefs. On the other hand, in liberal democracies where some people live in information ghettos — that is, they seek information that concur with their own views even if there is open access to alternative sources of information, there may be little or no advancement in their epistemic beliefs. These questions are not yet understood. In this study, we want to specifically explore the impact of encountering conflicting or consistent information. How would it influence a voter's support for a political party? How may it change perceptions of political knowledge and underlying beliefs about information coming from mainstream and online media? Additionally, how do voters cope with conflicting information?

The Study

The study employed a pre-test/post-test experimental design to study the effects of encountering conflicting or consistent information during election campaigning on the issue of foreign labour, one of the most debated topics among candidates and voters. In order to test the effects of conflicting information, the experimental method was chosen so as to manipulate the exposure of consistent or conflicting information to different groups of participants. The design of the experiment was informed by Kienhues, Stadtler and Bromme's study (2011). In the Kienhues, Stadtler and Bromme (2011) experiment, encounters with conflicting information led to advances in the participants' epistemic beliefs about medical information, that is, exposure to conflicting information made the subjects more informed about medicine and how to acquire such knowledge. This is an interesting result, as it demonstrates the potential of the Internet as a tool for learning (Tsai, 2004).

In our study, 60 eligible voters, recruited according to sampling criteria of gender, race, and household type using the 2010 population census, were randomly assigned to two groups of 30 people: the Conflicting Information Group and the Consistent Information Group. Table 1 shows the demographic breakdown of subjects in each group.

For the purpose of this study, the topic of "foreign labour" was chosen, from which information presenting consistent and conflicting perspectives (in this context, pro and/or anti-foreign labour perspectives) were collated from multiple information sources, including mainstream media sources and blogs.

The experiment, which took place between 28 April (a day after Nomination Day) and 7 May (Polling Day) 2011, was divided into

Table 1. Demographic breakdown of participants in each group

	%	Quota
Gender		
Male	49	15
Female	51	15
Total	**100**	**30**
Race		
Chinese	74	22
Malay	13	4
Indian	9	3
Others	3	1
Total	**100**	**30**
Household		
HDB	84	25
Private	16	5
Total	**100**	**30**

the following parts:

(a) General questionnaire

Subjects in both groups had to answer a general questionnaire at the beginning of the experiment, including questions such as age, gender, race, education, housing type, frequency of web usage, web proficiency, perceived level of political knowledge, media usage preferences (whether mainstream or online media) and political participation. These questions were asked to assess potential effects of these factors on the results. A test was done to examine if there were differences between the Conflicting Information and Consistent Information Groups on these factors. No significant differences were found. This shows that any differences found between the two groups are results of the experiment and not of prior differences between the two groups.

(b) Scenario

Subjects were then introduced to a scenario (see Appendix in this chapter) about a fictional friend who lives in a constituency that is being contested. In this scenario, an issue involving opposing views from the contesting political parties, various information sources, and the electorate has become a key discussion point in the constituency. This friend is asking for an opinion from the subject. Subjects were then asked to advise their friend by answering the following four questions:

1. You would advise that information about the issue should influence your friend's support for the parties involved. (More likely yes; More likely no; I don't know)
2. On a scale of 1–5, how certain are you of this decision? (1 being Very Uncertain and 5 being Very Certain)
3. On a scale of 1–5, how certain are you that experts could answer Question 1? (1 being Very Uncertain and 5 being Very Certain)
4. On a scale of 1–5, how much do you think you know about the topic compared to an average person? (1 being Very Little and 5 being Very Much)

(c) Pre-exposure test

When the subjects had answered questions based on the scenario, they were asked to answer eight questions concerning their epistemic beliefs on the foreign labour issue, that is, concerning the nature of knowledge about the topic. The questions were adopted using Kienhues, Stadtler and Bromme's (2011) 8-item scale on topic-specific epistemic beliefs. These items ask whether or not people felt that the information task relating to a certain topic is easily solvable. In other words, they measure whether "participants did not believe in a single correct and easy answer" or whether they think there is "a clear cut solvability of the task" (p. 197). The questions are:

1. I think it is justifiable that there are different opinions on this topic.
2. If a group of experts had to answer this question, they would have known the right decision.
3. If people hold different views on this topic, one opinion is correct and the other is wrong.

4. I don't think that it is possible for there to be more than one right opinion on this topic.
5. I feel that it is possible to find out the truth on this topic.
6. In my opinion, everybody performing this online search will arrive at the same answer.
7. In my opinion, there is no way to decide which solution is the best one.
8. I do not doubt that there is one right answer to this question, even though I did not find it.

(d) The experiment: Exposure to conflicting/consistent information:
   After responding to the scenario, subjects were given a webpage containing links to different preselected websites from both mainstream and alternative new media containing consistent or conflicting perspectives about the foreign labour issue. The Conflicting Information Group was exposed to a webpage that presented links to information which would present conflicting perspectives on the issue. The Consistent Information Group was divided into two sub-groups, with one sub-group exposed to webpages whose content carried consistent perspectives with positive valence towards the issue of foreign labour, and the other sub-group presented with a webpage with consistent perspectives that were anti-foreign labour in nature. Table 2 shows the links used for each group of subjects. All subjects were then given twenty to thirty minutes to browse the webpages provided and were told they could click the links freely or read information on a page for as long as they wanted within the time frame.

(e) Post-exposure test
   After browsing the linked pages, subjects answered the same set of questions in (b) and (c).

(f) Interview with Conflicting Information Group
   The final part of the study was a 20-minute interview of subjects in the Conflicting Information Group. The aim of the interview is to understand potential coping strategies and the

Table 2.   Links to consistent or conflicting information in each group

	Title	Source	Link
Conflicting information	Foreigners help create good jobs for S'poreans: PM (Pro)	*The Straits Times*	http://www.straitstimes.com/GeneralElection/News/Story/STIStory_659474.html
	Singapore gains from inflow of foreigners: PM Lee (Pro)	Channel News Asia	http://www.channelnewsasia.com/stories/singaporelocalnews/view/1077857/1/.html
	Foreign Talents in Singapore (Pro, Anti)	James Seng's blog	http://james.seng.sg/2008/02/28/foreign-talents-in-singapore/
	The PAP's flawed immigration, foreign talent and foreign worker policies (Anti)	The Online Citizen	http://theonlinecitizen.com/2011/02/the-pap%E2%80%99s-flawed-immigration-foreign-talent-and-foreign-worker-policies/
	Thoughts on Foreign Talent (Anti)	Mr Wang Says So	http://mrwangsaysso.blogspot.com/2007/02/thoughts-on-foreign-talent.html
Consistent, pro-foreign labour information	Foreigners help create good jobs for S'poreans: PM	*The Straits Times*	http://www.straitstimes.com/GeneralElection/News/Story/STIStory_659474.html
	Singapore gains from inflow of foreigners: PM Lee	Channel News Asia	http://www.channelnewsasia.com/stories/singaporelocalnews/view/1077857/1/.html
	S'pore needs foreign talent to stay competitive	My Paper	http://www.asiaone.com/News/AsiaOne+News/Singapore/Story/A1Story20110224-265029.html
	Foreign Talent Policy Here to Stay: Lee Kuan Yew	*The Business Times*	http://yaleglobal.yale.edu/content/foreign-talent-policy-here-stay-lee-kuan-yew
	Foreign Talents in Singapore	James Seng's blog	http://james.seng.sg/2008/02/28/foreign-talents-in-singapore/

(Continued)

Table 2. (*Continued*)

	Title	Source	Link
Consistent anti-foreign	The PAP's flawed immigration, foreign talent and foreign worker policies	The Online Citizen	http://theonlinecitizen.com/2011/02/the-pap%E2%80%99s-flawed-immigration-foreign-talent-and-foreign-worker-policies/
	Thoughts on Foreign Talent	Mr Wang Says So	http://mrwangsaysso.blogspot.com/2007/02/thoughts-on-foreign-talent.html
	More good years for foreigners?	The Temasek Review	http://www.temasekreview.com/2011/04/24/more-good-years-for-foreigners/
	New Citizen: I am too important to do NS	The Temasek Review	http://www.temasekreview.com/2011/04/10/new-citizen-i-am-too-important-to-do-ns/

impacts of reading different perspectives on the issue. A semi-structured interview guide was used, with a focus on clarifying the types of conflicting information noticed by participants, their consonance, and their coping strategies and impacts of such information.

Findings and Discussion

Conflicting Information Leads to Shifts in Epistemic Beliefs

Table 3 (which deals with all questions except Question 1) and Table 4 (which deals with Question 1) show the results for the Conflicting Information Group, Consistent Information Group (Anti-foreign Labour), and Consistent Information Group (Pro-foreign Labour).

For the Conflicting Information Group, four questions received significantly different answers (shaded in the table) between the pre-test and post-test: Q2, Q3, Q4 and Q8. The result for Question 8 (I don't think that it is possible for there to be more than one right opinion on this topic.) shows that after encountering conflicting information about the issue, participants were more likely to feel it was possible for more than one right opinion on the issue. The finding on Question 1 (You would advise that information about the issue should influence your friend's support for the parties involved.) shows that they were more certain after exposure to conflicting information that the issue was significant enough to determine support for a political party. In other words, participants who encountered conflicting information became more likely to think that it was possible that there was more than one right opinion on the topic, and may also decide that the issue was prominent enough to determine support for political parties.

Participants were more certain after exposure to conflicting information about how they will advise their friends in terms of supporting particular political parties (Question 2), more certain of the knowledge of experts on the issue (Question 3), and also felt that they knew more about the topic than before (Question 4). These results imply that an individual may look to the thoughts of

Table 3. Statistical test for significance differences in pre-test and post-test answers

		Conflicting Information Group		Consistent Information Group (anti-foreign labour)		Consistent Information Group (pro-foreign labour)	
		Z	1-tailed	Z	1-tailed	Z	1-tailed
Question 2	On a scale of 1–5, how certain are you of this decision?	−2.179	0.01	−1.730	0.04	−1.134	0.13
Question 3	On a scale of 1–5, how certain are you that experts could answer Question 9?	−3.120	0.00	−1.540	0.06	−1.633	0.05
Question 4	On a scale of 1–5, how much do you think you know about the topic compared to an average person?	−1.730	0.04	−1.155	0.12	−0.414	0.34
Question 5	I think it is justifiable that there are different opinions on this topic.	0.000	0.50	−0.343	0.37	−0.707	0.24
Question 6	If a group of experts had to answer this question, they would have known the right decision.	−0.263	0.40	−1.000	0.16	−1.098	0.14
Question 7	If people hold different views on this topic, one opinion is correct and the other is wrong.	−0.042	0.48	−0.351	0.36	−0.378	0.35

(Continued)

Table 3. *(Continued)*

		Conflicting Information Group		Consistent Information Group (anti-foreign labour)		Consistent Information Group (pro-foreign labour)	
		Z	1-tailed	Z	1-tailed	Z	1-tailed
Question 8	I don't think that it is possible for there to be more than one right opinion on this topic.	**−2.246**	**0.01**	**−1.811**	**0.04**	−0.707	0.24
Question 9	I feel that it is possible to find out the truth on this topic.	−0.632	0.26	−0.879	0.19	−0.707	0.24
Question 10	In my opinion, everybody performing this online search will arrive at the same answer.	−0.180	0.43	−0.525	0.30	−0.973	0.17
Question 11	In my opinion, there is no way to decide which solution is the best one.	−1.056	0.15	−0.731	0.23	−0.577	0.28
Question 12	I do not doubt that there is one right answer to this question, even though I did not find it.	−0.909	0.18	−0.689	0.25	−1.414	0.08

Note: The significant results are highlighted in bold.

opinion leaders as a result of encountering conflicting information, and can also become more resolute in their opinions on the topic even though they will acknowledge that there is more than one way to think about the issue. Additionally, they will also have a heightened opinion of their knowledge about the topic. This also means that

Table 4. χ^2 goodness of fit tests significance differences in pre-test and post-test answers for Question 1 (You would advise that information about the issue should influence your friend's support for the parties involved)

	Conflicting Information Group	Consistent Information Group (Anti Foreign Labour)	Consistent Information Group (Pro Foreign Labour)
Chi-Square	8.373	6.643	The χ^2 goodness of fit test was not conducted as a cross tabulation of pre-test and post-test answers did not show changes in the responses. All participants in this group did not change their responses to the question after the test.
df	2	2	
Asymp. Sig.	**0.015**	**0.036**	

Note: The significant results are highlighted in bold.

receiving different information from different sources can lead to greater advancement of knowledge as perceived by participants. In other words, the exposure to conflicting information may lead to more critical thinking, or greater deliberation about the issue and participants may also arrive at a more definite conclusion.

Varying Impacts of Consistent Information with Differing Valence

For those in the Consistent Information Group who were exposed to pro-foreign labour information, significant differences were found only for Question 3. Participants in this group became more certain of the opinions of experts (Question 3). Comparing the result with those of the Conflicting Information Group, this means that the views of opinion leaders are still important, although participants may be looking to opinion leaders in a different way. For the Conflicting Information Group, where participants had to reconcile conflicting information, they may be looking to opinion leaders to help them address the dissonances. For the Consistent Information Group, opinion leaders may be sought because their views are still important to either affirm or refute the information being read.

For those in the Consistent Information Group who were exposed to anti-foreign labour information, Question 8 (I don't think that it is possible for there to be more than one right opinion on this topic.) saw a statistically significant difference after exposure. Unlike participants who read Conflicting Information, participants in this sub-group felt more strongly that it was not possible for more than one right opinion on the issue. In other words, participants actually became more single-minded after reading articles that were not just giving them consistent, but also anti-foreign labour information.

Comparing the results across all three groups, the findings demonstrate that the presentation of information containing multi-faceted perspectives (even if they may be conflicting) is likely to lead to greater tolerance of opinions, whereas information with negative valence (in this case, anti-foreign labour) may stoke sentiments among voters, shifting their responses towards the perception that there was only one "right" opinion. Instead of advancing their epistemic beliefs, reading information with negative valence led them to views that there was only one "right" opinion instead. This was not the case for the Consistent Information Group that is pro-foreign labour. This could perhaps be explained as pro-foreign labour perspectives were not new to participants prior to the experiment, as they were already disseminated in mainstream media. Yet participants who encountered consistent, anti-foreign labour information were different, in shifting towards the perception that there was only one "right" opinion even though they may also have read pro-foreign labour perspectives in mainstream media as well as before the experiment. The results show that in the context of Singapore, the valence of information (and not just consistency of the message) may be quite important in shaping the epistemic beliefs of voters, which may eventually shape their opinions on various issues. Information are only reconciled, or processed by individuals, when they are presented, and individuals do not always process previously-read information together with the information being read currently. As most participants were exposed to pro-foreign labour information via mainstream media before the experiment, it could also be possible that when they encountered anti-foreign labour information, perceived as "new" information, they accept such "new" information without the opportunity to critically think or doubt their epistemic beliefs. This highlights the danger of prolonged exposure to information that presents homogenous and one-sided perspectives.

As the electorate matures politically and with greater interest in political participation using various media channels, the findings imply the importance of making available information with multiple perspectives, even though they may be contradictory. As shown in the study, multiple information (even if conflicting) can advance beliefs in knowledge, that is believing more strongly that there was more than one way to examine the issue, and generate a more informed opinion. We can make the inference that as a result, voters can become more tolerant of different perspectives and be better able to engage in political deliberation with others of different opinions. With the penetration of online media in the everyday lives of the electorate, it therefore becomes important that perspectives on an issue are not divided along the lines of mainstream media and alternative online media or represented by only either of them. According to the results of the experiment, having such a broad spectrum of information will also result in greater tolerance for different opinions.

Increased Certainty in Support for a Party

For Conflicting Information Group participants who were already certain that the issue was important enough to influence support for a party, the position was maintained even after going through the conflicting views presented to them. However, those who were uncertain whether the issue was substantial enough to influence support for a party moved towards certainty in this decision. This did not take on any particular valence, as these participants shifted from saying "I don't know" before encountering the information to "yes" or "no" after reading the information in almost equal proportions. The finding has important implications for those who may previously be undecided or neutral on their support for certain parties — the swing voters. Exposure to conflicting information may be significant in influencing them towards supporting or not supporting political parties. Such a shift in certainty of the decision did not show any significant direction: exposure to conflicting information meant an increase in certainty towards the issue, but it is not always positive. Nevertheless, this finding also means that encountering conflicting information can create more informed voters who are also more committed to the parties they support.

Interestingly, while encountering consistent, pro-foreign labour information did not generate any significant influence towards supporting (or not supporting) political parties, anti-foreign labour information did just the opposite. Those in the Consistent Information Group who were exposed to anti-foreign labour information were more certain in the post-test that the foreign labour issue should influence their friend's support for a political party, rather than saying that they do not know. Interestingly, a statistically significant number of those who in the pre-test did not think that the issue mattered enough to influence party support changed their position in the post-test.

This may be associated with information that participants considered to be the views of political parties. Pro-foreign labour information was disseminated to explain the Peoples' Action Party (PAP)'s policy decisions on foreign labour. In contrast, anti-foreign labour information which provides critiques of such policies are often raised by opposition parties. The findings imply that although both types of information (pro and anti-foreign labour) are consistent, they do not generate the same outcomes. Specifically, anti-foreign labour information can trigger greater certainty by participants to support, or not support political parties. This could be because the types of messages received by the pro-foreign labour Consistent Group may be more focused on the policy of foreign labour itself, whereas the types of messages received by the anti-foreign labour Consistent Group may point them to the abilities and functions of political parties — hence influencing them in thinking with greater certainty that the issue was significant enough to determine their support (or non-support) of political parties.

Along with the earlier outcome where participants became more single-minded, information with negative valence also worked to elevate the significance of the issue to the extent that it would influence their support for a political party.

An Increase in Perceived Political Knowledge

Compared to those in the Consistent Information Groups, those in the Conflicting Information Group also significantly perceived themselves as being more knowledgeable about the topic after the experiment. In the experiment, when both types of information were presented (as conflicting information), participants had the task of reconciling them and this required additional processing on the part of the individual participant compared to reading one type of information on one type of media. The result also suggests that the additional work of processing conflicting information results in heightened awareness by the participants of their own political knowledge.

From the post-experiment interviews, it became clear that beyond the perceived level of increase in knowledge, the exposure to conflicting information also led to other impacts, which may trigger further actions. The post-experiment interview provides further qualitative insights (Figure 2). Of 30 participants in the group, nine (30%) indicated in the interviews that the exposure to information presenting conflicting information on the issue of foreign labour engendered second thoughts about their own original views on the matter. Another 20% were inspired to seek further validation on the issue, either by attending political rallies, talking to friends or family about it, or reading more about the topic. Also another 20% said that it made them consider or think about the issue differently. Some 17% of participants said that the presentation and existence of conflicting views raised doubts in their minds about the sources of information, in that these sources may not be objective in presenting a comprehensive picture of the issue. This points to the possibility that when participants are exposed to conflicting information, they may become more discerning of the media, and have greater media literacy. Doubts about the political parties and their abilities to

What was the most significant impact for you?

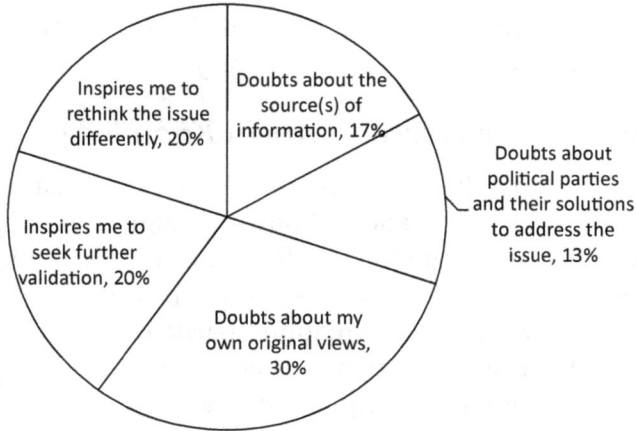

Figure 2: Impact of conflicting information according to post-test interviews of participants in the Conflicting Information Group

address the issue were prevalent for the remaining participants (13%). This suggests that encountering conflicting information may cause participants to think about the complexity and depth of the issue, and therefore raise scepticism about the abilities of political parties to resolve the issue.

Coping Strategies and Increased Scepticism towards Information Sources

The post-experiment interview asked participants in the Conflicting Information Group a number of open-ended questions relating to the impacts and how they would deal with conflicting information, and how this might influence what they believed about the sources of information. These open-ended responses are then coded into broad categories. Some of the coping strategies may be similar to the impacts of conflicting information, as some of the responses may be both an impact and a coping strategy.

The most mentioned strategy for coping with conflicting information was to seek diverse sources of information (30% of all strategies mentioned), such as newspapers, books, forums, and blogs. Looking to one's personal networks of friends, close colleagues, and family members followed, accounting for 20% of strategies mentioned. Participants also acknowledged that they would seek further clarifications by writing in to political parties or discussion forums in new or mainstream media. The opinions of experts also mattered, as a way to cope with conflicting information. Such experts may be academic and industry experts perceived to possess authoritative knowledge on the subject, but may also include mentors of participants. Other strategies include making personal observations by attending rallies, or seeking reliable sources of information. Figure 3 shows the detailed breakdown of responses.

It is worth noting here that seeking reliable sources of information was not almost as important as seeking diverse sources of information. This may be because one of the most obvious impacts of conflicting information for participants is the increase in scepticism towards information sources (Figure 4).

As a result, the "reliability" of information sources was already questioned by the majority of participants (70%) — translating into an emphasis on having diversity, rather than reliability, of information sources. With the rise of new media presenting diverse and conflicting perspectives, it becomes increasingly crucial to

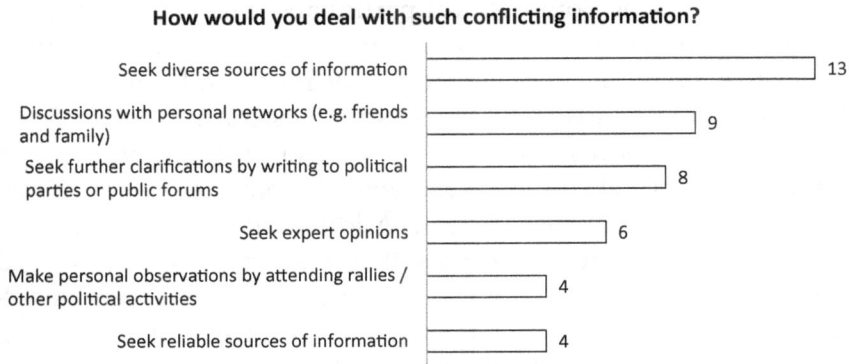

How would you deal with such conflicting information?

Strategy	Value
Seek diverse sources of information	13
Discussions with personal networks (e.g. friends and family)	9
Seek further clarifications by writing to political parties or public forums	8
Seek expert opinions	6
Make personal observations by attending rallies / other political activities	4
Seek reliable sources of information	4

Figure 3: Strategies to cope with conflicting information by participants according to post-test interviews of participants in the Conflicting Information Group

**How does this influence your beliefs about the sources
of information?**

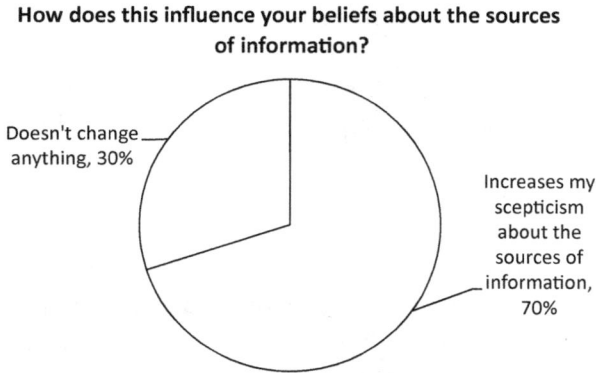

Doesn't change
anything, 30%

Increases my
scepticism
about the
sources of
information,
70%

Figure 4: Impact on beliefs about information sources according to post-test interviews of participants in the Conflicting Information Group

provide a wide range of perspectives on topics of interest, such as the issue of foreign labour in this case. The finding also provides some implications for mainstream media as voter perceptions of what constitutes authoritative information sources may be more complex than before.

Conclusion

With the use of online media to engage in political campaigning and discussions by both political parties and citizens, voters must process higher amounts of information complexity. This study shows that such information complexity, resulting from having to process divergent and conflicting perspectives, can have a significant and positive impact on voters. Those who were uncertain if an issue was important enough to influence support for a party shifted towards certainty in the decision. Additionally, having exposure to conflicting information also resulted in an increase in perceived political knowledge on the issue. The increase in perceived knowledge triggers further actions, such as a reconsideration of their own original views on the matter, and breeding doubts about the sources of information. This also presents opportunities for parties to engage voters, as an open dialogue to clarify conflicting information received by voters would be welcome. Voters presented with conflicting and divergent views may also be more tolerant of different opinions compared to those presented only with information with negative valence (in this case, information with anti-foreign labour perspectives). In other words, voters who are regularly exposed to information with multiple valences from various sources are also likely to be more tolerant and open to differing perspectives.

Other than looking to personal networks and/or experts, voters may engage in political participation as a result of trying to cope with conflicting information. Almost a quarter (20%) of participants in the Conflicting Information Group said they were inspired to seek further clarifications (Figure 2). This could be in the form of participation in public forums, writing to the political parties concerned, or making personal observations by attending rallies. In seeking information during electioneering, voters may also emphasise information sources for diversity instead of just reliability.

The results discussed were derived from an experiment to test voters' response to conflicting information. Although the nationwide survey shows that the presence of conflicting information as perceived by the general electorate may not be high (Figure 1), this may be because respondents do not feel that they have been exposed to alternative media or information enough to make any conclusive response to the question. At the same time, from the nationwide survey it was found that only 21% of respondents actually use alternative media for information on the election. However, as the electorate matures with their use of online media, the perceived presence of conflicting information and its impacts are expected to grow. The study provides preliminary indications of what such impacts may be, even for other countries with a similar media situation where the mainstream media is highly regulated, and where there is a relatively low usage of alternative media for political information.

The findings also have implications for voters who actively seek knowledge to make an informed voting decision. Knowledge is an integral part of informed decision-making in functioning democracies, and in the process voters also have an opportunity to advance their epistemic beliefs as well as media literacy. Particularly in a media-controlled environment, voters may find very clear distinctions between the types of information on different media platforms. In this context, the types of knowledge constructed by voters, depending on their consumption of information from which media platforms, may be quite discrete, and one can expect different impacts as a result. For instance, if they live in information ghettos where they choose to read only information that reinforce their own views, they may become more singular in their epistemic beliefs, even though they may have free access to alternative information. However, for those who do choose to take in different views, they can become more knowledgeable, informed, advance their epistemic beliefs and therefore shape the knowledge constructed. Additionally, in an attempt to reconcile conflicting information, they may also become active citizens by engaging in actions such as seek expert opinions, attend rallies and political events, or discuss the issue with their personal networks.

Appendix

The Scenario

You have a good friend who lives in a constituency that is currently being contested. The issue of foreign labour has been a hot topic in the coming election, with strong arguments for and against the issue. Your friend has been processing these divergent views, but still unsure if such information should influence his support for the parties involved. Your friend is similar to you in age, educational background, and has no preference for any particular political party or views. This friend is asking for an opinion from you. Advise your friend by answering the questions below:

You would advise that information about the issue should influence your friend's support for the parties involved.

☐ More likely yes   ☐ More likely no   ☐ I don't know

On a scale of 1-5, how certain are you of this decision? [Very uncertain (1) to Very certain (5)]

On a scale of 1-5, how certain are you that experts could answer Question 1? [Very uncertain (1) to Very certain (5)]

On a scale of 1-5, how much do you think you know about the topic compared to an average person? [Very little (1) to Very much (5)]

References

Cantwell, J. "Resolving Conflicting Information", *Journal of Logic, Language, and Information*, 7, (1998): 191–220.

Cozzens, M.D. and N.S. Contractor. "The Effect of Conflicting Information on Media Skepticism", *Communication Research*, 14(4), (1987): 437–51.

Eysenbach, G., J. Powell, O. Kuss, and E.R. Sa. "Empirical Studies Assessing the Quality of Health Information for Consumers on the World Wide Web: A Systematic Review", *The Journal of the American Medical Association*, 287(20), (2002): 2691–700.

IDA. "Annual survey on infocomm usage in households and by individuals for 2009", Infocomm Development Authority of Singapore (2010): Available at http://www.ida.gov.sg/doc/Publications/Publications_Level3/Survey2009/HH2009ES.pdf (accessed 15 September 2011).

IDA. "Annual Survey on Infocomm Usage in Households for 2010", Infocomm Development Authority of Singapore (2011) Available at http://www.ida.gov.sg/doc/Publications/Publications_Level3/Survey2010/HH2010ES.pdf (accessed 15 September 2011).

Kienhues, D., M. Stadtler, and R. Bromme. "Dealing with Conflicting or Consistent Information on the Web: When Expert Information Breeds Laypersons' Doubts about Experts", *Learning and Instruction*, 21(2), (2011): 193–204.

King, P.M. and K.S. Kitchener. *Developing Reflective Judgment: Understanding and Promoting Intellectual Growth and Critical Thinking in Adolescents and Adults* (San Francisco: Jossey-Bass, 1994).

Lee, T. and C. Kan. "Blogospheric Pressures in Singapore: Internet Discourses and the 2006 General Election", *Continuum: Journal of Media and Cultural Studies*, 23(6), (2009): 871–86.

Perry, W.G. *Patterns of Development in Thought and Values of Students in a Liberal Arts College: A Validation of a Scheme* (Cambridge, MA: Bureau of Study: Counsel, Harvard University, 1968).

Tan, T.H. "Singapore's Print Media Policy: A National Success?" In *Management of Success: Singapore Revisited*, Chong, T. (ed.). (Singapore: Institute of Southeast Asian Studies, 2010).

Tan, T.T. and A. Mahizhnan. "Subverting seriousness and other misdemeanours: Modes of resistance against OB markers in the 2006 Singapore General Election". Presented at the 17th Annual Conference of the Asian Media Information and Communication Centre (AMIC) on Changing Media, Changing Societies: Media and the Millennium Development Goals, Manila, Philippines, 14–17 July 2008 Available at http://www.spp.nus.edu.sg/ips/docs/pub/pa_TTHAM_Subverting%20Seriousness_AMIC_July%202008.pdf (accessed 7 September 2011).

Tsai, C.C. "Beyond Cognitive and Metacognitive Tools: The Use of the Internet as an 'Epistemological' Tool for Instruction", *British Journal of Educational Technology*, 35, (2004): 525–36.

Venkat, P.R. "Singapore Economy Expanded 4.8% in 2011", *Asia Business, The Wall Street Journal*, 31 December 2011 Available at http://online.wsj.com/article/SB10001424052970204720204577132040862931660.html?mod=googlenews_wsj (accessed 16 January 2012).

Yin X., J. Han, and P.S. Yu. "Truth Discovery with Multiple Conflicting Information Providers on the Web", *IEEE Transactions on Knowledge and Data Engineering*, 20(6), (2008): 796–808.

11

THE SILENCE OF THE MAJORITY: POLITICAL TALK DURING ELECTION TIME

Weiyu Zhang

Abstract

During the 2011 General Election, Singaporeans, on average, did not talk much about the elections. If we only consider talking with family and friends, Singaporeans, on average, sometimes talked about the elections. The lowest frequency was found in talking with people met online. In addition, Singaporeans who talked about the elections found that they disagreed with their fellow discussants only rarely or sometimes. Despite this lack of political talk and disagreement, political talk was perceived to be the second most important information source as well as the third most influential source on voting decisions. However, the trustworthiness of talking was lower than not only mass media but also party sources and alternative websites. Political talk is often linked to demographic factors. People who are 30 years old or younger were more engaged in political talk (including frequency, importance, trustworthiness, and influence) than those who are older than 30. It is consistently shown that engagement in political talk was higher among people who have higher education and income. Almost half (49.6%) of the respondents refused to reveal their voting decisions but those who were willing to say they voted for the opposition were more engaged in political talk than the others. When people who said they voted for People's Action Party (PAP) talked about the elections, they encountered more disagreement than the others.

From the early days of communication research both mass media and interpersonal interaction have been recognised as two major sources of influence on shaping people's attitudes and behaviour (for example, "two-step flow" in Katz and Lazarsfeld, 1955; see below for more on their study). However, as mass media became dominant information sources between the 1970s and 1990s, researchers seem to underestimate the importance of interpersonal talk (Eveland and Thomson, 2006). Recent research revealed that everyday talk, besides its independent impact on people, could also mediate or moderate the influence of mass media (Hardy and Scheufele, 2005; Zhang, 2012). The emergence of new media such as the Internet and mobile phones has greatly expanded the channels through which people can directly communicate with each other. For instance, social media such as Facebook allow users to exchange information and opinions at any time, from any place even when they are not together physically. The prominence of new media in people's everyday life suggests that interpersonal talk can have a greater effect now than in a mass-media-dominated age. In order to separate these new channels of political talk from the tradition of face-to-face interpersonal communication, this paper defines political talk as the exchange of information and opinions regarding political issues among individuals through the format of oral conversation, or "word of mouth".

In addition to the potential influence of interpersonal talk, normative concerns justify a close examination of everyday talk on political and public issues. From a tradition of participatory democracy (Mutz, 2006), political talk is considered as a form of active citizenry, which not only informs but also motivates ordinary citizens to participate in democratic processes. From the perspective of deliberative democracy, political talk is part of a society's larger deliberative system (Mansbridge, 1999). Political talk contributes to public deliberation (Guttmann and Thompson, 1996), during which interests are articulated, disagreements are exchanged, preferences are reshaped, and public opinion is rationalised.

While most of the research on political talk is conducted in liberal democracies, we have seen a burgeoning effort to fully understand interpersonal communication in other political systems such as those in transition or those that involve authoritarian components. As Lee pointed out, "political discussions occur in all kind of contexts" (2009, p. 380), perhaps with different frequency, degree of publicity, and potential influence. It is particularly interesting to study political talk when media is government-controlled. When mass media is not completely free, political talk serves as a crucial channel for alternative viewpoints. This chapter analyses political talk during election time in Singapore. After reviewing previous research on political talk and its influence, a description of the amount of political talk with various social peers and the amount of disagreement encountered is provided. Perceived importance and trustworthiness of political talk during election time is compared with mass media, party sources, and online sources. In addition, the demographic factors are linked to political talk. Finally, an examination of voters supporting different parties and their political talk is reported. The policy implications of these findings are discussed at the end of this chapter.

Political Talk and its Influence

In the classic model of "two-step flow", Katz and Lazarsfeld (1955) explained how ideas influence people. The first step is when ideas are transmitted from mass media to opinion leaders, who often pay close attention to the media content that is related to their interests. The second step involves interpersonal talk, in which ideas are transmitted from opinion leaders, often with their personal interpretation of the ideas, to the larger public. Hence political information presented in mass media does not directly influence the population but rather has to go through a second step when opinion leaders talk to others. This model suggests that interpersonal talk has always been an influential part of political communication. However, as mass media became widely adopted and the modern society increasingly fragmented, a direct influence of mass media on people's attitudes and behaviours was confirmed in many cases. The sequential model of two-step flow does not seem to apply any more. Instead, researchers found that interpersonal talk and mass media do not have to go through each other, with each having its independent impact (McLeod, Scheufele, and Moy, 1999). Furthermore, the effects of mass media depend on whether the information presented is consistent with that in interpersonal talk. When interpersonal talk is consistent with mass media coverage on an issue, the effects of mass media are amplified whereas if it is contradictory, the effects are compromised.

In general, political talk is shown to render desirable consequences according to previous research. Political discussion has direct and positive effects on political participation and knowledge (Eveland and Thompson, 2006; McLeod, Scheufele, and Moy, 1999; Straits, 1991). Political discussion also shapes political attitudes and opinions (Kim, Wyatt, and Katz, 1999; Lalljee and Evans, 1998). In addition, political discussion interacts with media to influence participatory behaviour. "[I]nterpersonal discussion plays a role in the reception and processing of political news when it comes to translating mass-mediated messages into meaningful individual action" (Scheufele, 2002, pp. 57, 58).

Theorists of deliberative democracy (Habermas, 1996), however, argue that not all political discussions qualify as deliberative talk. For political talk to be considered deliberative (open, equal, inclusive, and rational), it also has to fulfil certain conditions and have characteristics consistent with the norms of deliberative democracy (Moy and Gastil, 2006). One such condition is political disagreement. On the one hand, everyday political talk often lacks disagreement: people tend to talk to like-minded others and avoid conflicts (Eliasoph, 1998; Mutz, 2006; Schudson, 1997). On the other, social relationships are not based purely on similarity in political views; people do not choose their fellow discussants simply because of their similarities (Huckfeldt, 2001; Huckfeldt, Johnson, and Sprague, 2004). As a result, it is common for people to encounter political disagreement in their social networks (Beck, 1991; Ikeda and Huckfeldt, 2001).

Not only are the findings on the amount of disagreement in everyday political talk mixed, so is the evidence on the impact of political disagreement. Some research has shown that disagreeing with others facilitates the learning of political information

(Kwak *et al.*, 2005) and leads to political tolerance (Mutz, 2006). Other studies have found that disagreement can lead to attitudinal ambivalence (Priester and Petty, 2001; Visser and Mirabile, 2004), that is, uncertainty about whether one should hold favourable or unfavourable attitude towards an issue. This in turn undermines participation (Huckfeldt, Johnson, and Sprague, 2004; Mutz, 2002, 2006; Nir, 2005).

The studies mentioned above are carried out in liberal democracies. Studies on political discussion from other types of political systems are scarce. Research from Hong Kong shows that there is a positive correlation between amount of political discussion and support for democratisation (Sing, 2005). Ordinary political conversation with family and friends is found to be positively related to expression of a minority opinion, political knowledge, and likelihood of voting (Lee, 2005; 2009). In Singapore and Taiwan, political discussion is also correlated with political participation and this positive effect is stronger among people who consume more political news (Zhang, 2012). In terms of political disagreement, Lee (2009) finds that the positive correlation between political talk and knowledge is stronger among those who experience more disagreement in discussion. However, the positive impact of political talk on opinion expression and voting does not differ among people who have encountered different amounts of disagreement in their political talk.

Singapore serves as an interesting context to study political talk. The hybrid features of the Singapore political system make it hard to classify it along the authoritarian-democratic spectrum. On one hand, Singapore has the basic democratic mechanism of elections, which grant all citizens the right to vote in a system that has been free of fraud. However, between elections and after the government is elected, the style of governance is authoritarian. For example, the mass media including newspapers, radio and television are under close control of the government through a combination of economic measures (for example, management shares), administrative means (for example, appointing top editors), legal tools (for example, suing foreign journalists under a very broadly defined defamation law), and ideological apparatus (for example, various social programmes to build consensus) (Ang and Yeo, 1998; George, 2005; Rodan, 2004). As a result, the ruling party's overwhelming grip on power has not been challenged substantially and it has been in power since the independence of the country in 1965. Against this backdrop of controlled mass communication channels, political talk becomes even more important in Singapore compared to countries with free media and a free flow of information. Interpersonal channels then become one of the few venues through which alternative viewpoints are disseminated and engaged. The recent emergence of new media, social media in particular, has largely enhanced the ability of ordinary citizens to talk to each other directly. They are no longer confined to face-to-face settings and the political conversations can take place at any time.

Therefore, this chapter poses the following research questions in order to provide a relatively comprehensive description about political talk during election time in Singapore:

1. How much did Singaporeans talk about the elections and disagree with each other?
2. How did Singaporeans perceive the importance and trustworthiness of political talk?
3. What were the relationships between demographic factors (age, gender, race, education, and income) and political talk and disagreement?
4. What were the differences between voters who voted differently in terms of their political talk and disagreement?

Measurements

The findings are based on a national representative survey of 2,000 citizens of voting age. The key variables that are measured are discussed below.

1. *Political talk.* Respondents were asked to indicate on a 5-point scale (1 never, 2 rarely, 3 sometimes, 4 often, 5 very often) how often they discussed the elections with the following groups: (1) family

members; (2) friends; (3) colleagues at work, and (4) people they meet online. The four items were averaged to form an index of frequency of political talk. The mean was found to be 2.25.[1]

2. *Political disagreement*. Respondents were asked to indicate, when they discuss the elections with the four parties mentioned above, how often they disagreed with their fellow discussants. The same 5-point scale as mentioned above was used. The four items were averaged to form an index of amount of political disagreement with a mean of 2.42.[2]

3. *Perceived importance*. Respondents were asked to indicate on a 5-point scale (1 unimportant, 2 of little importance, 3 moderately important, 4 important, 5 very important) how important they thought the following were as sources of information about the recent election: (1) TV stations and their websites; (2) radio; (3) newspapers and their websites; (4) political party websites; (5) political party brochures, newspapers and other publication; (6) going to political party election rallies; (7) Facebook; (8) microblogs such as Twitter, Weibo, and Plurk; (9) YouTube and other video websites; (10) online-only news websites and blogs such as The Online Citizen, Yawning Bread and Temasek Review; (11) mobile phone SMSs; and (12) talking with others.

4. *Perceived trustworthiness*. Respondents were asked to indicate on a 5-point scale (1 untrustworthy, 2 a little trustworthy, 3 moderately trustworthy, 4 trustworthy, 5 very trustworthy) how trustworthy each of the 12 sources mentioned above was for them as a source of information about the election.

5. *Perceived influence on voting*. Respondents were asked to indicate on a 5-point scale (1 no influence at all to 5 a lot of influence) during the elections, how much the following influenced how they decided to vote: (1) what they read in the newspapers; (2) what they heard

---

[1]SD = 0.90, Cronbach's alpha = 0.76
[2]SD = 0.89, Cronbach's alpha = 0.88

at the rallies; (3) what they saw on television; (4) what they read on party websites; (5) what they read on Facebook; (6) what they read on Twitter, Weibo, Plurk, and other microblogging websites; (7) what they read on the blogs and online-only news websites such as The Online Citizen, Yawning Bread and Temasek Review; (8) what they read in their SMSes; (9) what they read in their e-mails; (10) what their friends or colleagues told them; and (11) what family members told them.

6. *Voting.* Respondents were also asked to indicate their voting choices. In order to minimise the sensitivity of this question, they were told that "in talking to many people about elections, we often find that a lot of people were not able to vote, because they were not registered, they were sick, or they just did not have time". The voting choices included (1) I voted the opposition; (2) I voted the PAP; (3) I did not vote; and (4) refused to answer (this option was not read out to respondents).

7. *Demographics.* The sample is 53% female and has an average age of 45 years. About 78% of respondents are Chinese, 14% Malay, 7% Indian, and 2% others. About 48% of respondents were educated up to or higher than Junior College. About 48% of respondents have monthly household incomes lower than S$4,000.

Findings

The amount of political talk in general was not much (Figure 1). For every category of discussants our respondents talked to, the averages of political talk never exceeded 3 (equivalent to "sometimes" on our scale). Discussions with family and friends were more frequent than with colleagues and people met online. The respondents almost never discussed elections with people met online.

The amount of disagreement experienced during discussions on elections was not much either (Figure 2). While disagreement with friends, colleagues, and people met online was almost the same, it was found that disagreement with family members was the lowest. In all, discussing with and disagreeing with friends occurs

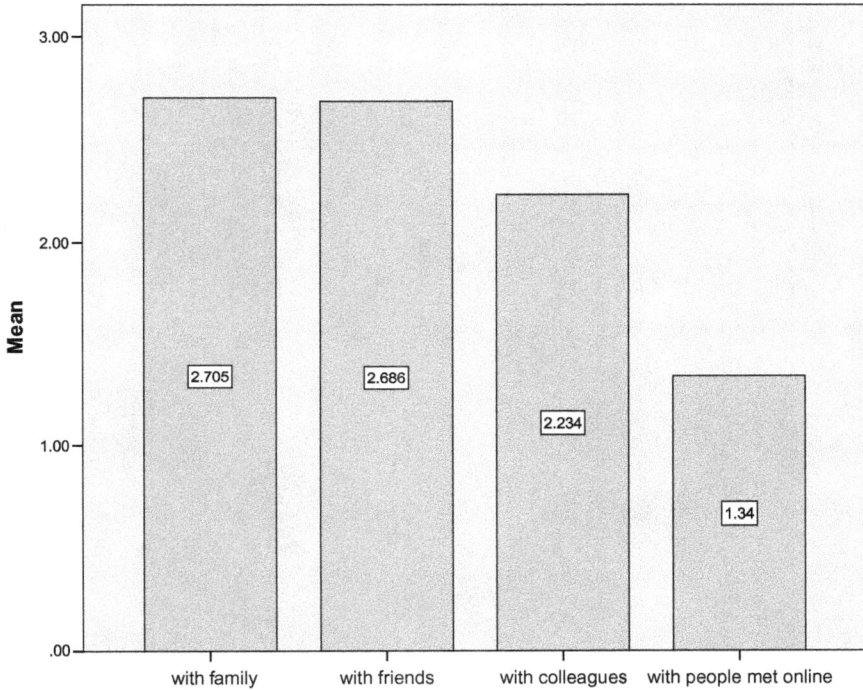

Figure 1: The average of amount of political talk

Note: Respondents were asked to indicate on a 5-point scale (1 never, 2 rarely, 3 sometimes, 4 often, 5 very often) how often they discussed the elections with these groups: (1) family members; (2) friends; (3) colleagues at work; and (4) people they meet online.

most frequently compared with other groups. What is interesting is that contradictory to popular wisdom, respondents talked about elections the least with people they met online although the amount of disagreement was no less than in other discussions.

During election time, talking with others was perceived as the second most important information source, only lower than traditional mass media (Figure 3). The importance of talking was perceived as almost the same with rallies. Political talk was clearly more important than some party sources such as party websites and party publications and all online sources including Facebook, microblogs,

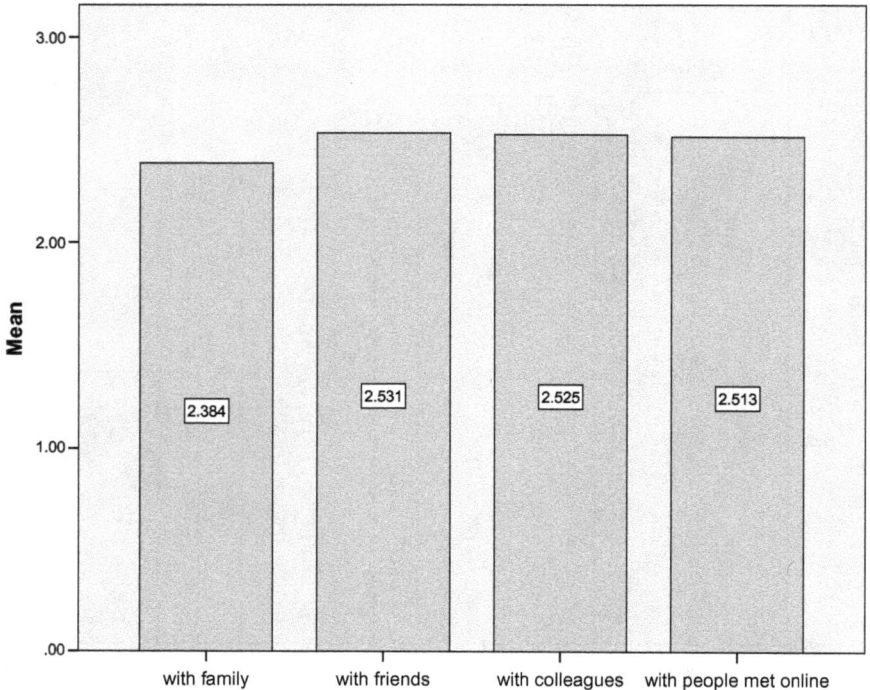

Figure 2: The average of amount of political disagreement

Note: Respondents were asked to indicate on a 5-point scale (1 never, 2 rarely, 3 sometimes, 4 often, 5 very often) when they discuss the elections with the four parties mentioned above, how often they disagreed with these groups: (1) family members; (2) friends; (3) colleagues at work; and (4) people they meet online.

video websites, and alternative websites. This comparison clearly indicates that political talk was an important communication mode during the elections.

However, talking with others was perceived as not very trustworthy compared with most of the other information sources (Figure 4). It was clearly less trustworthy than traditional mass media, including TV, radio, and newspapers. It was not considered as trustworthy as party sources and alternative websites. It was slightly more trustworthy than many online sources such as Facebook, microblogs, and video websites. It can be summarised

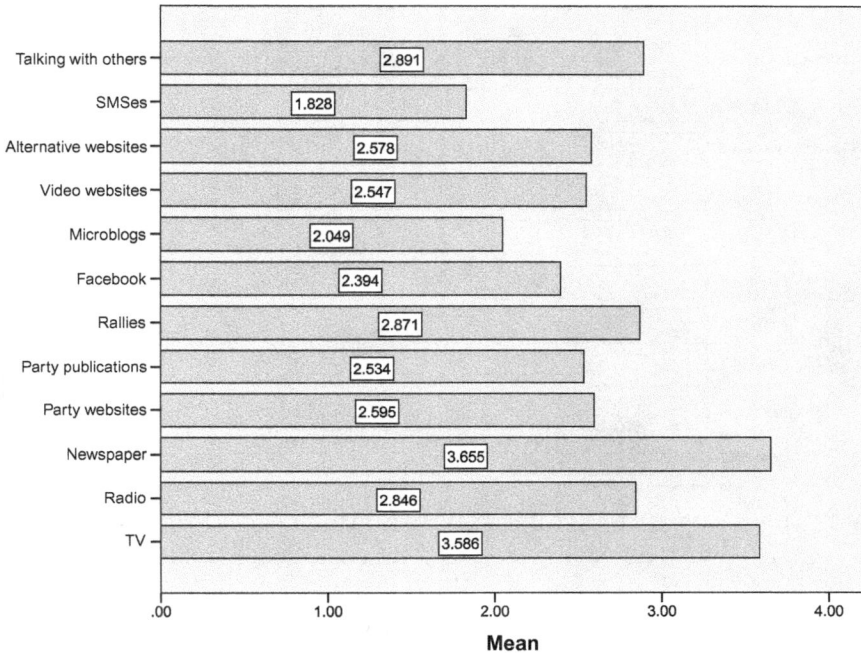

Figure 3: The perceived importance of information sources

Note: Respondents were asked to indicate on a 5-point scale (1 unimportant, 2 of little importance, 3 moderately important, 4 important, 5 very important) how important they thought the following were as sources of information about the recent election: (1) TV stations and their websites; (2) radio; (3) newspapers and their websites; (4) political party websites; (5) political party brochures, newspapers and other publications; (6) going to political party election rallies; (7) Facebook; (8) microblogs such as Twitter, Weibo, and Plurk; (9) YouTube and other video websites; (10) online-only news websites and blogs such as The Online Citizen, Yawning Bread and Temasek Review; (11) mobile phone SMSes; and (12) talking with others.

that respondents considered political talk an important information source but did not trust it much.

In terms of the perceived influence on respondents' voting decisions, almost all information sources did not show a large amount of influence as all the averages were lower than 3, which is the midpoint of the scale (Figure 5). Mass media were still perceived as the most influential among all the sources. Talking with

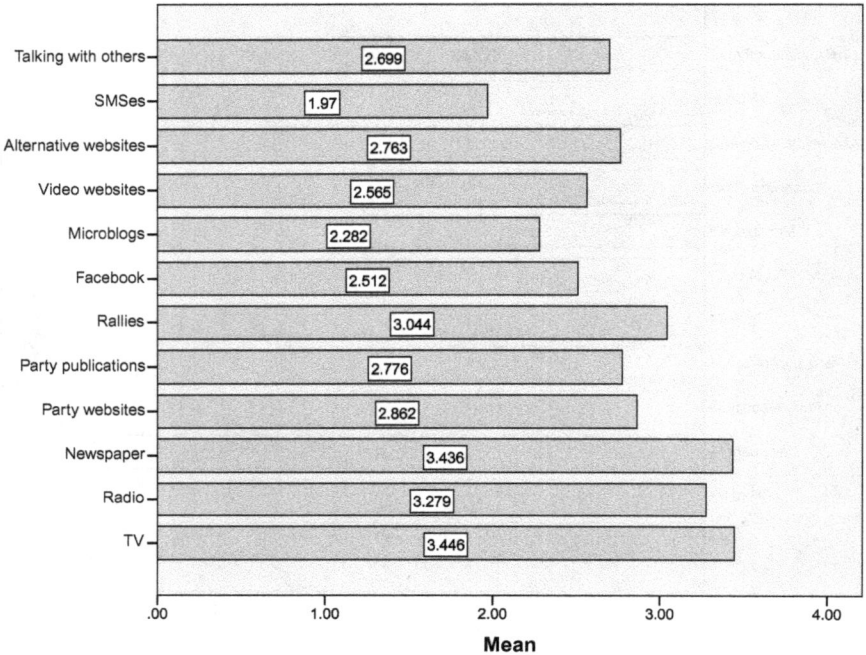

Figure 4:   The perceived trustworthiness of information sources

Note: Respondents were asked to indicate on a 5-point scale (1 untrustworthy, 2 a little trustworthy, 3 moderately trustworthy, 4 trustworthy, 5 very trustworthy) how trustworthy each of the 12 sources mentioned above was for them as a source of information about the election.

either family members or friends and colleagues was the third most influential source, which was lower than mass media and rallies but higher than online sources.

Statistical tests[3] were done to show the relationship between gender and age and political talk variables. Males talked more about the elections than females[4] and perceived more influence from friends and colleagues on their voting decisions.[5] People who

---

[3]T-tests were carried out.
[4]$t = 2.118$, $p < 0.05$
[5]$t = 2.453$, $p < 0.05$

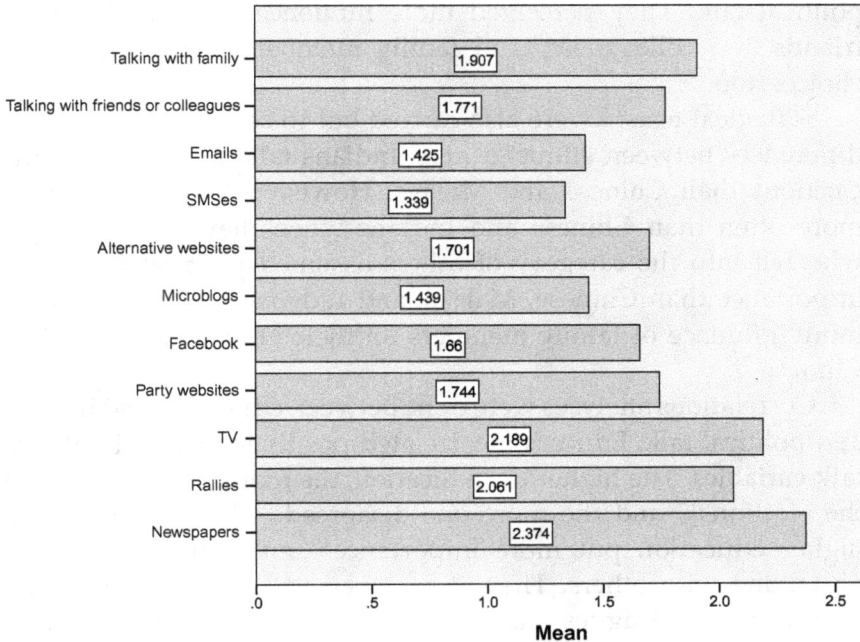

Figure 5: The perceived influence of information sources on voting decisions

Note: Respondents were asked to indicate on a 5-point scale (1 no influence at all to 5 a lot of influence) during the elections, how much the following influenced how they decided to vote: (1) what they read in the newspapers; (2) what they heard at the rallies; (3) what they saw on television; (4) what they read on party websites; (5) what they read on Facebook; (6) what they read on Twitter, Weibo, Plurk and other microblogging websites; (7) what they read on the blogs and online-only news websites such as The Online Citizen, Yawning Bread and Temasek Review; (8) what they read in their SMSes; (9) what they read in their emails; (10) what their friends or colleagues told them; and (11) what family members told them.

are 30 years old or younger, compared with those older than 30, talked more about the elections[6] and disagreed more when talking.[7] They also attributed more importance[8] and trustworthiness[9] to

---

[6]$t = 7.125$, $p < 0.001$
[7]$t = 3.140$, $p < 0.001$
[8]$t = 6.658$, $p < 0.001$
[9]$t = 3.064$, $p < 0.01$

political talk. They perceived more influence from talking with friends and colleagues[10] and family members[11] on their voting choices, too.

Statistical tests[12] were also carried out to see if there were any differences between ethnic groups. Indians talked more about the elections than Chinese and Malays. However, Malays disagreed more often than Chinese and Indians when they talked. People who fell into the category of others assigned political talk more importance than Chinese, Malays, and Indians. Malays perceived more influence of family members on their voting decisions than Chinese.

Correlations analyses were done between education and income and political talk. Education correlated positively with all political talk variables. The higher the education, the more one talked about the elections[13] and the more one disagreed.[14] Respondents with higher education put more importance[15] and trustworthiness[16] on talking with others. They also perceived more influence from friends and colleagues[17] and family members[18] on their voting decisions.

Income also correlated positively with most political talk variables except for disagreement. The higher one's income, the more one talked about the elections.[19] Respondents with higher incomes put more importance[20] and trustworthiness[21] on talking with others.

---

[10] $t = 10.168$, $p < 0.001$
[11] $t = 10.290$, $p < 0.001$
[12] A series of ANOVA with post-hoc tests were used. Findings reported here are all significant with a p value lower than 0.05.
[13] $r = 0.402$, $p < 0.001$
[14] $t = 0.087$, $p < 0.001$
[15] $r = 0.264$, $p < 0.001$
[16] $r = 0.181$, $p < 0.001$
[17] $r = 0.258$, $p < 0.001$
[18] $r = 0.225$, $p < 0.001$
[19] $r = 0.340$, $p < 0.001$
[20] $r = 0.187$, $p < 0.001$
[21] $r = 0.143$, $p < 0.001$

They also perceived more influence from friends and colleagues[22] and family members[23] on their voting decisions.

A final analysis[24] was made to see whether political talk had anything to do with one's voting decision. Among the respondents, 49.6% refused to say whom they voted for. People who said they voted for the opposition talked more about the elections than everyone else, including those who said they voted for the People's Action Party (PAP), who said they did not vote, and who refused to answer. They also attributed more importance to political talk than everyone else. They assigned political talk more trustworthiness than people who said they voted for PAP and people who refused to answer. They perceived more influence from talking to friends and colleagues on their voting decision than everyone else, and more influence from talking to family members than people who said they voted for PAP and who refused to answer. However, people who said they voted for PAP disagreed more often than people who said they voted for the opposition and those who refused to answer.

Discussion and Conclusion

This chapter concludes that Singaporeans, on average, did not talk much about the elections. With family and friends, Singaporeans, on average, sometimes talked about the elections. This low level of political talk could arise from Singaporeans not being very politicised. Elections also tend to be one-sided, though increasingly less so, and therefore there are also fewer points of contention to discuss. In addition, Singaporeans who talked about the elections found that they disagreed with their fellow discussants only rarely or sometimes. The lowest frequency of political talk is found in talking with people met online. Contrary to the conventional wisdom that

---

[22]$r = 0.134, p < 0.001$
[23]$r = 0.129, p < 0.001$
[24]Post-hoc statistics from ANOVA were used to test the differences. Findings reported here are significant with a p value lower than 0.05.

the Internet enables and encourages diverse discussions, voters seem to be hesitant to engage in political discussions with peers they meet in cyberspace. It suggests that Singaporeans might not trust strangers who are hiding behind anonymity, and this lack of trust prevents them from talking about the rather sensitive topic of elections. As prominent as new media are, this finding implies that facilitating discussions with existing social contacts rather than complete strangers is where new media show the most potential.

Despite this lack of political talk and disagreement, political talk was perceived to be the second most important information source (only lower than traditional mass media) as well as the third most influential source on voting decisions (lower than traditional mass media and slightly lower than rallies). However, the trustworthiness of talking was lower than not only mass media but also party sources (including rallies) and online sources. The findings suggest that voters rely on political talk to gauge the social norms in their networks, although they recognise that political talk might not be trustworthy. Rumour and gossip might function as cues of social pressure, even though voters do not trust such information to be true. If false information is not clarified in traditional mass media that are most important and trustworthy to voters, it could become a factor that influences voters' decisions.

A second conclusion is that the salience of political talk, though generally low, is often linked to demographic factors. People who are 30 years old or younger were more engaged in political talk (including frequency, importance, trustworthiness, and influence) than those who are older than 30. It is consistently shown that engagement in political talk was higher among people with higher education and income. This finding suggests that different segments of the population engage in different amounts of political talk. Actively involving the vocal portion of public in the political process might help to shape the viewpoints circulated in everyday political talk.

A final conclusion is that people who said they voted for the opposition were more engaged in political talk than the others. However, it is interesting to note that when people who said they voted for PAP talked about the elections, they encountered more disagreement than the others. This finding suggests that the self-reported supporters of the opposition are more vocal in expressing their opposition not only with their fellow opposition supporters but also with the PAP supporters. In contrast, most PAP supporters simply do not voice their support that often. Therefore, when the self-reported PAP supporters are involved in political talk, they find themselves outnumbered by the opposition supporters and have to disagree more often.

These findings also point to certain practical implications. First, despite the significant influence of traditional mass media during election time, talking with others is still important, although not frequent. The power of "word of mouth" should not be underestimated, especially in the new media era. Research has shown that generally direct interpersonal communication between politicians and citizens and among citizens themselves helps to increase political knowledge, and in some cases, political participation. If political participation is preferred over political apathy, then building an environment where political discussions are encouraged and political differences that stem from such discussions are managed appropriately would be a conducive approach. Given the proliferation of new media in Singapore, the future promises more, rather than less, political talk.

References

Ang, P.H. and T.M. Yeo, *Mass Media Laws and Regulations in Singapore* (Singapore: Asian Media Information and Communication Centre, 1998).

Beck, P.A. "Voters' Intermediation Environments in the 1988 Presidential Contest", *Public Opinion Quarterly*, 55, (1991): 371–94.

Eliasoph, N. *Avoiding Politics* (New York: Cambridge University Press, 1998).

Eveland, W.P. and T. Thomson, "Is it Talking, Thinking, or Both? A Lagged Dependent Variable Model of Discussion Effects on Political Knowledge", *Journal of Communication*, 56(3), (2006): 523–42.

George, C. "Calibrated Coercion and the Maintenance of Hegemony in Singapore", *Asia Research Institute Working Paper Series No. 48*, 2005

Available at http://www.ari.nus.edu.sg/docs/wps/wps05_048.pdf (accessed 21 September 2011).

Guttmann, A. and D. Thompson. *Democracy and Disagreement* (Cambridge, MA: Harvard University Press, 1996).

Habermas, J. *Between Facts and Norms* (Cambridge, MA: MIT Press, 1996).

Hardy, B.W. and D.A. Scheufele. "Examining Differential Gains from Internet Use: Comparing the Moderating Role of Talk and Online Interactions", *Journal of Communication*, 55(1), (2005): 71–84.

Huckfeldt, R. "The Social Communication of Political Expertise", *American Journal of Political Science*, 45, (2001): 425–38.

Huckfeldt, R. and J.D. Sprague. *Citizens, Politics, and Social Communication* (New York: Cambridge University Press, 1995).

Ikeda, K. and R. Huckfeldt. "Political Communication and Disagreement among Citizens in Japan and the United States", *Political Behavior*, 23(1), (2001): 23–51.

Katz, E. and P. Lazarsfeld. *Personal Influence* (Glencoe, IL: Free Press, 1955).

Kim, J., R.O. Wyatt, and E. Katz. "News, Talk, Opinion, Participation: The Part Played by Conversation in Deliberative Democracy", *Political Communication*, 16, (1999): 361–85.

Kwak, N., Williams, A.E., Wang, X. and Lee, H. "Talking Politics and Engaging Politics: An Examination of the Interactive Relationships between Structural Features of Political Talk and Discussion Engagement", *Communication Research*, 32(1), (2005): 87–111.

Lalljee, M. and G. Evans. "Political Talk and the Stability and Consistency of Political Orientation", *British Journal of Social Psychology*, 37, (1998): 203–12.

Lee, F.L.F. "Ordinary Political Conversation and Public Opinion Expression: Is Existence of Discord Necessary?", *Journalism & Mass Communication Quarterly*, 82(4), (2005): 891–909.

Lee, F.L.F. "The Impact of Political Discussion in a Democratizing Society: The Moderating Role of Disagreement and Support for Democracy", *Communication Research*, 36(3), (2009): 379–99.

Mansbridge, J. "Everyday Talk in the Deliberative System". In *Deliberative Politics: Essays on Democracy and Disagreement*, Stephen, M. (ed.), (New York: Oxford University Press, 1999).

McLeod, J.M., D.A. Scheufele, and P. Moy. "Community, Communication, and Participation: The Role of Mass Media and Interpersonal Discussion in Local Political Participation", *Political Communication*, 16(3), (1999): 315–36.

Moy, P. and J. Gastil. "Predicting Deliberative Conversation: The Impact of Discussion Networks, Media Use, and Political Cognitions", *Political Communication*, 23(4), (2006): 443–60.

Mutz, D.C. "The Consequences of Cross-cutting Networks for Political Participation", *American Journal of Political Science*, 46(4), (2002): 838–55.

Mutz, D.C. *Hearing the Other Side* (New York: Cambridge University Press, 2006).

Nir, L. "Ambivalent Social Networks and Their Consequences for Participation". *International Journal of Public Opinion Research*, 17(4), (2005): 422–42.

Priester, J.R. and R.E. Petty. "Extending the Bases of Subjective Attitudinal Ambivalence: Interpersonal and Intrapersonal Antecedents of Evaluative Tension", *Journal of Personality and Social Psychology*, 80(1), (2001): 19–34.

Rodan, G. *Transparency and Authoritarian Rule in Southeast Asia* (London and New York: RoutledgeCurzon, 2004).

Scheufele, D.A. "Examining Differential Gains from Mass Media and Their Implications for Participatory Behavior", *Communication Research*, 29(1), (2002): 46–65.

Schudson, M. "Why Conversation is Not the Soul of Democracy", *Critical Studies in Mass Communication*, 14, (1997): 297–309.

Sing, M. "Public Support for Democracy in Hong Kong", *Democratization*, 12(2), (2005): 244–61.

Straits, B.C. "Bringing Strong Ties Back in: Interpersonal Gateways to Political Information and Influence", *Public Opinion Quarterly*, 55(3), (1991): 432–48.

Visser, P.S. and R.R. Mirabile. "Attitudes in the Social Context: The Impact of Social Network Composition on Individual-level Attitude Strength", *Journal of Personality and Social Psychology*, 87(6), (2004): 779–95.

Zhang, W. "The Effects of Political News Use, Political Discussion and Authoritarian Orientation on Political Participation: Evidences from Singapore and Taiwan", *Asian Journal of Communication*, 22(5), (2012): 474–92.

CONCLUSION

Tan Tarn How

This book explores the theme of new media and its relationship with the 2011 Singapore General Election. It makes important contributions in three areas: how media use is related to political participation, political traits, demographics and voting; how stakeholders such as voters, bloggers and political parties use the Internet and mobile telephony; and how theoretical understanding about new media needs to be expanded, especially in their interaction with one another and with voters, that goes beyond the particularities of this election. In this concluding chapter, we focus on the need for, and scope of, further research that will deepen our understanding of the new media and its impact on electoral politics in Singapore and elsewhere.

Of the two chapters in the first section — the impact of new media on political participation and voting — are *Not Quite an "Internet" Election: Survey of Media Use of Voters* and *Different But Not That Different: New Media's Impact on Young Voters' Political Participation*, the first overturns most pundits' prediction with the key conclusion that media as a whole — and even more so, new media — had an unexpectedly low impact on voting during the campaign period. Telling evidence from the survey revealed that most people had already decided who they would vote for even before the campaign started.

The other chapter fills out the picture. These two chapters provide insights about the differences between consumers and non-consumers of alternative media, and the differences between young voters and the rest of the population. They raise the question of whether there is any impact of mainstream and alternative media in the long period between elections and if so, how it occurs. This also leads to the question as to whether all forms of media would play a greater role as politics in Singapore gets less monolithic, elections more competitive and media more diverse, as many observers believe. As for young voters, it would be worthwhile to investigate whether the differences found between them and older voters are generational (that is, they remain the same even as they get older) or is a simple artefact of youth (that is, they become like their parents as they grow older). If the differences are generational it would mean that they would remain as the cohort grows older. Consequently the complexion of politics will evolve qualitatively with each election. The role of media in such changes would be of particular interest.

The second set of chapters on how stakeholders such as voters, bloggers and political parties use the Internet and mobile telephony includes *Legal Landmines and OB Markers: Survival Strategies of Alternative Media*. Despite the rise of social media with greater immediacy such as Facebook and Twitter, blogs will continue to play an important role as sites of extended reporting and opinion writing, especially those offering alternative discourses. The tensions discussed in the chapter will continue to loom large since it appears that there would be little rollback of the regulations. The challenges bloggers face are as much regulatory as of reach. According to our survey alternative blogs received a readership comprising only a fifth of the population. Whether they will gain more mindshare and space for expression in the light of the political landscape mentioned above deserves to be studied in the coming elections.

The second chapter in the set, *Untapped Potential: Internet Use by Political Parties*, raises the very intriguing and perplexing question of why the online reach of political parties is so low, and why they have invested so little and have been so unimaginative in tapping these cheap and powerful platforms. The chapter on the equalising effects of Twitter (discussed below) makes the question even more perplexing. This situation is in stark contrast to what is often seen in many other countries where the empowerment of minor parties brought about by the Internet has allowed them to overcome the odds of resource scarcity and political control. The authors give good reasons for the state of affairs, but a full explication would probably come only from a study which includes interviews with the parties themselves on their online strategies, or the lack thereof. This would be a fruitful line of research.

The third chapter in this set is *Pro, Anti, Neutral: Political Blogs and their Sentiments*. The content analysis of political blogs found that they are not as anti-PAP or anti-government as claimed by many and feared by the ruling party. It suggests a move in the blogosphere from being an outpost and redoubt of anti-government and anti-PAP sentiment towards a "normalisation" of discourse online, that is, one more reflective and representative of political opinion offline. Why it is nevertheless perceived by many that the "anti" blogs have more traction or indeed if they have would be worth investigating.

The chapter *The Silence of the Majority: Political Talk during Election Time* rounds up this set. That Singaporeans are not very political is shown by the headline finding that political talk is very low. That political talk is low outside of elections is probably a result of the low political interest among Singaporeans. But in light of the fact that voting is compulsory, why there is so little political talk *during an election* is a puzzle. Additionally, the finding that people tend to talk less rather than more with strangers online seemingly contradicts the belief that the Internet engenders democracy by encouraging political discussion. Furthermore, in less democratic countries where fear comes into play, the absence of a disinhibition effect provided by the cover of anonymity is also puzzling. The author provides good explanations of these counter-intuitive findings, but they merit more research.

Some of above chapters also make theoretical contributions. For instance, the *Pro, Anti, Neutral* chapter shows the democratising role of the blogosphere. However, the chapters in the last and third set focus primarily on theoretical questions. *David vs Goliath: Twitter's Role in Equalising Big-Party Dominance* adds to the field of normalisation versus equalisation studies. If Twitter becomes more widely used in future elections, this will undoubtedly have a greater impact on parties and voters. Whether equalisation would be found in other platforms such as Facebook and blogs and Instagram, and how the other kind of normalisation mentioned above (in terms of discourse online and its representativeness of offline sentiment) comes into play are interesting questions to pursue. Whether the smaller political parties will start to harness the "David effect" of online media also remains to be seen.

Who Calls the Shots? Agenda Setting in Mainstream and Alternative Media takes an innovative methodological approach, analysing the mutual effects that online mainstream and online alternative media have on one another in their coverage of election issues. It makes an important contribution to the literature. In this modern fast-paced online world, it is not surprising that one is watching the other watching one, but the authors provide solid proof that neither side does nor can afford to ignore the other in the battle for eyeballs and mindshare.

Lifting the Veil of Ignorance: Internet's Impact on Knowledge Gap reveals the important democratic role of the Internet and the alternative discourses in increasing the political knowledge of voters. Often dismissed as mis- or dis-information, political blogs and websites actually provide a needed balance to the pro-establishment mainstream media. It would be interesting to investigate more deeply where the knowledge gap exists, how and when people are exposed to alternative information, and how this relates to new and old media use, political participation, and voting. For less democratic nations like Singapore, where media is not as diverse as elsewhere, this question is of special interest.

Squaring Political Circles: Coping with Conflicting Information provides an instructive complement to the previous chapter by showing through an experimental design that it is precisely the exposure to conflicting information similar to what could be read in mainstream and alternative media that helps to raise media literacy. Participants who are given more than one side of a story are empowered to decide the importance of the issues at hand and also gain confidence in their judgement. Similar to questions raised from the previous chapter, areas of future research would include real world studies on encounters with conflicting information online, such as whether and how that information is sought or chanced upon and the effects of that information. As consumption of mainstream media moves to new media platforms (strongly indicated by the survey data for this book) from print and television sets, the opportunities for such encounters would increase because crossing over from one source of information to an alternate and alternative source of information is but a matter of a mouse click.

The chapter *The Leap from the Virtual to the Real: Facebook Use and Political Participation* underlines the relationship between online participation via the use of social networking platforms and offline participation. Which way the cause and effect works remains to be answered. Mobilisation by Facebook and other platforms also deserves further investigation.

In summary, the book gives a wide variety of snapshots of what happened in 2011 when new media was a part of the political landscape and what happens in general when new media is consumed by voters. The introductory chapter uses the metaphor of Rashomon Effect to highlight that different people had different views of new media and its impact. Another apt metaphor that covers this whole book is that of the proverbial elephant whose complete and accurate image is a challenge to create. Each of these chapters provides a different part of that image which together helps to piece a clearer and more complete picture of this strange beast called the Internet. It is part of the value of the studies taken as a whole that they do not all point to one tendency. Most notably, while some chapters such as those on Twitter and Facebook show the democratising potential of the Internet, others such as those on political talk and political parties' online efforts suggest that the potential is still unmet. Further studies will no doubt add to the clarity and comprehensiveness even if it is the nature of this animal that it will continue to evolve and change in form and function.

What changes are expected in the media and political landscape in the future? First, as the Internet and related platforms become even more ubiquitous in this self-declared Smart Nation, information seeking and delivery behaviour will change dramatically. For instance, more people will be accessing both mainstream and alternative media online. Voters can thus move from reading mainstream to alternative material without having to put down their newspaper first before turning on their mobiles or switching on their computers. Second, the chasm between mainstream media and alternative media as it existed in the early stages of the new media development will narrow because information can no longer be contained or sanitised by one central control or authority. Third, the "prosumer" role of consumers will increase substantially because of the ease with which each consumer can now reach others. Fourth, the vertical conversation that characterised the communication channels all these decades will now be greatly augmented by horizontal channels that facilitate unfettered communication between citizens. All of these developments, individually and collectively, will alter the role and impact of media in politics. That, in turn, is highly likely to alter the face of politics in Singapore. Though the 2011 General Election was *not* an "Internet" election, the future ones may well be.

APPENDIX 1

Background on Survey

The survey aimed to find out the use of media for information about the 2011 General Election. Two thousand Singaporeans aged 21 and above were interviewed between 24 May (two weeks after Polling Day) to 17 July 2011. Random stratified sampling was used. The sample satisfied quotas for race, age, and gender according to the 2010 population census. The interviews were conducted in English, Chinese, and Malay.

The interviews were conducted using Computer-Assisted Telephone Interview (CATI) by a commercial survey company. Each interview was about 25 minutes.

The 50 questions in the survey asked about demographics; use of offline and online media, and mainstream and alternative media; attitudes towards media and media control; political traits; political participation; and voting behaviour:

1. Demographics:
   a. Age
   b. Gender
   c. Race
   d. Education
   e. Housing
   f. Family income
   g. Constituency where respondent lived

2. Political traits

    a. Political interest
    b. Political knowledge
    c. Political talk
    d. Political orientation
    e. Political efficacy
    f. Political cynicism

3. Political participation

    a. Online participation
    b. Offline participation

4. Voting behaviour

    a. Voting preference
    b. Media influence on voting
    c. Revealing candidate choice
    d. When it was decided who to vote for

5. Media consumption
   (Radio, Newspapers, Television, Online main stream media, Foreign news websites, Facebook pages of political parties, alternative online news websites/blogs in Singapore)

    a. Duration
    b. Viral content
    c. Party websites/Facebook pages

6. Attitudes towards media

    a. Importance of media
    b. Trust in media
    c. Media control
    d. Bias/fairness of media

7. Exposure to conflicting information

    a. Incidence of encounters
    b. Types of media with conflicting information

8. Facebook

    a. Importance
    b. Usage

9. Microblogs
   a. Type used
   b. Frequency of usage
10. Mobile phone
   a. Ownership
   b. Type of use
11. Youths
   a. Party parents voted for
   b. Education level of parents

The survey questionnaire can be accessed at http://lkyspp.nus.edu.sg/ips/wp-content/uploads/sites/2/2014/08/Questionnare_Final.pdf

Breakdown of the survey data

1. Age Group

	Total	Percentage (%)
21–29	334	16.7
30–39	324	16.2
40–49	495	24.75
50+	847	42.35
Total	**2,000**	**100**

2. Gender

	Total	Percentage (%)
Male	945	47.25
Female	1,055	52.75
Total	**2,000**	**100**

3. Education

	Total	Percentage (%)
Primary or lower	400	20
Secondary (Upper/Lower secondary)	863	43.15
Polytechnic/Diploma	340	17
University	397	19.85
Total	**2,000**	**100**

4. Housing Type

	Total	Percentage (%)
1–3 room	375	18.75
4 room	713	35.65
5 room and exec flats/HUDC/Others	597	29.85
Condo/Private flats/Landed property	299	14.95
Refused to answer	16	0.8
Total	**2,000**	**100**

APPENDIX 2

Fact Sheet on the 2011 General Election

Singapore's eleventh General Election since independence was held on 7 May 2011. Seven political parties contested for 87 parliamentary seats in 27 electoral divisions, of which 12 were single-member seats representing Single Member Constituencies (SMC) and 15 were multiple-member divisions called Group Representation Constituencies (GRC). Some 2.35 million people were eligible to vote. Opposition parties fielded candidates in all but one of the constituencies — the five-member Tanjong Pagar GRC.

The PAP won 81 seats. It also won 60.1% of the valid votes cast, the lowest since independence. The opposition won six seats (all by the Workers' Party), the most since 1991. This election was also the first time that an opposition party won a GRC.

The timeline is as follows:

19 April	Dissolution of Parliament
27 April	Nomination day
6 May	Cooling-off day
7 May	Polling day
11 May	Overseas vote counting

The parties and their performance are shown below:

Party Name	Candidates Fielded	Wards Contested				Seats Won	% of Valid Votes Won in Contested Wards
		SMC	4 member GRC	5 member GRC	6 member GRC		
People's Action Party (PAP)	87.	12	2	11	2	81	60.1%
Workers' Party	23	4	1	3	—	6	46.6%
Singapore People's Party (SPP)	7	2	—	1	—	0	41.4%
National Solidarity Party (NSP)	24	4	—	4	—	0	39.2%
Singapore Democratic Party (SDP)	11	2	1	1	—	0	36.8%
Reform Party (RP)	11	—	—	1	1	0	31.8%
Singapore Democratic Alliance (SDA)	7	1	—	—	1	0	30.1%

ABOUT THE CONTRIBUTORS

1. Editors — Tan Tarn How, Arun Mahizhnan, Ang Peng Hwa

Mr Tan Tarn How is a Senior Research Fellow at the Institute of Policy Studies. His research areas are in arts and cultural policy and media and Internet policy. He has written on the development of the arts in Singapore, in particular, fostering partnerships between the people, private and public sectors, on the creative industries in Singapore, China and Korea, on cultural policy in Singapore, and on arts censorship. He has also carried out research on the management and regulation of media in Singapore, the impact of the Internet and social media on society, the role of new and old media in the 2008 Malaysian election and the 2006 and 2011 Singapore elections, and the way in which the Internet and social media has influenced the development of civil society and democratic development. He is working on a book on Flourishing Life, which examines issues arising from instrumental economics-oriented thinking in politics, society and education. He was a journalist for nearly one and half decades before joining IPS. He has also been a teacher and television scriptwriter, and is a playwright and arts activist.

Mr Arun Mahizhnan is Special Research Adviser at the Institute of Policy Studies. He advises the Director on IPS' research projects and undertakes selected special projects. Currently, he is leading the effort to publish Singapore Chronicles, a 50-volume book series to commemorate the 50th anniversary of Singapore's Independence. He was previously Deputy Director and the head of the Arts Culture and Media cluster in IPS. His past research interests also included business issues such as regionalisation of the Singapore economy, and development of entrepreneurship.

Mr Arun is concurrently an Adjunct Professor at the Wee Kim Wee School of Communication and Information at the Nanyang Technological University, Singapore.

Before joining IPS in 1991, he had worked in both the public and private sectors for 20 years, mostly in public communication fields.

Ang Peng Hwa is Professor at the Wee Kim Wee School of Communication and Information, Nanyang Technological University, Singapore and President-Elect of the International Communication Association 2015. His research interests lie in media law and policy and he has consulted on the subject for the governments of Singapore, Thailand and Bhutan.

He is the author of *Ordering Chaos: Regulating the Internet* (Thomson, 2005), which argues that the Internet can be, is being and should be regulated. He was a member of 40-strong Working Group on Internet Governance that was appointed by then UN Secretary-General Kofi Annan to prepare a report for the 2005 World Summit on the Information Society.

A lawyer by training, he worked as a journalist before going on to pursue a Master's in communication management at the University of Southern California and a Ph.D. in the mass media at Michigan State University.

In 2000, he was awarded a Fulbright fellowship at Harvard University; in 2001, he was a visiting scholar at Oxford University. Ang recently stepped down as chairman of the regional non-profit media organisation Asian Media Information and Communication Centre (AMIC), and is one of the two vice-presidents of the Consumers' Association of Singapore (CASE), and legal advisor to the Advertising Standards Authority of Singapore (ASAS).

2. Not quite an "Internet" Election: Survey of Media Use of Voters — Tan Tarn How and Arun Mahizhnan (editors) (see page 259)

3. Legal Landmines and OB Markers: Survival Strategies of Alternative Media — Cherian George

Cherian George, an Associate Professor at Hong Kong Baptist University's School of Communication, is a Singaporean writer and academic engaged in journalism research, education and advocacy. He is also an Adjunct Senior Research Fellow at the Institute of Policy Studies, and serves as Director of the Asia Journalism Fellowship, a mid-career sabbatical programme of Temasek Foundation and Nanyang Technological University in Singapore. His research centres on journalism and democracy, and includes freedom of expression issues, media controls in diverse political contexts, alternative media, and the impact of religious intolerance. He is the author of three books: *Singapore: The Air-Conditioned Nation* (2000); *Contentious Journalism and the Internet: Towards Democratic Discourse in Malaysia and Singapore* (2006); and *Freedom From The Press: Journalism and State Power in Singapore* (2012). (www.cheriangeorge.net)

4. Untapped Potential: Internet Use by Political Parties — Debbie Goh and Natalie Pang and
Pro, Anti, Neutral: Political Blogs and their Sentiments — Natalie Pang and Debbie Goh

Debbie Goh is an assistant professor in the Division of Journalism and Publishing at the Wee Kim Wee School of Communication and Information. She received her Ph.D. in Mass Communication from Indiana University's School of Journalism. Her research focuses on gender and ICTs, the digital divide, and media framing. Her work has won top paper awards from the International Communication Association and the Association for Education in Journalism and Mass Communication. These include "Who We Are and What We Want: A Feminist Standpoint Approach to Defining Effective ICT Use for West Virginian Women" and "It's the Gays' Fault: News and HIV as weapons against homosexuality in Singapore." Prior to joining NTU, Debbie was an adjunct lecturer at West Virginia University P.I Reed School of Journalism, where she taught specialized news reporting. She also taught new media and society at the WVU Honors College. Professionally, Debbie has worked as a journalist for Singapore's *The Straits Times* newspaper, and as editor for magazines and newsletters in Indiana and West Virginia. She is also an alumni of the WKWSCI.

Natalie Pang is an Assistant Professor at Wee Kim Wee School of Communication and Information, and Principal Investigator at the Centre of Social Media Innovations for Communities (COSMIC) at Nanyang Technological University. She obtained her Ph.D. in Information Management from Monash University in 2009, where her research was also awarded the Vice Chancellor's Commendation for Doctoral Thesis Excellence and the Faculty of IT Doctoral Medal. She is a social media and technological effects researcher, and has won a top paper award at ISIC: The Information Behaviour Conference, the leading conference on information behaviour. Her research in social media involves: social media information design and processing, social media and information behaviour in the contexts of uncertainty and crises, and social media and participatory documentation and civic engagement. Her other area of research examines technological effects in marginalised communities such as older adults and people with special needs. Natalie teaches courses in social informatics, information management, qualitative research methods, information behaviour, and records management.

5. Who Calls the Shots? Agenda Setting in Mainstream and Alternative Media — Paul Wu Horng-Jyh, Randolph Tan Gee Kwang and Carol Soon

Dr Paul Wu Horng-Jyh is the Head of Information and Communication Technology Programme at the School of Science & Technology, SIM University. He completed his Ph.D. in the University of Michigan and his research interest lies in cognitive architecture, computational linguistics, technology start-up, digital archives, knowledge management and system science. His work has been published in peer-reviewed journals such as *Journal of Information Science, New Review of Hypermedia and Multimedia* and *Computer & Mathematics with Application.* Prior to joining the SIM University, Dr Wu was a Senior Fellow in Wee Kim Wee School of Communication and Information, Nanyang Technological University. Dr Wu also holds patents in data search and data quality services.

Randolph Tan Gee Kwang is Associate Professor and Director at the Centre for Applied Research at SIM University (UniSIM). He also currently serves as a nominated Member of Parliament. He received his Bachelor's degree in Economics, and his Ph.D. in theoretical econometrics, both from Monash University. He was Head of Business Analytics at UniSIM from 2010 to 2011, and subsequently headed the Business programme until September 2012. His current research interest is in the area of labour economics, with a focus on manpower issues in the Singapore economy. Prior to joining UniSIM, he was at NTU, where he taught courses in statistics, econometrics, multivariate analysis, time series analysis and applied economics. From 2006–2009, he produced labour market forecasts for the Singapore economy on behalf of NTU's Economic Growth Centre. He has also conducted research into the properties of test statistics in linear simultaneous structural equation models, the modelling of housing markets, and multi-factor productivity analysis.

Dr Carol Soon is Research Fellow at the Institute of Policy Studies and her research interests include digital engagement, how individuals and organizations leverage new media to engender political and social change, and Singapore as a digital village. Her research has been published in peer-reviewed journals such as the *Journal of Computer-Mediated Communication, Information Communication & Society, Asian Journal of Communication, Journal of Information Technology and Politics*, and *Social Science* and *Computer Review*. She is currently Co-Investigator of a project on deliberative governance. Dr Soon teaches a module on new media and politics at the University Scholars Programme in NUS. In 2012, she was Visiting Research Fellow at the Asia Research Centre, Murdoch University, with support from the Australian Endeavour Award. She is a Member of the Media Literacy Council and Associate Editor with the *Media Asia Journal*.

6. Different but not that Different: New Media's Impact on Young Voters' Political Participation — Trisha T.C. Lin and Alice Y.H. Hong

Trisha T.C. Lin (Ph.D., University of Hawaii, Manoa) is an assistant professor at Wee Kim Wee School of Communication and Information, Nanyang Technological University, Singapore. Trisha's research focuses on interactive digital media, mobile media and communication, and new media convergence. She was granted the 2004 Australia Asia Executive Award by the Australian Government to study digital TV in Australia as a visiting scholar at University of New South Wales. As a former TV professional, she has published research articles regarding emerging audiovisual technologies, such as mobile TV, IPTV, social TV and multi-screen TV. Realizing the significance of mobile technologies, she works on projects in location-based mobile advertising, mobile dependency, and mobile health. She has publications in top communication journals such as *New Media & Society*, *Telecommunications Policy*, *Environmental Communication*, *Asian Journal of Communication* and *Chinese Journal of Communication*. Aside from teaching and research duties, Trisha serves as the Marketing and Publicity Committee Chair of Chinese Communication Association, the Director of Chinese Language Media Workshop (co-organized by WKWSCI and Singapore Press Holdings), as well as the Lianhe Zaobao's new media columnist.

Alice Y.H. Hong is a Professor at the Graduate Institute of Mass Communication, Fu Jen Catholic University, Taiwan. She received her Ph.D. degree from the University of Wisconsin-Madison in 1996, and was a research fellow at the Asian Communication Research Centre (ACRC), Nanyang Technological University, Singapore in 2009. She has many years of practical experience in election campaigning and is also a reviewer of many renowned academic journals in Taiwan and in the U.S. She has broad research interests and her areas of specialization include Internet marketing, election campaigning, advertising effects, and quantitative research methods.

7. The Leap from the Virtual to the Real: Facebook Use and Political Participation — Marko M. Skoric

Marko M. Skoric is Associate Professor at the Department of Media and Communication, City University of Hong Kong. Previously, he was Assistant Professor at the Wee Kim Wee School of Communication and Information, Nanyang Technological University, Singapore. He holds a Ph.D. in Communication from the University of Michigan, and a B.Sc. in Psychology from the University College London, UK. Marko's teaching and research interests are focused on new media and social change, with particular emphasis on civic and political implications of new communication technologies.

Dr. Skoric's research has appeared in peer-reviewed journals such as *Journal of Computer-Mediated Communication, CyberPsychology, Behavior & Social Networking*, and *Computers in Human Behavior*. His recent work includes a "big data" analysis of 2011 Singapore General Election tweets and research on social media and political polarization during the Occupy Central protests in Hong Kong in 2014.

Dr. Skoric's chairs the *International Conference for e-Democracy and Open Government Asia* (CeDEM Asia)   and *New Media and Citizenship in Asia* series of International Communication Association (ICA) preconferences. His research and comments have appeared in the international news media, including *The BBC, The Economist* and *The Washington Post*, and his study on video games was cited by the Supreme Court of the United States (*Brown v. Entertainment Merchants Assn*).

8. David vs Goliath: Twitter's Role in Equalizing Big-Party Dominance — Xu Xiaoge

Dr. Xu Xiaoge is the founder of Mobile Studies International (mobile2studies.com). Before joining Botswana International University of Science and Technology as professor of mobile studies, he worked at University of Nottingham (China Campus), Nanyang

Technological University (Singapore), City University of Hong Kong, and Xinhua News Agency. His expertise lies largely in mobile studies and journalism studies. Besides his journal articles and books, Prof. Xu has also been offering media consultancy and training services to the media industry in Asia and beyond.

9. Lifting the Veil of Ignorance: Internet's Impact on Knowledge Gap — Debbie Goh (see page 261)

10. Squaring Political Circles: Coping with Conflicting Information — Natalie Pang (see page 261)

11. The Silence of the Majority: Political Talk During Election Time — Weiyu Zhang

Weiyu Zhang is Associate Professor at the Department of Communication and New Media, National University of Singapore. She holds a Ph.D. in Communication from Annenberg School for Communication, University of Pennsylvania. Her research focuses on civic engagement and ICTs, with an emphasis on Asia. Her published works have appeared in *Journal of Communication, Communication Theory, Communication Research, Journal of Computer-Mediated Communication, Information, Communication, & Society, International Communication Gazette, Computers & Education, Computers in Human Behavior*, and many others. Her recent project is to develop and examine an online platform for citizen deliberation.

www.ingramcontent.com/pod-product-compliance
Lightning Source LLC
Chambersburg PA
CBHW050337270326
41926CB00016B/3500